Places for People

Places for People

HOTELS MOTELS
RESTAURANTS BARS
CLUBS
COMMUNITY RECREATION FACILITIES
CAMPS
PARKS PLAZAS PLAYGROUNDS

EXAMPLES OF OUTSTANDING ACHIEVEMENT
SELECTED FOR PUBLICATION BY
THE EDITORS OF *ARCHITECTURAL RECORD*

(AR) AN ARCHITECTURAL RECORD BOOK

EDITED BY JEANNE M. DAVERN
DESIGNED BY JAN V. WHITE

McGRAW-HILL BOOK COMPANY
NEW YORK

NEW YORK
ST. LOUIS
SAN FRANCISCO
AUCKLAND
DÜSSELDORF
JOHANNESBURG
KUALA LUMPUR
LONDON
MEXICO
MONTREAL
NEW DELHI
PANAMA
PARIS
SÃO PAULO
SINGAPORE
SYDNEY
TOKYO
TORONTO

Architectural Record Series

Architectural Record Books:
Hospitals, Clinics and Health Centers
Campus Planning and Design
Interior Spaces Designed by Architects
Houses Architects Design for Themselves
Techniques of Successful Practice, 2/e
Office Building Design, 2/e
Apartments, Townhouses and Condominiums, 2/e
Great Houses for View Sites, Beach Sites, Sites in the Woods,
    Meadow Sites, Small Sites, Sloping Sites,
    Steep Sites, and Flat Sites
Places for People: Hotels,
    Motels, Restaurants, Bars, Clubs,
    Community Recreation Facilities,
    Camps, Parks, Plazas, Playgrounds

Other Architectural Record Series Books:
Ayers: Specifications: for Architecture, Engineering, and Construction
Feldman: Building Design for Maintainability
Heery: Time, Cost, and Architecture
Hopf: Designer's Guide to OSHA

The editors for this book were Jeremy Robinson and Hugn S. Donlan.

It was set in Optima by Monotype Composition Co., Inc.
It was printed by Halliday Lithograph Corporation and bound
by The Book Press.

34567890 HDHD 7854321098

Library of Congress Cataloging in Publication Data
Main entry under title:
Places for people.
    "An Architectural record book."
    Includes index.
    1. Hotels, taverns, etc. 2. Motels.
3. Restaurants, lunch rooms, etc. 4. Recreation
areas. I. Davern, Jeanne M.
NA7840.P55   725'.2   76-14979
ISBN 0-07-002201-1

Contents

Preface   ix

Index   240

SECTION ONE: PLACES TO STAY

Introduction   1

1. The new "grand hotels"   2

Hyatt Regency Hotel, San Francisco, California   4
Architect: John Portman and Associates

The Century Plaza, Los Angeles, California   12
Architect: Minoru Yamasaki and Associates

Crown Center Hotel, Kansas City, Missouri   16
Architect: Harry Weese and Associates

Hyatt Regency Hotel, Houston, Texas   22
Architect: JVIII, a joint venture of Koetter Tharp and Cowell,
Caudill Rowlett Scott and Neuhaus + Taylor

2. The new "small hotels"   32

"Planning hotels that pay"   34
An article by William B. Tabler

"Planning hotels that work"   37
An article by Alan H. Lapidus

Mansion Inn Hotel, Sacramento, California   42
Architect: Dreyfuss and Blackford

Village Inn Motor Hotel, Birmingham, Michigan   43
Architect: O'Dell/Hewlett & Luckenbach, Inc. (successors to Luckenbach/Durkee and Associates)

King of the Road Motor Inn, Nashville, Tennessee   44
Architect: Hugh Newell Jacobsen

Fenway North Motor Hotel, Revere, Massachusetts   46
Architect: Salsberg and LeBlanc

Waimea Village Inn, Waimea, Hawaii   48
Architect: Thomas O. Wells and Associates

3. Resort hotels / on the water   50

El Conquistador Hotel, Punta Gorda, Puerto Rico   52
Architect: Jose de la Torre
Hotel consultant: Morris Lapidus Associates

Martinique Hilton, Martinique, French West Indies   56
Architect: Charles Rameau
Consulting Architect: Warner Burns Toan Lunde

Waiohai Resort Hotel, Poipu Beach, Kauai, Hawaii   60
Architect: Vladimir Ossipoff

Kona Hilton Hotel, Kona, Hawaii   61
Architect: Wimberly Whisenand Allison and Tong

Hotel Tahara'a Intercontinental, Papeete, Tahiti   62
Architect: Wimberly Whisenand Allison and Tong

Amathus Beach Hotel, Limassol, Cyprus   64
Architect: The Architects Collaborative, Inc. and Colakides & Associates

Travelodge Motor Hotel, Pacific Marina, Alameda, California   66
Architect: Campbell & Wong and Associates

The Place by the Sea, Atlantic Beach, Florida   68
Architect: William Morgan

Sheraton-Islander Inn, Newport, Rhode Island   72
Architect: Warner Burns Toan Lunde

4. Resort hotels / in snow country   76
Flaine, a ski resort near Chamonix, France   78
Architect: Marcel Breuer

Ski resort, Avoriaz, France   82
Architect: Atelier d'Architecture

Northstar-at-Tahoe, California   88
Architect: Bull Field Volkmann Stockwell
Site feasibility, land planning: Eckbo, Dean, Austin & Williams

Kirkwood Meadows Lodge, Lake Kirkwood, California   94
Architect: Bull Field Volkmann Stockwell

Elkhorn at Sun Valley, Sun Valley, Idaho   96
Master planning: Sasaki Walker Associates
Architect: Killingsworth, Brady & Associates

5. Lodges that invite conferences   104
Playboy Resort Hotel, Lake Geneva, Wisconsin   106
Architect: Robert L. Taege & Associates

Kah-nee-ta Lodge, Warm Springs, Oregon   108
Architect: Wolff Zimmer Gunsul Frasca Ritter

Asilomar, Pacific Grove, California   112
Architect: John Carl Warnecke and Associates

Sunriver Lodge, Bend, Oregon   114
Architect: George T. Rockrise & Associates

Salishan Lodge, Gleneden Beach, Oregon   117
Architect: John Storrs

"Planning successful resort hotels"   123
An article by Alan H. Lapidus

SECTION TWO: PLACES TO EAT, DRINK, ENJOY!

Introduction   128

1. Restaurants and bars   130

Restaurant, Toronto Squash Club   132
Architect: Neish, Owen, Rowland & Roy

Noodles Restaurant, Toronto   134
Architect: C. Blakeway Millar

American Restaurant, Kansas City   136
Architect: Warren Platner Associates

Downtowner Motor Inn, Kansas City   138
Architect: Urban Architects

Le Monde Restaurant, TWA, JFK, New York City   140
Architect: Warren Platner

Boston Madison Square Garden Club, Boston   142
Architect: Keith Kroeger and Leonard Perfido

Clydes Bar, Washington, D.C.   144
Architect: Hugh Newell Jacobsen

Caesar's Palace, Tokyo   146
Architect: Paolo Riani

Mid Gad Valley Restaurant, Alta Canyon, Utah   150
Architect: Enteleki Architecture, Planning, Research

Phases Restaurant, Bernardston, Massachusetts   152
Architect: Drummey Rosane Anderson

Borel Restaurant, San Mateo, California   154
Architect: Robinson & Mills

2. Clubs   156

Jacaranda Country Club, Plantation, Florida   158
Architect: Donald Singer

Montauk Golf and Racquet Club, Montauk Point, Long Island   162
Architect: Richard Foster

Palmetto Dunes Clubhouse, Hilton Head, South Carolina   165
Architect: Copelin and Lee

Tennis Club, East Hampton, Long Island   166
Architect: George Nemeny

Mill Valley Tennis Club, Mill Valley, California   168
Architect: John Louis Field

SECTION THREE: PLACES TO PLAY

Introduction   170

1. Community recreation facilities   172

Roxbury Branch, YMCA, Boston   174
Architect: The Architects Collaborative

Clinton Youth and Family Center, New York City   178
Architect: James Stewart Polshek, Waldredo Toscanini

Portland Jewish Community Center, Portland, Oregon   182
Architect: Wolff Zimmer Gunsel Frasca Ritter

Cochise Visitor Center, near Willcox, Arizona   185
Architect: Dinsmore, Kulseth & Riggs

Drake's Beach Facilities Building, Point Reyes National Seashore, California   186
Architect: Worley K. Wong, John Carden Campbell

Bedford Stuyvesant Community Pool, New York City   188
Architect: Morris Lapidus Associates

Coal Street Pool, Wilkes-Barre, Pennsylvania   190
Architect: Bohlin and Powell

2. Camps   196

Camp Louise, Girl Scouts of America, Columbia County, Pennsylvania   198
Architect: Bohlin and Powell

Camp Lane, near Mapleton, Oregon   204
Architect: Unthank, Seder & Poticha

Airpark Lodge, Reelfoot Lake State Park, Tiptonville, Tennessee   206
Architect: Gassner/Nathan/Browne

Milldale Camps, Reisterstown, Maryland   209
Architect: RTKL, Inc.

3. Parks, Plazas and Playgrounds   210

Inwood Hill Park Nature Trails, New York City   212
Architect: Richard G. Stein and Associates

"Designing the urban landscape: New concepts of urban open space developed in projects by M. Paul Friedberg and Associates"   214
Watertown East Development and Con Ed Park and Visitor Center   214
Harlem River Bronx State Park   216
Wall Street Plaza and Mobile Video Park   218
Private Children's Playground and Ward's Island Park, New York City   220

4. The 50th State: "Test for the Landscape of Tourism"   222

Oahu   226
Hawaii   230
Maui   234
Kauai   236
Molokai   238

Preface

Places for People is a sequel to the best-selling ARCHITECTURAL RECORD book of all time, *Motels, Hotels Restaurants and Bars,* first published in 1945 and after two editions now out of print. The sequel contains only new material, and sections on design and planning for various kinds of recreational needs have been added. But the origins and intent of this volume are identical to those described by the editor of the earlier book, the late James S. Hornbeck, in his introduction to the 1953 edition:

"What makes for success in a motel, hotel, restaurant or bar? Why do people stop and enter the Sunrise when they might choose the Sunset next door? Part of the answer to these questions is by nature managerial, but an equally important part is inherently physical. In this book our concern is with the significance of the design of the physical plant, and in showing the reader how good design can benefit both the owner and the public. The text and illustrations were first published in ARCHITECTURAL RECORD on the two-fold basis that only architects possess the rounded training, technical know-how and artistic imagination necessary to make such buildings equally satisfying to both management and customer, and that good design pays off in increased profit to the owner."

"In making this volume available both to the general public and the design profession," Mr. Hornbeck added, "the editors of ARCHITECTURAL RECORD hope that it will achieve three objectives: first, they hope that owners of motels, hotels, restaurants and bars who read these pages will be persuaded that a high level of design pays. Second, the editors hope prospective investors in such projects will recognize the business wisdom of engaging professional architectural talent early in the game. Finally, we hope that architects will find this book a useful guide to contemporary examples of considerable merit."

I can think of no better words to introduce *Places for People,* a new collection selected from material representing eight years of research and study by the editors of ARCHITECTURAL RECORD. The new book offers impressive affirmation of the belief expressed in the introduction to the earlier volume that "the case for competent design will become better understood as competition increases."

Indeed, not only is the case for competent design better understood, it is being transmuted into a demand for *spectacular* design. Places to stay, places to eat and drink, and places to play are being conceived as events in themselves rather than merely as *containers* for events. Whether they hope to attract business people or vacationers or both (and more and more there is a mix of those objectives), places designed for people to *enjoy* while they attend conventions, hold business conferences *or* vacation are leading their more mundane competitors all over the world. Not only do the most successful operations now seek to attract *both* business and vacation customers, but more and more those customers count on mixing business with pleasure—and vice versa.

There is good news about places to stay in the recent architecture of hotels and motels. The proliferation of identical (and mundane) accommodations for transients assumed to be interested only in a good night's sleep before they move on has begun to give way before competition from "places to stay" which offer something more; and the trend is accelerating as evidence mounts that the "something more" attracts more customers even for overnight stays as well as more customers for longer stays and more business travel with family holidays attached.

The distinction between in-city and along-the-highway accommodations is no longer so clearcut, and the choice of accommodations both in the city and on the road is far wider. The downtown motel is now a standard building type, and an increasing number of motels along the highway could (and do) double as resort hotels. The amenities both expected and supplied in new hotels and motels are steadily increasing. But above all, the long-distance mobility made possible by air travel, and encouraged by shorter work weeks, shorter work years and shorter work lifetimes have stimulated the development of tourist "destination areas" of many different kinds in as many different locales around the world as could hope to lure a tourist for business or pleasure—and, most often these days, both.

And a new generation of "grand hotels" is creating new in-city "tourist destination areas." Time was when the "grand hotel" was a stage setting for the idle rich. Now it is a stage setting for business promotion—conventions and tourism. The idea that you could design a hotel so that people got a kick out of their surroundings, and that it could be good business to do it, probably got its commercial start in the brashly fantastic hotels designed for the fantasy world of Miami Beach in the Fifties by Architect Morris Lapidus. Architect Minoru Yamasaki's Century Plaza in Los Angeles (1964) adapted the concept to more worldly tastes, and the spectacular series of hotels by Architect John Portman that began with the Atlanta Hyatt Regency (1965) has effectively institutionalized the idea that the hotel you stay at may be one of the things you come to see—and to experience. The new grand hotels are places for people to notice, enjoy and remember.

And there are new "small hotels" which are not bound by the kind of prescriptive architectural standards which make motels in Florida look and seem exactly like motels in Nebraska or Montana. Whether in town or on the road, the examples shown herein reflect the many ways in which their architecture can provide them with their own special identity, making them attractive places to stay—"something more" than acceptable overnight accommodations.

Resort hotels, which these days are among the most successful convention hotels, have been capitalizing on splendid sites on the water and in mountain areas selected to lure the world's seemingly endless proliferation of skiers. Some of the most effective adaptations of modern architecture to site and region, climate and function, are to be found among resort areas designed in recent years. Examples in this book are testimony to the variety that such adaptations can produce on varying sites in many parts of the world.

An increasing number of hostelries are especially planned to combine conference facilities with the atmosphere and recreational facilities of a resort, and the examples selected for inclusion here show how effectively these objectives can be combined.

Restaurants and bars have always been stage sets—whether places to see and be seen or romantic hiding places; but only fairly recently, with some few notable exceptions, have they been deliberately *designed* as stage sets.

Most people like a good meal (according to their widely varying lights as to what *is* a good meal); but those for whom gourmet cooking (or *any* cooking) is the principal lure of eating out are a tiny (and probably shrinking) band. Not only convenience and functional comfort, but a setting which provides a sense of occasion—whether it's "fast food" with the kids or New Year's Eve in a nightclub—are increasingly required for any establishment to compete effectively in the increasingly competitive world of restaurants, bars and clubs. Examples selected for this book offer convincing illustrations of this thesis.

From neighborhood centers to national parks, community facilities for recreation have come to play an ever more significant part in the leisure activities of Americans of all ages. And the use of such facilities has come to be ever more a *part* of daily life rather than a *departure* from it. The lunch-hour or after-work swim or tennis game, the family bowling, skiing or boating outing have become quite ordinary aspects of contemporary life; and more and more facilities are designed to accommodate them.

The quickened public interest in and concern for the natural environment are also encouraging the planning of new kinds of parks and playgrounds, both in and out of cities and towns; and there are the creative beginnings of very large-scale recreational planning both for preservation and enjoyment of America's natural wonders.

The third section of this book, "Places to Play," contains a sampling of the wide range of facilities which are being developed in response to the burgeoning new demand for easily accessible leisure-time activities.

More and more, the efforts of architects are directed in all their work toward responding more consciously to the psychological as well as the physical needs of the users of buildings. This collection reflects the increasing degree to which architects are designing buildings which are in the fullest sense "places for people."

—Jeanne M. Davern

Part One

There is good news about places to stay
in the recent Architecture of Hotels
and Motels. The proliferation of identical
(and mundane) accommodations for transients
assumed to be interested only in a good
night's sleep before they move on has begun
to give way before competition from "places
to stay" which offer something more. And
the trend is accelerating as evidence mounts
that the "something more" attracts more
customers even for overnight stays as well
as more customers for *longer* stays and more
business travel with *family holidays* attached.

Places to stay

Places To Stay

1

The new

"Grand Hotels"

All photos Alexandre Georges except as noted

HYATT REGENCY HOTEL

San Francisco, California
John Portman and Associates

The dramatic space pictured above is the eye-dazzling 17-story lobby of the new Hyatt Regency San Francisco hotel for which John Portman & Associates were architects. In a city where great interior spaces are something of a tradition and have been surprising and delighting people for half a century and more, this lofty and lively space is in the great tradition of such famed earlier examples as the Palace Hotel's Garden Court, the rotunda of the City Hall, the crystalline lobby of the Crown Zellerbach Building and the court of the old City of Paris store. There is no question that John Portman succeeded in making the "people space" he intended: people throng to it, in obvious enjoyment of its effect on them.

When plans for development of the commercial parcel of the Golden Gateway Redevelopment Area along San Francisco's waterfront were announced in 1967, only one aspect of the plan was uncontested and uncriticized: the design for the hotel which was to be a part of the office building-shop complex. True, there was discussion of the building's orientation to the north, and the suggestion was made that it might more appropriately occupy the proposed site of the fourth office building; but, by and large, the hotel design proposal was taken as a happy one and was agreeable to all, including local design professionals. Now that the hotel is complete and in use, there is no disputing the correctness of that 1967 appraisal and acceptance; it is a smashing success.

All photos Alexandre Georges except as noted

The hotel—the Hyatt Regency San Francisco—is one of five buildings in Embarcadero Center, the last parcel to be sold in the fabulous Golden Gateway Redevelopment Project. The site cost its developers—David Rockefeller and Associates, Trammell Crow, PIC Realty Corporation and architect John Portman, Jr.—$11.5 million in 1966, a high price then even though the site was unique. The sale was conditioned on acceptance of certain requirements of the Redevelopment Agency: that the development include only commercial facilities; that it accept and work with the already established concept of buildings rising from a two-story base topped by a landscaped plaza; that the developer provide a ground level site for recreational-cultural uses; and that one per cent of construction costs be allocated for works of art on public view. The developers, too, made conditions: Their design proposal exceeded by far the 23-story height limit set by the Agency (in line with existing city policy). No one had expected either such height (one building was to be 60 stories high) or such density. To permit the project, the Agency had to alter its criteria, and it did. The first building was a 46-story office building; the 20-story hotel followed; a 31-story office building is underway.

The hotel is an extraordinary building. Two of its sides rise conventionally from the streets they abut. The north face, however, slopes back at a 45 degree angle and on the bias, giving the building wall an unusual dynamic effect which varies with the light and the view point.

Joshua Freiwald

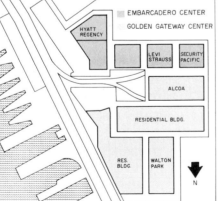

1 Elevator lobby
2 Escalator
3 Entrance
4 Meeting room
5 Ballroom

EMBARCADERO CENTER
GOLDEN GATEWAY CENTER

HYATT REGENCY

LEVI STRAUSS

SECURITY PACIFIC

ALCOA

RESIDENTIAL BLDG.

RES. BLDG.

WALTON PARK

N

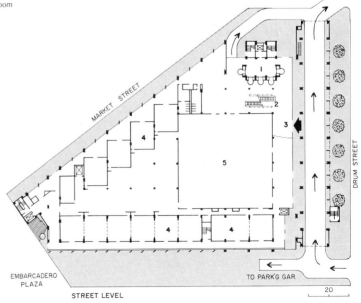

MARKET STREET

DRUM STREET

EMBARCADERO PLAZA

TO PARK'G GAR.

STREET LEVEL

20

The hotel's unique site—adjacent to a newly created plaza, near the landmark Ferry Building (far left of photo at left), and at the foot of the city's main thoroughfare, Market Street—is part of the Golden Gateway Redevelopment Area. A porte-cochère along the Drumm Street side provides the principal entrance to the hotel.

7

The building's exterior, however, is only prelude to the spectacular space inside, 17 stories high, daylighted by a narrow skylight, molded and modulated by the planes which enclose it, perpendicular on one side, sharply angled on the other. The asymmetry of this great volume of space and the reverse-ziggurat effect of its projecting balconies creates an exciting, dramatic and tantalizing effect. The focal point for this stupendous space, the cynosure without which it would not be complete, is a great hollow sphere standing on three massive legs in a pool of quiet water, curved tubes of gold anodized aluminum making a web of intersecting pentagons, stacked and rotated about a central axis. Enigmatic, arresting, endlessly fascinating, this masterpiece by former San Francisco architect (now a sculptor in Rome) Charles O. Perry brings the whole interior into scale. It is 40 feet high, 35 feet in diameter. Anything smaller would have been lost in the vast space. Anything less open than this golden maze would have made the space mundane. Sculpture and building complement each other with rare affinity.

Joshua Freiwald

One does not become aware of this great space gradually. The sudden surprise of the first view of it was carefully planned; whether by elevator or by escalator from the street level entrance, the arriving guest turns unsuspecting toward the light and is overwhelmed by what he sees. The sheer volume of the lobby is breathtaking; and then the variety of more tangible amenities asserts itself. Trees, shrubs, flowers, water; the patterned paving on the floor; unusual places to sit; small changes in floor level—this is not barrier-free design; the handicapped may view but would find it difficult to use this lobby; the trellis "roofs" over the restaurants and lounges: all these bring the awesome dimensions into human proportions and make it—as John Portman, the architect and the developer, intended—a place for people. People are always there, doing all the things the lobby asks them to do. Guests get changing perspectives of the lobby as they use the exposed glass-cage elevators and walk along the balconies to their rooms. Once in their rooms, those lucky enough to be on the north side have terraced balconies from which to view the new Embarcadero Plaza and the Bay beyond.

Other Portman-designed hotels (in Atlanta and Chicago) have had atrium lobbies, but not with the asymmetrical configuration of the San Francisco hotel—"a geometric nightmare," structural engineer Stanley Steinberg calls it. He designed it as a series of modified A-frames connected at the top, so apparently simple it seems more dream than nightmare, indistinguishable from the architecture but maintaining its structural integrity. He also had to contend with exceptional foundation problems, since the site was once part of the Bay and has an unusually high water table. The building rests on a concrete mat on pre-stressed concrete piles.

The huge lobby—it is 170 feet high by 170 feet wide, and 300 feet long—was not without other problems, after the structural solution was assured. To reconcile the atrium concept with city and state fire laws, architects and engineers worked very closely with San Francisco building department officials from the beginning, especially with engineers Robert Levy and Alfred Goldberg who, while they "gave nothing," as Steinberg says, helped to work out "equivalent safety" measures to make the design acceptable. The building is fully sprinklered; there is an early alarm system; a smoke exhaust system is located directly under the skylight; and two smoke towers—one at each end of the building—are provided. Furthermore, because the corridors are open to view, any room fire would be detectable much sooner, says Steinberg, than in the usual hotel corridor.

Designed primarily for conventions, the 840-room hotel works for other functions as well. Its ballroom on the street level can be independently entered, and its meeting rooms, pleasantly ranged on the perimeter of the lower floors, can also be used without entering the lobby. Three entrances serve the hotel, on the west, east and south sides.

HYATT REGENCY SAN FRANCISCO, San Francisco, California. Architect: *John Portman & Associates—John Portman, Jr.,* architect in charge. Engineers: *John Portman & Associates* (structural), *Harding Miller Lawson & Associates* (soils), *Britt Alderman, Jr. & Associates* (mechanical), *Morris E. Harrison & Associates* (electrical). Consultants: *John Blume* (static and seismic analyst), *William Lam* (lighting), *John Portman & Associates* (interiors, public spaces; graphics), *Elster's* (guest rooms; kitchens). General contractor: *Jones-Allen-Dillingham.*

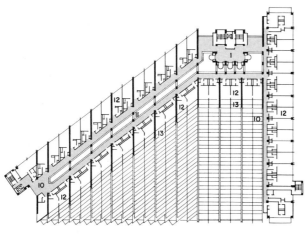

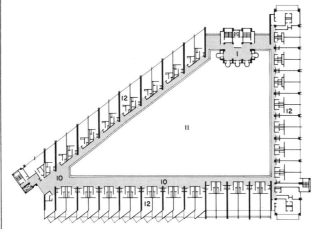

Joshua Freiwald

1 Elevator Lobby
2 Escalator
3 Offices
4 Desk
5 Seating "pyramid"
6 Eclipse by Charles Perry
7 Shops
8 Restaurant
9 Cocktail Lounge
10 Balcony
11 Atrium
12 Guest rooms
13 Terrace

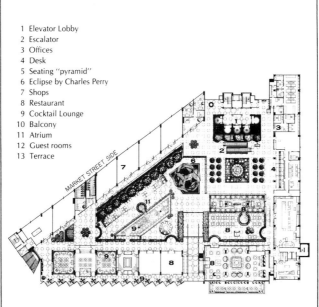

Joshua Freiwald

There are six restaurants and cocktail lounges on the lobby level, three of them situated in the main line of traffic through the lobby mall or in the circulation pattern around the mall. These eating and drinking places are like sidewalk cafes— part of the Portman premise that the lobby is designed for people. The "Other Trellis" is an eyecatching sunken lounge, open to view of and from the mall, in which translucent tables, illuminated from within, contrast with brilliant red carpet and upholstery. Three other cocktail lounges open off the lobby, one of which, "13 Views" (left), faces the Embarcadero Plaza and its controversial fountain. This lounge consists of 13 glass enclosed bays, each with table and chairs. Opposite these bays are shops and a nightclub.

CENTURY PLAZA HOTEL

Los Angeles, California
Minoru Yamasaki and Associates

The Century Plaza Hotel is a glamorous paradox, a luxury resort on a mid-city site, designed to attract conventions and large events without interfering with the relaxed atmosphere of a resort. The site is exceptional: a six-acre plot in Century City, Aluminum Corporation of America's unique city-in-a-city development on a former movie studio lot, once far from the center of Los Angeles, now completely surrounded by the city. Of the six acres, the hotel occupies three; the rest are used for handsomely landscaped grounds and resort facilities. The marked drop-off of the site from the boulevard accounts for the hotel's deceptively simple solution to the complex problem of segregating activities from the lobby out to the terrace and swimming pool and up through 13 floors of rooms, the emphasis is on the individual guest; below the lobby are two floors designed specifically for the diverse activities of people in groups. The plaza level flows out to an open court and becomes a lively part of the hotel's dramatic entrance. The 20-story, 800-guest-room building is a steel frame and post-tensioned concrete structure with exterior walls of anodized aluminum panels, precast concrete and cement plaster finish. The architectural contract did not include selection of interior colors and furnishings.

CENTURY PLAZA HOTEL, Century City, Los Angeles, California. Architects: *Minoru Yamasaki and Associates.* Structural engineers: *Worthington, Skilling, Helle and Jackson.* Consultants: acoustics—*Bolt, Beranek & Newman, Inc.;* electrical—*Oldman, Inc.;* lighting—*Wheel-Garon, Inc.;* elevators—*Jaros, Baum & Bolles;* interiors—*Donald A. Robbins* for Western Supply and Service Co. Landscape architect: *Robert Herrick Carter.* Contractor: *George A. Fuller Company.*

The hotel is on a six-acre site in Century City, the huge new city-in-a-city being developed by Alcoa on the former Twentieth Century-Fox lot in Los Angeles. Few city hotels have had so open a site or so splendid a view: to the Pacific Ocean on the west, over the panorama of Los Angeles to the east.

Lobby is 24 feet high, daylighted from two sides, and opens out to a garden terrace with lake and fountains. Lounge area is recessed below lobby level. Registration desk is in arcade beyond lobby.

Photos by Julius Shulman

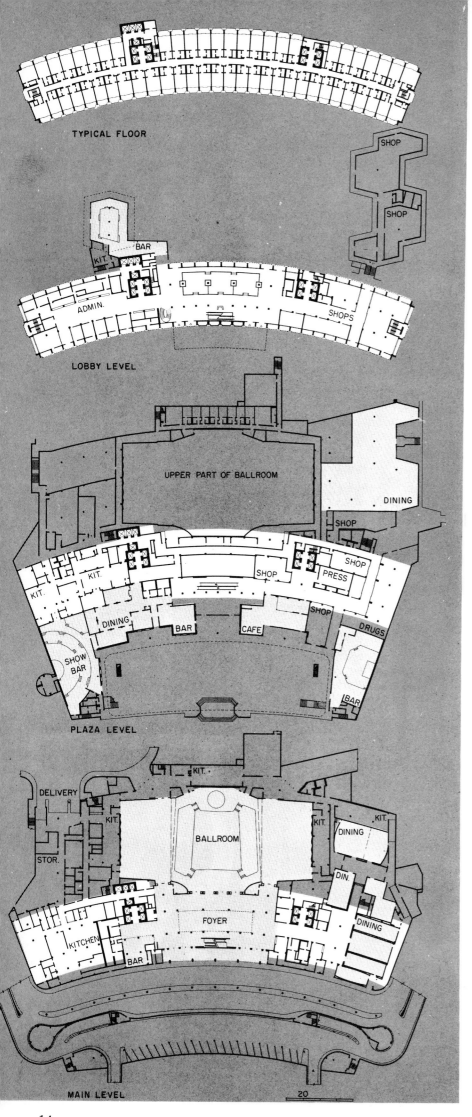

TYPICAL FLOOR

SHOP

SHOP

BAR

KIT.

ADMIN.

SHOPS

LOBBY LEVEL

UPPER PART OF BALLROOM

DINING

SHOP

KIT.

KIT.

SHOP

SHOP

PRESS

SHOP

DINING

BAR

CAFE

SHOP

DRUGS

SHOW
BAR

BAR

PLAZA LEVEL

DELIVERY

KIT.

KIT.

KIT.

KIT.

DINING

BALLROOM

STOR.

DIN.

FOYER

DINING

KITCHEN

BAR

MAIN LEVEL   20

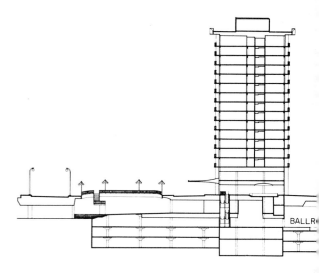

BALLR

Century Plaza does what many other
hotels cannot do: it separates the individual guest and the conventioneer (or
special-event guest) without stigmatiz-
ing either. Yamasaki says "the hole on
one side of the main north-south
boulevard through Century City was the
key" to the ingenious solution which
places all convention meeting and
exhibit rooms, and the grand ballroom,
on the California floor, one level below
grade, and provides a handsome motor
entrance direct to the ballroom foyer.
Two floors of parking provide spaces for
1,000 cars. The ballroom—largest in
the West—can be partitioned into three
large rooms. The center section contains a large stage and orchestra pit;
seating in this section is in tiers.

14

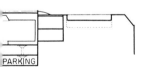

The garden side is all resort hotel: lake with islands for table service from the Garden Bar (below, left), a glass-walled pavilion whose roof cantilevers from graceful columns; swimming pool and putting green; park-like landscaping and specialty shops. Guest room design also suggests a resort: rooms are large enough to provide a parlor area next to the 16-foot-long balcony.

CROWN CENTER HOTEL

Kansas City, Missouri
Harry Weese and Associates

The 730-room Crown Center Hotel is perched upon a limestone outcrop on the western edge of the Crown Center development. Its elements are superbly organized around the rockface and part of the rock itself is exposed indoors. Master planner Edward Larrabee Barnes and Harry Weese, the architect of the hotel, originally wanted it to be a horizontal structure following the contours of the rock. Thus both sides of the square would have been controlled by the concept of medium-rise massing implicit in Barnes' office complex and his master plan.

Western International Hotels, the firm operating the hotel, has such a hotel in its chain—the beautifully designed medium-rise Camino Real in Mexico City. This operator's experience with horizontal as opposed to vertical circulation has not been entirely satisfactory, however, since hotel guests and staff appear to prefer quick elevator rides coupled with short walks, to slow hikes with or without baggage or food carts through long corridors.

After Western International shot down Weese's various medium-rise schemes, both he and Barnes had to accept the fact that medium-rise Crown Center was to have at least one tower. (The laws of economics and practicality will bring more towers later on. The high- and low-rise apartment complex was first conceived as a series of horizontal terraces.)

Once Weese began to design the kind of tower-podium structure which hotel operators favor, within the constraints of the rock outcrop, he was on his way to the creation of a remarkable building. The five-story high podium element literally backs into the rock. Here are the spaces which typically form the guest room tower base—lobby, shops, ballroom, restaurants, kitchens and service areas, with extensive garage space adjacent and below. The V-shaped 14-story tower begins at the top of the rock, approximately 70 feet above the level of the surrounding streets. What is splendid about the architecture of this hotel is the spatial transition from the lobby through the indoor rock garden to the outdoor garden, swimming pool and roof terraces shown in the plot plan (right). From the street (opposite page), the massing is spectacular.

CROWN CENTER HOTEL, Kansas City, Mo. Owner: *Crown Center Redevelopment Corporation*. Architect: *Harry Weese and Associates*. Associated architects: *Marshall and Brown*. Project managers: *Concordia Management Services*—project manager: *W. M. Flanagan*, hotel coordinator: *E. A. Balys*. Engineers: *Jack Gillum and Associates* (structural); *TEC* (mechanical/electrical); *R. C. Coffeen & Associates* (acoustical); *Donald Bliss* (lighting). Consultants: *PBNL Architects, Inc.* (interior design); *Landscape Associates* (landscape architecture); *Harper and George* (graphics). General contractor: *Eldridge & Son Construction Co., Inc.*

At the corner of the guest room tower is a glass-walled elevator shaft, a design device which must delight more guests than it terrifies, judging from the frequency with which it now appears in luxury hotels. At the top of the shaft is a restaurant with a panoramic view, another essential of the modern hotel. The north face of the guest room tower is set back behind the podium. The podium roof contains tennis courts, a putting green and badminton and shuffleboard facilities. The steel and glass canopy (right) shelters the principal entrance. At the rear of this photo is Union Station. Should rail travel revive, the hotel will benefit.

Hedrich-Blessing Photos

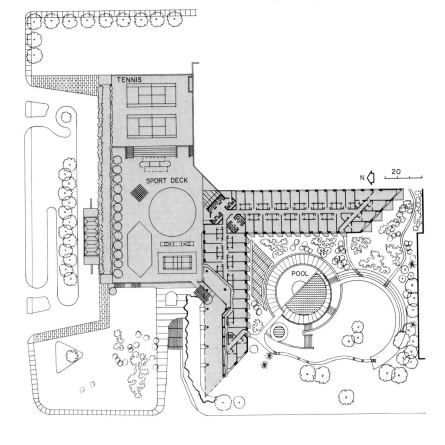

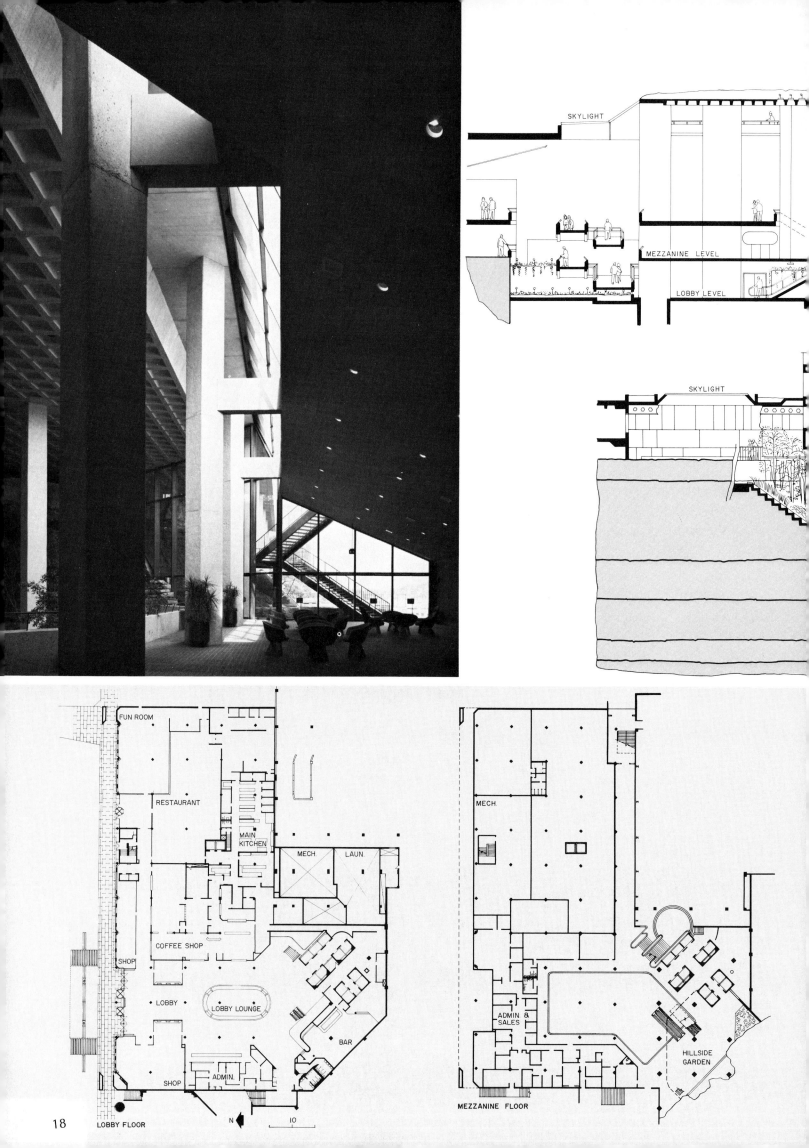

SKYLIGHT

MEZZANINE LEVEL

LOBBY LEVEL

SKYLIGHT

FUN ROOM

RESTAURANT

MAIN KITCHEN

MECH. | LAUN.

COFFEE SHOP

SHOP

LOBBY

LOBBY LOUNGE

BAR

SHOP | ADMIN.

MECH.

ADMIN & SALES

HILLSIDE GARDEN

MEZZANINE FLOOR

LOBBY FLOOR

N

10

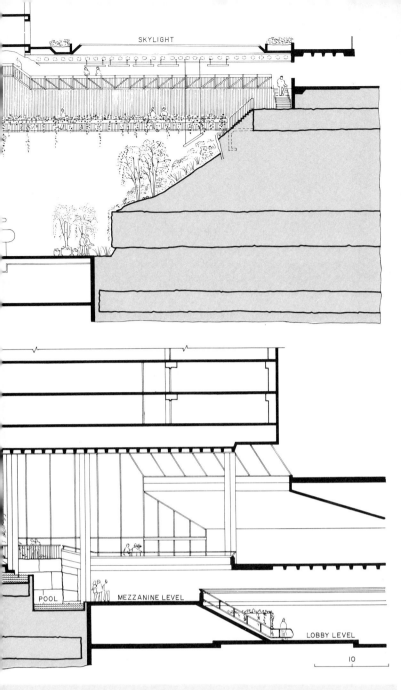

SKYLIGHT

POOL

MEZZANINE LEVEL

LOBBY LEVEL

10

The indoor rock garden and waterfall (above) can be seen at the rear of the lobby seating photo (below), and in the sections (left) and is adjacent to the general lobby (opposite page). Guests may take a winding stair through the garden and emerge at an upstairs cocktail lounge which overlooks this splendid conservatory, or cross a bridge spanning the cascades which leads either to the outdoor pool or the sports deck. Robert L. Shaheen of Landscape Associates constructed the garden and selected the plant materials.

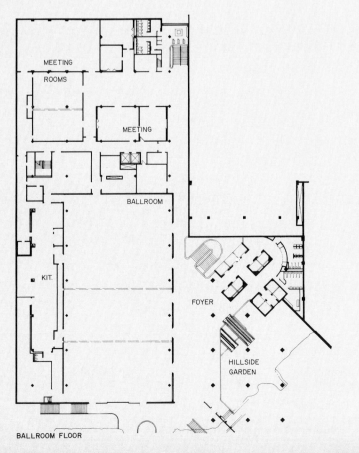

MEETING
ROOMS

MEETING

BALLROOM

KIT.

FOYER

HILLSIDE
GARDEN

BALLROOM FLOOR

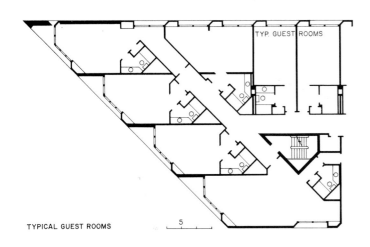

TYPICAL GUEST ROOMS

5

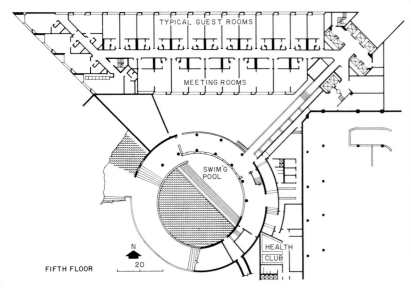

TYPICAL GUEST ROOMS

MEETING ROOMS

SWIM'G POOL

HEALTH CLUB

FIFTH FLOOR

N

20

The sports facilities form an in-town resort which for elegance of arrange-ment—in the purely architectural sense of the phrase—is unmatched by any U.S. luxury hotel. The pool and its outdoor garden are sheltered by the two wings of the tower. The top of the indoor garden is circumscribed by the pool. The circular pool terraces are the principal means of transition between the indoor and the outdoor gardens. Ingenious circulation networks, including a marvelous bridge, separate swimmers, sports deck users, visitors and service.

The tapestry (left and above) is made of undyed wools and mineral rocks in a diamond pattern which deliberately echoes Weese's use of the 45-degree angle as his geometric basis for the design of the hotel. Designed by Helen Anselevicius, it faces the glassed-in elevators which appear beyond the main staircase (right). The stair connects the main lobby with the ballroom floor.

HYATT REGENCY HOTEL

Houston, Texas
JVIII, a joint venture of Koetter Tharp and Cowell, Caudill Rowlett Scott, Neuhaus + Taylor

Located in the heart of Houston's business district, the 30-story, 1,020-room Hyatt Regency Hotel can be justly credited with enhancing the city's flourishing convention business.

Developed by a joint venture client, the hotel was also designed by a joint venture: JVIII, consisting of three firms: Koetter Tharp & Cowell; Caudill Rowlett Scott; and Neuhaus & Taylor. The client consists of The Houston National Company, a subsidiary of Tenneco Realty, Incorporated, and the PIC Realty Corporation, a subsidiary of The Prudential Life Insurance Company. Together, these joint ventures are responsible for a complex including the Hyatt hotel, a 15-story public parking garage and a 47-story office building (below, extreme left) known as 1100 Milam. Linked on three

levels, the buildings are related in color—a bronze tone—to the nearby Tenneco building; the complex is in this way further distinguished from the rest of the light-colored downtown buildings such as One Shell Plaza (SOM) shown extreme right, page 23.

There is also a functional connection between the buildings in that the parking garage accommodates central mechanical services in its penthouse, providing the entire complex with hot and chilled water. This realized some economies, and speeded construction.

With a second-stage office tower planned, it is clear that the hotel—at the convergence of major circulation patterns—is the prominent service center, as well as the most likely oasis, for a growing business community.

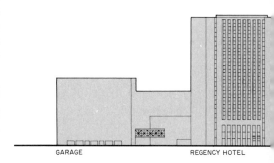

GARAGE   REGENCY HOTEL

Julius Shulman

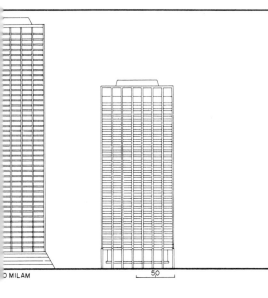

O MILAM

50

Reinforcing the relationship between the hotel and its business neighbors is its connection physically by underground and overhead linkages in the downtown center. A tunnel already existed between the Tenneco building and the hotel site; it was later extended to the garage. The skywalk system (one level above grade) reflects a decision of the building owners to protect people from weather without forcing them into burrows beneath the ground. The bridges also have the advantage of being about half the price of tunnel construction. The strong three-way interlacing of buildings exposes them to every form of traffic, an important factor in their commercial success. The buildings thus are related by circulation routes and by colors and materials. The brick paving of the hotel lobby floor is taken up by inlaid brick strips to break up the concrete surface of the parking garage. The office building's ground floor will be paved in the same brick.

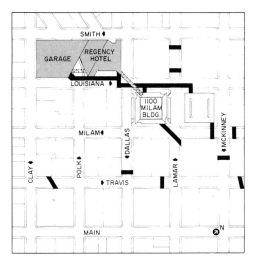

In a city where cars prevail and outdoor spaces are bland and even hostile because of climate conditions, the soaring, light, 30-story atrium of the Houston Hyatt Regency is more than a trademark; it is a much needed amenity, more so than in a city such as San Francisco, where one almost reluctantly leaves the outdoors for the handsome indoor environment of the San Francisco Hyatt Regency, pages 4–11.

In contrast to downtown Houston, this hotel's park-like lobby attracts; it contains trees up to 40 feet high, and colorful flowers border a conversation pit recessed 18 inches into the main floor. Seating arrangements for groups or people alone are supported on teakwood decking. Natural light is admitted through two skylights (photo, below right), and through a 55-foot high clear glass wall running between the columns on the main entrance side of the building (extreme left).

The triangular floor plan (below) with elevators at the apex shows how pedestrian and vehicular traffic is separated, with pedestrian access oriented to the office structures. Auto traffic to the hotel can discharge passengers and proceed either on its way or to the garage, where parking is provided for 2700 cars. Below grade parking is provided for another 300 cars.

The elevator lobby is served by two lines of glass-sided cabs, four overlooking the atrium and three providing views of the city. Shafts are lined with rows of clear lamps.

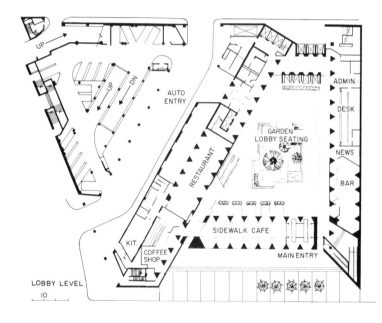

LOBBY LEVEL
10

In this essentially convention hotel, where the emphasis is on public activities and social functions, the public facilities have been placed on the first four levels, all entered from the atrium. Located here are the ballroom, meeting rooms, exhibition space, shops, a variety of bars and restaurants, and the all-important behind-the-scenes functions: kitchens, management offices, laundry, storage, loading docks, etc., all convenient to the spaces they serve, but neatly contained—never visible to the public.

From the ground floor, one perceives much about the public space above, often delineated by irregular cantilevered portions of the balconies (photo right, and pages 24–25). Foyer space adjacent to the ballroom and meeting rooms, for instance, is defined this way. This expresses one activity; the regular, more tranquil uniformity of guest room floor balconies expresses another.

The photo at right also shows the Window Box, a gourmet dining room set in a two-story cantilevered greenhouse. The projecting glass windows give diners a full view of the atrium, while affording immediate recognition of this space for people on the main floor. Gold chain mail hanging from the ceiling divides the space into three zones which can be lighted separately. This allows the room to accommodate small and large numbers.

Moving from space to space brings the guests over and over again in contact with the atrium, in a "see and be seen" environment.

Even people passing through the lobby skywalk on their way between the parking building and the office building are drawn into the life of the hotel, without interfering with its normal activities.

The architects describe their design goals for the interior of the hotel as "natural, warm materials, clear and fresh colors, intimacy within large spaces, dynamic light—both natural and man-made, park-like character, easy elegance. The rhythm of the building column creates unity between the various interior spaces. The triangular brick column form marches through the public areas modulating space, nesting seating, creating intimacy while recalling the fact that this variety lives within one hotel."

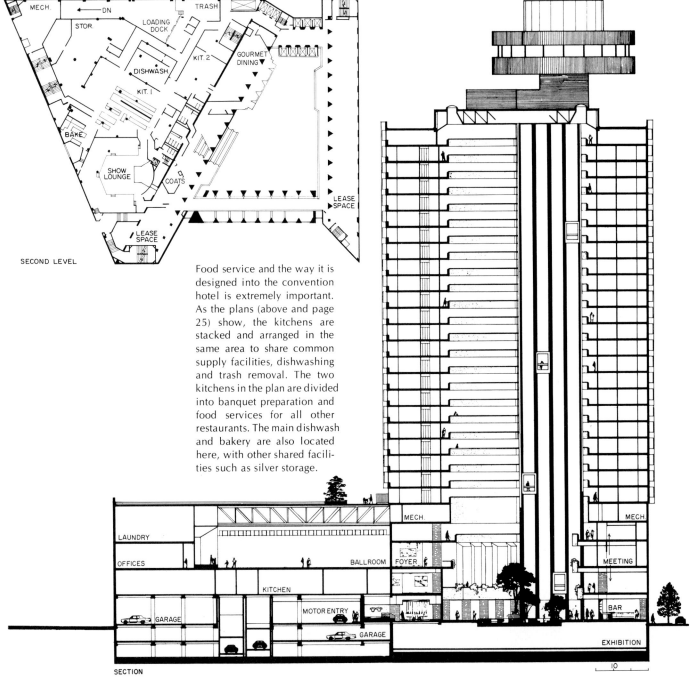

Food service and the way it is designed into the convention hotel is extremely important. As the plans (above and page 25) show, the kitchens are stacked and arranged in the same area to share common supply facilities, dishwashing and trash removal. The two kitchens in the plan are divided into banquet preparation and food services for all other restaurants. The main dishwash and bakery are also located here, with other shared facilities such as silver storage.

Served by two glass elevators with views outside the building, the "Spindletop" revolving cocktail lounge (photo and plan, below top) does offer an excellent view of the city, unhampered by buildings too close at hand. Subdued lighting and deep hues were selected to enhance the nighttime view of Houston. Meals are not offered here, but a small kitchen is available for sandwich preparation. Restrooms, reached by stairs, are located one level below.

In contrast to the low-keyed intimacy of the rooftop lounge is the 30,000-sq-ft-ballroom (bottom photo) on the third level (plan). Reached by escalators from the ground floor, it will accommodate 2000 persons. The setting can only be described as electric, with red plush walls and carpeting combining with a ceiling treatment of projecting sonotubes electrostatically sprayed with red fuzz to give a velvet-like appearance.

Movable walls can divide the space into three smaller rooms for minor functions, and a staging kitchen is provided adjacent to the ballroom, and just above the banquet portion of the main kitchen.

Available for closed-circuit television or stage productions, the ballroom can also supplement the hotel's 30,000-sq-ft exhibit space converted from the below-grade parking garage. Displays brought to the ballroom are conveyed in a 24-ft-long freight elevator opening directly to a large service corridor on the perimeter of the main room. The elevator will accommodate panel trucks and hearses, common exhibits for the auto shows booked into the hotel. The architects say that without this exhibit potential, the hotel would have to turn down many of the large shows that come to Houston.

Numerous meeting rooms, essential to convention hotels, are provided on levels three and four, with the area on the fourth level surrounding the ballroom devoted to the management office requirements.

Among the many restaurants in the hotel is the ground floor sidewalk cafe (photo below right), defined by pairs of bricked triangular columns along the main entrance elevation (see extreme left, photo on page 24). Overlooking the street, the cafe opens into the

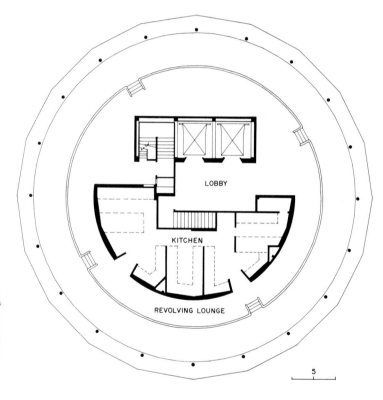

Alexandre Georges

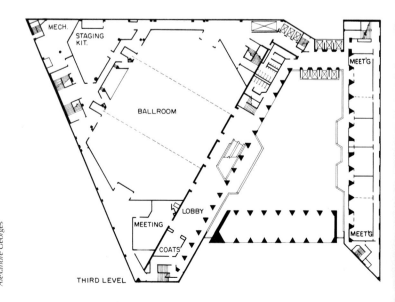

THIRD LEVEL

atrium with projecting fingers (photo right); it is recessed to the 18-inch level of the atrium's conversation area, reinforcing its kinship to the "park." Trees filter the morning sun in the restaurant, which is furnished in butcher block tables set with brightly colored service.

The interiors of this hotel are integral to the building concept, according to Charles Lawrence of CRS and Marc Tucker of Neuhaus + Taylor, who said, "we agreed early in the design process that the interiors should be an extension of the building design."

This is the first Hyatt Regency Hotel to be totally designed by one group. JVIII had responsibility for all interiors, including the guest rooms, which seem to be rarely within the province of hotel architects.

Julius Shulman photos

Since many informal meetings take place in a convention hotel's guest rooms, advantage has been taken in this hotel of angled window bays to create seating groups facing away from the hottest rays of the sun. Guest rooms begin at the sixth level, with the typical layout shown below right in the plan.

At this particular floor, rooms on one side of the building open to a wide terrace containing the swimming pool. Cabana guest rooms on the terrace side of the building are screened from the pool area, developing their own private outdoor space with access to the larger public terrace.

The color scheme in the rooms is basically vivid yellow and orange upholstery used with dark carpeting and light walls. In the bathrooms, marble counters double as bars. Contemporary room cabinetry features real wood used in the vertical planes, with plastic laminate on the horizontals. The architects designed the room interiors.

HYATT REGENCY HOTEL, Houston, Texas. Architects: JVIII, a joint venture of: Koetter, Tharp & Cowell; Caudill Rowlett Scott; Neuhaus + Taylor—partner-in-charge: Charles R. Sikes, Jr., Neuhaus + Taylor; project manager: A. William Modrall, Jr., Koetter, Tharp & Cowell; director of design: Charles E. Lawrence, Caudill Rowlett Scott; director of interiors: Marcus R. Tucker, Neuhaus + Taylor. Engineers: Walter P. Moore & Associates (structural), Chenault & Brady (mechanical). Consultants: William C. Lam & Associates (lighting), Dubose Gallery (art). General contractor: W. S. Bellows.

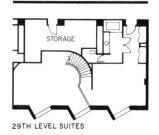

29TH LEVEL SUITES

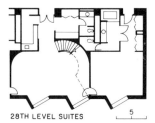

28TH LEVEL SUITES

The two top floors of the hotel are given over to suites, with two grand suites (see plans, left) with double-story living rooms (photo below). Architect Alan Lapidus says, truth be known, suites are not that expensive to build, and they are very useful in selling a convention. Since the cardinal rule on all hotels is that all rooms must be individually "keyed," the suites of the Houston Hyatt Regency contain bedrooms which can be separated for individual use. Guest rooms usually have to serve daytime business purposes, so they should be planned to function as living rooms, with dressing and bath areas well hidden.

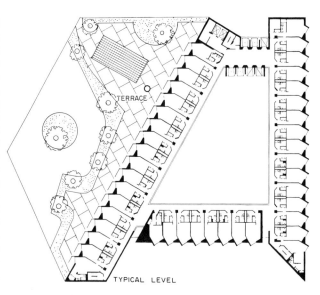

TERRACE

TYPICAL LEVEL

Alexandre Georges

30

Place's To Stay

2

The new

"Small Hotels"

PLANNING HOTELS THAT PAY

by William B. Tabler

It seems likely that William B. Tabler has been involved in the planning and design of more hotels than any architect in history. In nearly thirty years of practice since he founded the New York firm that bears his name, Mr. Tabler has been closely involved in the planning and design of more than 150 hotels around the world, for such major hotel corporations as Statler, Hilton, Inter-Continental, Stouffer, Sheraton and Sonesta among others.

To be sure, there has been some slowdown in the economy. But for any business, the telephone and mails are no substitute for face-to-face selling, face-to-face problem-solving—and businessmen are going to continue to criss-cross the country and need hotels to stay in. What's more, in today's business climate, more and more industry and trade group meetings are absolutely essential; and we see more and more hotels near airports and in the major convention or airport-hub cities built for this purpose.

Hotel companies do not build anymore; they manage

There is a pattern developing and that is the pattern of hotel companies—including the great old names—not to build hotels, but rather simply to manage hotels built by others. In most of the attractive resort areas in this country, the development of hotels is being handled by the real estate interests—people of firms like Laurance Rockefeller's; the Aga Khan, who has projects in Sardinia and North, West, and East Africa; Moshe Mayer, an Israeli entrepreneur; and Olin Corporation, which is planning a chain of lodges in East Africa. A similar pattern is developing in major commercial centers—except here hotels are being used as catalysts for commercial growth. For example, in Kansas City, Hallmark is developing a new industrial and commercial center around its plant, and built the Crown Center Hotel (pages 16–21), which is being operated for them by Western International. Similarly, the much-talked about Regency Hyatt in Atlanta was built by the architect, John Portman, as part of his downtown renewal program, and taken over by Hyatt fairly late in the game. One other example is the development of hotels as a catalyst to land sales in the area. Often a real estate developer with a large tract will build a hotel to make the land around it more valuable than it was before. If you look at Figure 1, this page, the breakdown of costs of a typical hotel, certain costs are fixed. One of the variable costs is the building itself, which means that the more the land costs, the more the developer is apt to cut from the cost of the building.

To get the business, architects must cut their own costs

Like hotel-keeping, architecture is being subjected to assaults from all sides, mostly because of costs. Many clients, including developers of hotels, are deeply concerned about the high cost of building.

Architects are trying and learning a variety of new techniques to reduce their costs and thus the fee they must charge; to remain competitive against foreign architects (who sometimes seem to be less costly, but who do not provide the same services; see Figure 2), and against the proliferating groups of designer-builders in the construction industry who try to persuade clients that they "can do it cheaper."

Don't misunderstand—I know that we cannot return to the days of the old Grand Hotels. But that does not mean we are doomed to mediocrity. We can build—with reasonable budgets—hotels that have style, that are appropriate to the cities in which they are located, that offer something special.

Conventionally, it takes a year to design a building of the scale of a hotel; but with experience and the efficiencies of computer drafting and spec writing we're able to get that time down to four months. (See Figure 3.)

Not every bulding can be designed that fast by every architect—but for our firm, experienced over many years in hotel design, that time frame is par for the course. With a construction time of one to two years,

Figure 1

	Underdeveloped areas	Developed areas	Overdeveloped areas
Land	1%	10%	20%
Site	5	1½	1
Building (construction)	60	50	40
Furniture, fixtures & equipment	15	15	15
Fees	5	5	5
Finance tax	10	10	10
Operating equipment	1	1½	2
Pre-opening	1	4	4
Inventory	1	1½	1½
Working capital	1	1½	1½
	100%	100%	100%

depending on the size and complexity of the project, we can get a hotel open for business in under two years from the decision to study the project. Initially, we prepare for a fee the mortgage package for the developer to take to banks and investors. It will take us one to two months to develop the package: program, schematics, memorandum specifications, cost estimate and rendering.

The point is that in any profession, architecture or hotel-keeping, you have to begin by making use of every labor- and cost-saving technique that's available. But most good architects use these efficiencies for what they are—tools of the trade; and do not mistake them for the end results of good architecture.

The financing of hotels is these days done pretty much by cut-and-dried formula

Within the tough-to-change economic parameters are some other facts of financial life that make it more difficult than it used to be to create a fine hotel. You don't need to be an experienced architect or developer to know that mortgage money is harder to get than ever. The conventional 60 per cent mortgage is a thing of the past. That was the old rule: if the hotel man put up 40 per cent

of the hotel cost, the banks would lend the other 60 per cent.

Now that the hotel companies have stopped building, it is often the developer of the downtown renewal, or the land speculator, who comes up with the equity money— and with different kinds of strings attached than the old hotel operator, whose goal was a good hotel, not a successful land speculation. That's one piece of bad news. Another:

The bank that takes the mortgage, even at today's very high interest rates, wants a piece of the action. In other words, today's smart and aggressive bankers don't just want to lend money in return for interest payments. Having decided that a project will be very successful, they demand, in return for the loan of the money, participation in its success.

The variable mortgage rate is another nice deal for the banker, and not such a good deal for the hotel man. A variable mortgage rate is one in which the interest rate charged on the outstanding portion of the loan is allowed to change with the prevailing market rate. This sounds fair—but it would never work to the advantage of the hotel owner.

One new financing scheme that works is the condominium hotel. This is a relatively

new technique, used by developers of housing projects as well as hotel developers. Essentially—and this, of course, drastically reduces both the equity money needed by the developer, and the mortgage—individual rooms in a hotel are sold each to a different owner. He has the use of the room when he wishes, and on other occasions it is rented by the hotel manager to transients.

This is most common in resort areas, but recently, this financing technique has been used to build hotels in convention cities. Here, the purchaser of rooms or suites may be a company that regularly makes a major presentation at trade shows in that city; or which needs a suite for visitors in its headquarters city; or needs a good address in major cities like New York or Chicago or Los Angeles.

What's needed in the financing and design of hotels is more imagination

One of the many problems of the hotel industry is that there are too few new ideas. The "wunderkind" of the hotel business these days is Trammell Crow, the young Texan who had the nerve to back a young Atlanta architect named John Portman who wanted to build a hotel with a 21-story atrium court—an idea which clearly was extravagant and inefficient and against all the rules of hotel development, except that it worked. Trammell Crow comes up with a new wrinkle per week; one of his newest is persuading cities that they need a hotel and should finance the hotel with municipal revenue bonds at low interest, much as states give industries free land and a big tax break if they locate their new plant in the state. He's also good at finding men with land and persuading them to put in the land as equity if he builds a hotel there, a cost advantage (no land cost) which puts him in a very favorable position to profit from a new hotel.

The reason we need new imagination, new leadership, new concepts is that the only thing that has allowed the industry to keep going under the old ideas is inflation. As I mentioned earlier, construction costs are going up at a rate far in excess of general cost increases; one per cent per month is not uncommon. (For a breakdown of current costs and workable space allocations, see Figure 4.) The rate of inflation has been helping hotel construction. By the time a hotel is complete and ready for occupancy, room rates that would have been too steep at groundbreaking time have become reason-

Figure 2

Fees	(European)	(Tabler)
Architectural	5-6%	5%
Structural	1-2	Incl.
Mechanical	2-2½	Incl.
Quantity surveyor	2-2½	
Total	10-13%	5%
Additional services		
Continuous field representative	1-1½%	1%
Project management	2-5	1

Figure 3

Mortgage package		1 to 2 months
Preliminaries		1 to 2 months
Working drawings		2 to 4 months
	TOTAL	4 to 8 months
Construction		1 to 2 years

Figure 4

Room cost:	$1000 X room rate
Areas	Convention hotel area per room (450 sq ft BR + 250 sq ft Pub. & Serv. = 700 sq ft/Rm)
	Holiday Inn area per room (450 sq ft BR + 100 sq ft Pub. & Serv. = 550 sq ft/Rm.)
	Bedroom net area 50 per cent (225 sq ft of 450 sq ft)
	Banquet room net area (10 sq ft/person)
	Coffee shop net area (15 sq ft/person)
	Lounge-bar net area (20 sq ft/person)
	Dining room net area (20 sq ft/person)
Feasibility	Cost/sq ft X Rm/sq ft = Rm cost X 2 ÷ 1000 = Rm rate (example: $200/sq ft X 70 sq ft = $14,000 X 2 ÷ 1000 = $28)

able. When John Portman's 2000-room Times Square hotel opens, rooms will probably rent for $70 a night. It sounds unreasonable, but it may not be in three or four years.

Room rates may be $100 per day by 1980

There have been estimates that hotel room rates will double by 1980. And this estimate is made by one of the brightest men in the field, Stephen W. Brener of Helmsley-Spear, the New York City-based realtor. Mr. Brener feels we have reached the end of the line in using inflation to get convention hotels built. In fact, he sees a complete halt in construction of this building type, unless new financing means, coupled with supportive tax measures, are developed soon. Instead, Mr. Brener predicts more non-convention, luxury hotels will be built, with room rates probably reaching $100 per day by the 1980's. Personal incomes may have gone up some, but surely they will not have doubled. This means that to attract people, we will have to offer something better. And that something better begins with good design.

One example is the Century Plaza Hotel (pages 12–15) in Los Angeles designed by Minoru Yamasaki. The handsome garden behind this hotel forms its own environment, a quiet spot in the center of a rapidly developing area, and creates a view for half the rooms in the hotel.

Now this is not to say that special gardens or multi-story atriums are an essential part of the environment of the hotel of the future. Two or three hotels with atriums have a special appeal; when there are 200 of them an atrium will be nothing special. What we need are more fresh ideas for hotel environments. Unfortunately, developers may be reluctant to invest in extraordinary design as costs soar. Several developers of one lovely new hotel have recently suffered severe losses on it.

Where else do we begin when we try to do something better? Oddly enough, another hope is energy conservation. It's pretty hard to find anything good about the energy and fuel shortages with which we all have just begun to struggle . But many architects see in the energy problems that face us some better opportunities for design, for the reason that we think the energy crisis will make clear to many clients some basic engineering and cost analysis ideas which we have understood for some time.

We have, in recent years, forgotten some old truths of designing buildings: sun shading; siting of buildings so that the solar load is minimized. A typical rectangular hotel consumes perhaps a third more energy in air conditioning costs if its windows face east and west than it would with a north-south orientation. We've been saving too much money in our equipment and materials—because owners predictably (and this is notably true of hotel developers) keep pressing for lower, lower, lower first costs. As a result, our engineers have been pressed to specify lower-quality (and therefore cheaper) air conditioners, clear (and cheaper) glass where heat-absorbent or reflective glass should be used to cut solar load. We've been forced, by owner pressure, to skimp on insulation, and on sun shading (perhaps in the form of fins, or deep insets of the window).

The new factor—the new hope I see that from this present crisis may come better hotels—is life-cycle costing. It does cost more in first costs to use better glass, more efficient mechanical systems, to add as a design element some form of sun shading. But in the interests of conservation and because fuel and electric power are clearly going to become much more expensive very quickly, the whole cost equation of lower first costs vs. lower operating costs is changing.

Closely related is the question of appropriateness of a hotel to its city. The Plaza in New York with its 19th century ornateness, its plaza out front, its views of Central Park, seems somehow just right for New York.

Hotels like that do something that few new hotels do. These hotels reinforce the uniqueness of the city where they are. San Francisco is a city of not just great physical beauty, but of great spaces: in the Palace Hotel's Garden Court, the rotunda of City Hall, the crystalline lobby of the Crown Zellerbach building, and the court of the old City of Paris store. The 17-story lobby of the new Hyatt Regency San Francisco, by John Portman, is therefore in a tradition of great spaces, as the article on pages 4–11 recognizes. These are great people spaces.

Let me repeat a phrase I used earlier: I think that—at a time when more and more hotels (like more and more aspects of our life) are becoming standarized—we need more and more hotels that reinforce the character of the city in which they are built.

That takes good architects, and it takes good clients; clients who honor the character of the place where they want to build. Must our highest goal be the lowest common denominator? We must bring the hotel industry back from dullness and sameness.

PLANNING HOTELS THAT WORK

by Alan H. Lapidus

Architect Alan H. Lapidus is associated with his father in the firm of Morris Lapidus Associates, Architects, of New York and Miami Beach. The firm has become known around the world for its evocative and provocative hotels—worlds within worlds where attending a convention (or taking a vacation) is a very special event. In this article, Mr. Lapidus discusses some principles of successful design of convention hotels, with special reference to two of the firm's recent projects

All convention hotels have some things in common. One of them is traffic. A 400-room hotel has a maximum population of 800-900 people, usually 850. There may be people coming from some place else in the city to attend the convention. Local organizations may want to have a ball, while the convention is having meetings. If those two sources of traffic get together, it can be disastrous.

So early in the design we separate vehicular traffic patterns, which both project hotels shown here illustrate in their own way. In the Phoenix of Atlanta (overleaf) we bring it in on different levels. The upper level of that hotel is strictly for lobby traffic and totally separate from circulation for the convention facilities on the lower level.

Separate people from their hats and coats immediately. In both hotels, the check room is located on a floor adjacent to the convention room floor. We never put the hall and coat room on the same level. It's sheer chaos. Registration can occur on the level of the hall or on the entrance level, but never underestimate the convention registration process. Some 800 people looking for their name tags takes room.

All convention floors are subdivisible; that's axiomatic. One question always asked is: does it cost more to subdivide the hall many more times? The rule is one of proportion. If you divide too far, the proportion (number of rooms to cost) gets ridiculous; sliding partitions are very expensive. So is soundproofing; we can provide almost any level of sound control desired and the price is exactly proportional.

But the key to any convention hotel is absolute flexibility. The hotel should be able to have a state funeral in one area and a rock concert in another; and in one place be serving dinner, and in another having a dance. The flexibility is worth the cost. A hotel should not have to turn down one event because it's incompatible with another. Potential revenue dollars should not have to be sacrificed to save a few initial costs.

The complexities of food service can be simplified

Another absolute must is shown in both hotels described here: every eating place must be capable of being served independently, all at the same time, but totally differently.

In Atlanta, we have a separate kitchen for the convention hall; it is part of the main kitchen and all the kitchens are stacked, as they always should be. If they are on the same floor, they should always be in the same area to make the most efficient use of common supply areas, dishwash, etc.

A convention hall ballroom has to be 20- to 35-feet-high, while kitchen space has to be only 10-feet-high. In the Atlanta hotel, we're taking the extra 20 feet above the kitchen and using it as storage adjacent to the ballroom. If we can seat 800 people for dinner in 8000 sq ft and 1200 for a meeting in the same space, at dinner, the hotel must remove 1200 meeting chairs, bring out 800 dining chairs plus tables. That all has to go in and out often so it must be stored nearby.

If a hotel is big enough, there is a convention dishwash connected to the main one; otherwise dishes go back to the main dishwash. Even with a separate convention kitchen and dishwash, they should be in the same area with the main kitchen.

Every hotel is so different; there are rules of thumb concerning kitchens, but you still have to figure every individual instance. I do it this way: the kitchen area should be approximately half the area of the eating space and the number of guest rooms multiplied by two is the number of people the hotel should be able to feed at a sit-down dinner. Another rule of thumb is to tighten the service circulation. Eliminate long passages; wandering employees are an inefficiency.

In Atlanta, we have designed something special for room service because it is a big convention hotel; in convention hotels, you are going to get a big run on room service. So we developed what we call a flying kitchen; the idea was taken from an airline galley. In this case, we put the galley in a large elevator. There is no limit to the elevator size you can build; hoisting machinery is basically the same. To make a bigger cab and shaft adds practically no extra expense. Of course, elevators are always trailing their cables so you can put anything in the cab; we are installing warming ovens and chillers.

We have a standard airline type menu for breakfast, lunch and dinner. When room service gets the call, it is transmitted to an autowriter terminal in the elevator. A constantly revolving crew of waiters can deliver the order within ten minutes to any room.

Know what employees are doing, where and when

Depending on the class of service provided, figure on approximately one and a quarter to one and a half employees per guest room, including one maid for every 13-14 rooms. When you plan, you have to not only know how many employees the hotel will use but when they're doing what they do. Maids are

text continued on page 41

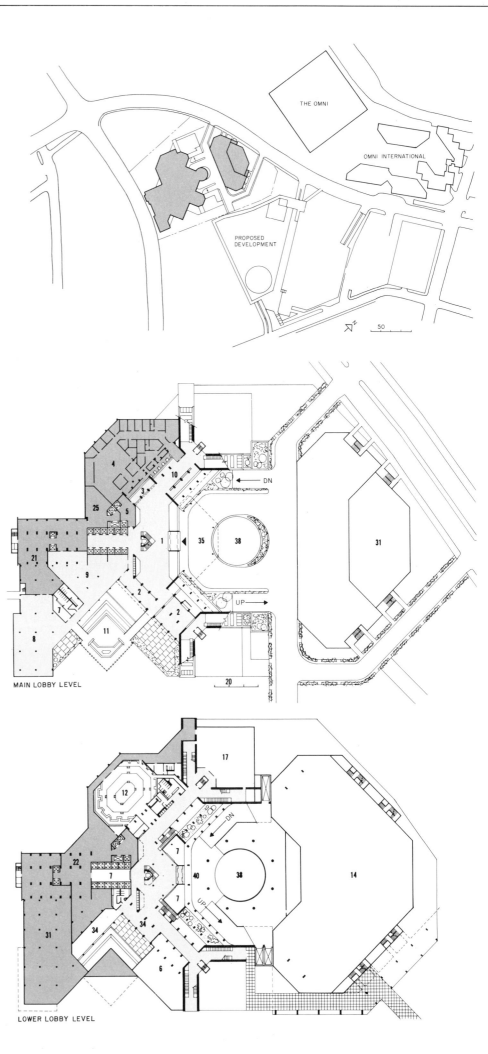

Extraordinary features need not cost more

According to the architect, perhaps the more significant feature of the 52-story Phoenix of Atlanta hotel is that, although the spaces are unique, there are no unconventional or unusual construction features employed. From the cost standpoint, this means that the hotel should cost approximately the same as any standard hotel of similar size: $31,000–$32,000 per room. This current project of Morris Lapidus Associates is proposed for the downtown Atlanta sports-convention-commercial complex (plan top right) being developed by Tom Cousins. Guests will enter the hotel under a large glass canopy which sweeps up to the full height of the building, affording spectacular views of the city from the elevator lobby on each floor. In contrast to this space, restaurants and bars are more intimate, designed as individual pavilions set in reflecting pools. The interplay of indoors and outdoors is important.

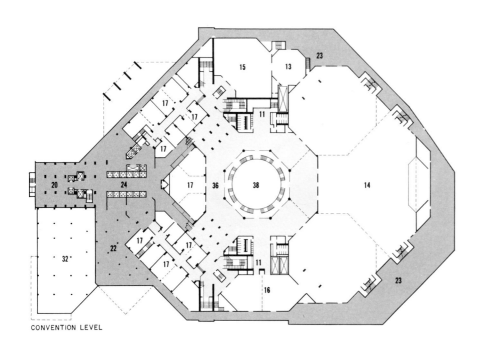

CONVENTION LEVEL

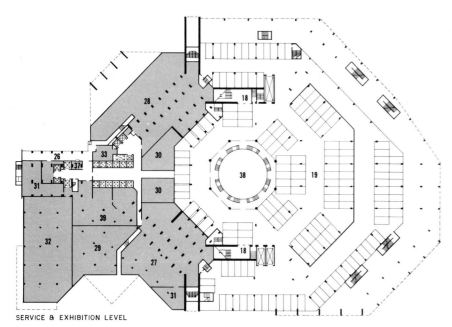

SERVICE & EXHIBITION LEVEL

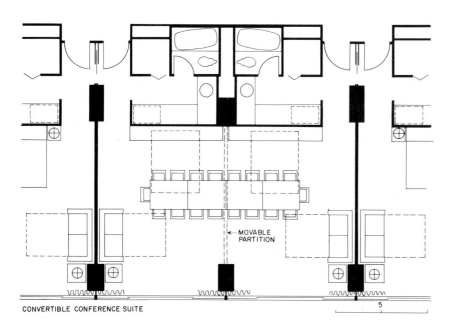

CONVERTIBLE CONFERENCE SUITE

← MOVABLE PARTITION

Breakdown of public areas—Phoenix of Atlanta
(Total 2,058 guest rooms)

Restaurants	Sq ft		Occupancy
Main Lobby			
Main restaurant	6,400		425
Coffee shop	5,000		400
Lobby bar	2,000		135
Mezzanine			
Gourmet restaurant	4,000		200
Lower lobby			
Snack bar	1,900		135
Ice cream parlor & cafe	1,000		75
Night club	5,625		375
Convention facilities	Sq ft	Mtg.	Banquet
Small ballroom 1	5,600	800	400
Small ballroom 2	4,200	600	300
Grand ballroom	40,500	5,785	2,900
Guest of honor room	5,300	758	380
TOTAL FOR 3 ADJOINING BALLROOMS	50,000	7,143	3,580
Preconvention foyer space	8,000		
TOTAL AREA OF CONTIGUOUS MTG. ROOMS	58,000		
21 additional meeting rooms average size—75 to 100 people	745		
Exhibition space (convertible to parking)	35,400		
Shops			
Main lobby floor	625		
Mezzanine	5,600		
Lower lobby	4,655		
TOTAL	9,800		

1	Main lobby	21	Main kitchen
2	Lobby lounge	22	Kitchen
3	Registration	23	Convention kitchen
4	Administration	24	Service pantry
5	Luggage holding	25	Room service
6	Shops & agencies	26	Loading dock
7	Check room	27	Employees' locker
8	Restaurant	28	Laundry/housekeeper
9	Coffee shop	29	Switchboard
10	Newsstand	30	Maintenance & stor.
11	Bar/cocktail lounge	31	Mechanical
12	Discotheque	32	Boiler room
13	Preconvention foyer	33	Trash
14	Grand ballroom	34	Snack bar
15	VIP ballroom	35	Main entry
16	Ballroom	36	Convention foyer
17	Meeting room	37	Receiving & control
18	Exhibition foyer	38	Open light well
19	Exhibition parking	39	Emp. cafeteria
20	Receiving kitchen	40	Convention entry

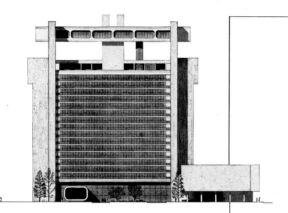

Traffic well-defined in small convention hotel

This small convention hotel proposed for Charleston, West Virginia is part of a major downtown renewal project, as are many new convention hotels being built today. As the plans at the right show, vehicular traffic for the hotel and convention businesses is separated, but interconnected. Inside, service circulation is tight, and designed—as all hotels should be—so that staff never cross public spaces in the performance of their duties. In the Charleston hotel, there is a straight line from receiving, with no other way out of the kitchen for employees and goods, than what is intended. Security and efficiency cannot be overemphasized in planning a hotel. Note the large service hall outside the convention hall. The size is sufficient to accommodate large rolling electric carts used during banquets. Dishes prepared in the main kitchen on the floor below are placed in the carts, which are plugged in near the ballroom doors for easy access by waiters.

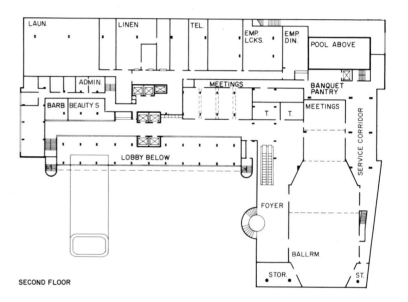

SECOND FLOOR

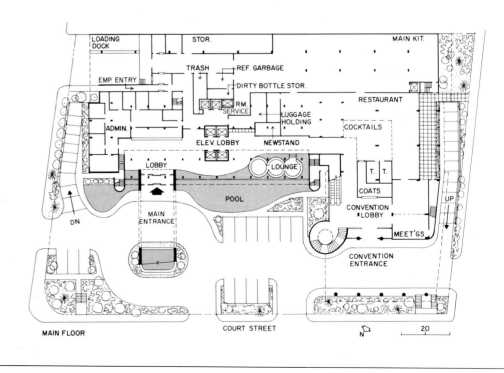

MAIN FLOOR

COURT STREET

N 20

text continued from page 37

trooping in the morning and should be through by mid-afternoon. The majority of dining room staff come on at night.

When a hotel starts to get sizable, remember the number of service elevators and what they are used for. There is usually heavy use for room service first thing in the morning. The maids also want to use the elevators in the morning. Part of the problem can be solved by having the maids charge their room carts the night before (each maid has her own cart). Therefore a service room on each floor capable of taking one cart for each 13 rooms should be provided for night storage.

The carts could also be brought down at night when the service elevators are empty, brought to housekeeping and charged. If carts are charged in the basement laundry and kept there overnight, you need a bigger holding area in the laundry and less on each floor.

Regardless, the carts must be left under absolute security or the towels and sheets will walk away. So if the cart room is on each floor, it has to be locked independent of the service elevator. You also need linen and trash chutes in the service area on each floor.

We recommend using one passenger elevator for service in the morning. This is a key-operated elevator with a two-way door that can connect to the service area; in the morning when there is a heavy run on room service generally there is not a run on passenger elevator service.

Parking space can do double duty if planned well

We took a portion of the parking garage in Atlanta, and applied electrical juncture boxes on the columns; we also ran lines for hot and cold water to fan coil units with cut-off valves so they will not run off the plant normally. When an exhibition space is needed, the hotel will paint the space, turn the valves so the fan coil units provide heating and air conditioning, and plug in spot lights. On that level are the loading docks, so heavy equipment can be brought right to the exhibit floor, through folding walls near the elevators.

Plan the rooms for business meetings

There is an enormous need for conference space in convention hotels. For the Phoenix of Atlanta, we found a way to provide the conference space, without sacrificing bedrooms.

On the second floor only, we paired rooms making the common wall a sliding partition (see plan); thus, we have ten conference suites, 18 by 27 ft 6 in. On the wall where we

would normally place the double bed, we will install an updated version of the old pull-down bed, in a handsome paneled wall unit. With the bed stored and the partition open, the hotel can rent the room during the day for meetings. Extra storage is provided on this floor for chairs and conference tables.

Make the most of ceremonial spaces, less of the rooms

When we do a hotel, we first separate the ceremonial spaces from the rest and concentrate on these. In other words, a room is a room. We try to make it as good, efficient and comfortable as possible, but I consider it idiocy to spend money on the rooms. Anything spent on the rooms is a repeat cost, so if you have 400 rooms and use a $100 detail in each, you have—for even a little hotel—a big extra expense you don't need.

In the Charleston project, we did not have the money for the kind of multi-story ceremonial lobby used in Atlanta, and we had only 400 rooms, so we took another ceremonial space: the cocktail lounge-restaurant. People can see this landmark all over the city of Charleston. It is visible; we wanted to pull that out and say this is "special." It is held aloft by the stair towers and mechanical tower, and connected to the top floor of the hotel by a glass elevator. It's a $200,000 premium we're spending, not very much divided by 400.

The cost is tremendous to put in a separate kitchen and restaurant such as this. It has to be very successful—if they're successful they work. When I designed the restaurant, I also designed the menu. I have to know exactly what will be served there, because that determines the kitchen. When I showed this to the client, I said it was going to be a broiling kitchen. There are no huge steam kettles, tremendous ovens, or extensive ranges. There is one line of broilers, so the restaurant will serve steaks, chops, lobster tails; with a radar range, fowl can be offered. Vegetables and basic soups that are prepared downstairs can be brought up and held.

But as I said, there is a cost for remoting a separate kitchen and dishwashing operation. The client cannot have an inexpensive restaurant on top. What usually pays for it is the liquor. The hotel will probably break even on the food, even with outrageous prices, but everyone will go to a restaurant like this for a drink, and liquor is the high profit item.

The guests will be a certain captive trade within the hotel, but if the developer can also have some kind of magnet to attract outsiders, he can make back his investment.

Roy Flamm

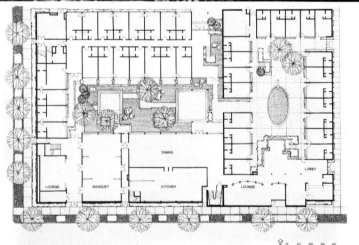

MANSION INN HOTEL

Sacramento, California
Dreyfuss and Blackford

Strategically located in downtown Sacramento near the state capitol, directly across from the governor's mansion (for which it is named), and at the intersection of a U.S. highway and a major city thoroughfare, Mansion Inn is designed to attract travelers, tourists and group meetings. Public rooms (restaurants, cocktail lounge, registration lobby) are on the highway side of the building. Built in two stages, the Inn turns away from traffic noise to two handsomely landscaped interior courts. Basement level has banquet facilities.

MANSION INN HOTEL, Sacramento, California. Architects: *Dreyfuss & Blackford*. Mechanical engineer: stage one—*Leonard Stecher*, stage two—*Daniel Yoshpe*. Landscape architect: *Robert Danielson*. General contractor: stage one—*E. A. Corum & Son*, stage two—*Charles F. Unger Costruction Company*.

Phil Fein & Associates

Simple materials (steel and wood frame, plaster and concrete block finish painted buff) and landscaping make main entrance inviting and dignified in keeping with governor's mansion opposite (far left, photo at left). Success of first 52-room unit around a swimming pool led to 66-room addition with new restaurant, banquet room and more parking.

Daniel Bartush photos

VILLAGE INN MOTOR HOTEL

Birmingham, Michigan
O'Dell/Hewlett & Luckenbach, Inc.
(successors to Luckenbach/Durkee and Associates)

This luxury motor hotel is located on the immediate outskirts of Birmingham, Michigan, along a busy and garish section of an eight-lane highway. The owner wanted acoustical privacy between guest rooms and public rooms because much of the hotel's business consists of meetings of various sizes. Accordingly, the guest rooms are on the upper floors, with meeting rooms on the ground floor, easily accessible from the lobby and from the parking area outside. An existing restaurant next door serves the hotel; and for snacks, vending machines are located on each floor. The simple building design, with its straightforward use of materials (brick veneer cavity walls for insulation, concrete for the projecting bays which enclose heating and cooling units) is welcome on the cluttered street.

VILLAGE INN MOTOR HOTEL, Birmingham, Michigan. Architects: *O'Dell/Hewlett & Luckenbach, Inc.* (successors to *Luckenbach/Durkee & Associates, Inc.*), *Basil Nemer,* associate architect. Consulting engineers: *McWilliam & Keckonen.* General contractor: *Englehart, Buettner & Holt, Inc.*

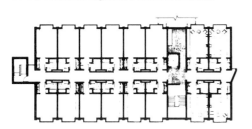

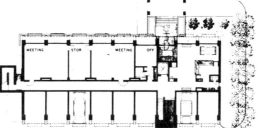

KING OF THE ROAD MOTOR INN

Nashville, Tennessee
Hugh Newell Jacobsen

Interiors of this motor inn were recognized for exceptional distinction with an *Architectural Record* award for "Record Interiors of 1971." No blizzard of neon greets the visitor here; nor is he delivered into a plastic-palmed Polynesia for dinner. Instead, the guest passes through a sequence of elegant but tasteful spaces, vivid in color, but detailed with restraint. The red, blue and white lobby space, right, and the dining room, far right, set the tone. In the private rooms and the suite, the theme is carried through in the same cheerful spirit. The tall cylinder opposite the bed contains TV, lighting and speakers while providing support for a specially-designed writing table. Furnishings, some designed by the architect, are selected with care and do much to enrich these spaces. Architects for the structure: Robinson Neil Bass & Associates.

Robert Lautman photos

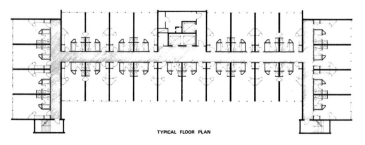

TYPICAL FLOOR PLAN

Louis Reens photos

FENWAY NORTH MOTOR HOTEL

Revere, Massachusetts
Salsberg and LeBlanc

Situated at the intersection of two main highways near Boston, this motor hotel includes, besides its 78 guest room units, facilities for meetings, for entertaining and for dining. The site slopes gently away from the main entrance, which is at street level. Three guest room units of 12 rooms each are placed around landscaped courts on the terraces. The site plan separates vehicular and pedestrian traffic by means of a system of covered footpaths which connect the living units with the main building. Automobile traffic and parking are permitted only on the perimeter of the site. Direct access from parking to guest units is through entrances at the end of each building. The main building contains registration lobby, meeting and lounge rooms and restaurant. The primary requirement for the motor hotel was that it provide an "inviting environment which would encourage guests to extend their stays."

FENWAY NORTH MOTOR HOTEL, Revere, Massachusets. Architects: *Salsberg & LeBlanc.* Structural engineer: *Benjamin Abrams.* Mechanical engineer: *Poley Abrams Corp.* Contractor: *Joseph Schneider.*

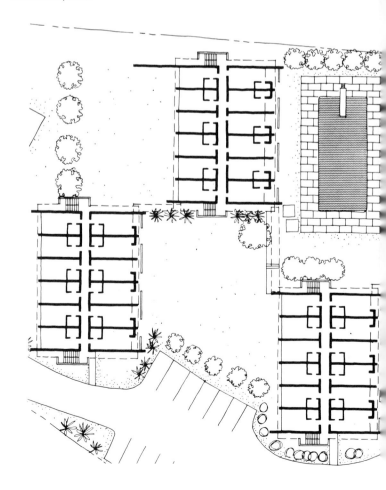

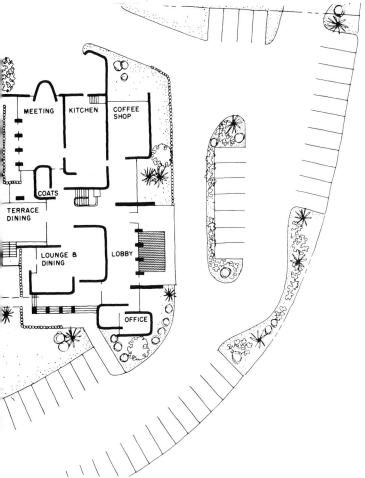

Buildings are reinforced concrete with concrete bearing walls. On the south side all rooms have balconies, extending their size and providing sun protection to ground floor units. Public rooms are all located in the main building, the activities they serve interrelated and supporting each other. Curved partitions are designed to reinforce the continuity of spaces.

WAIMEA VILLAGE INN

Waimea, Hawaii
Thomas O. Wells and Associates

Waimea Village Inn has none of the usual tropical resort trappings, but it is a resort nevertheless. By being what it really is, a country inn, it is more of a tourist attraction than it could possibly be otherwise. The inn is located in the village of Waimea, a small ranch town on the slopes of Mauna Kea on the island of Hawaii. Scale and character of the village are modest, and the problem of inserting a major building into this quiet environment was real. Two things were fortunate: the architect was very familiar with the town, having helped the people there in formulating guidelines for architectural and sign control and for maintaining the picturesque character and scale of the place; and the owner wanted the inn to be a place in which cowboys from the nearby Parker Ranch would feel as much at home as visitors from the mainland. Design became a matter of "nestling a dense development into the midst of small Hawaiian ranch houses and the village vegetable stand," according to the architect. In the damp, cool climate the same simple materials common to the town's smaller buildings made sense: wood treated with preservative against rot, clear waterproofing on cedar shingles, corrugated iron roofs. Breaking up the masses into smaller shapes, interspersing the buildings with small landscaped open spaces, smallpaned windows, simple railings, give the buildings the desired residential scale. The bar has become a local gathering place; the commercial building houses a country store. The Inn successfully fits into the character and the life of the town.

WAIMEA VILLAGE INN, Waimea, Hawaii. Architect: *Thomas O. Wells & Associates.* Engineers: *John A. Martin & Associates,* structural; *Ferris & Hamit, Inc.,* mechanical; *Bennett & Drane, Inc.,* electrical. Landscape architect: *George Walters.* Graphics: *Bruce Hopper.* Contractor: *Hawaiian Dredging & Construction Company,* Honolulu.

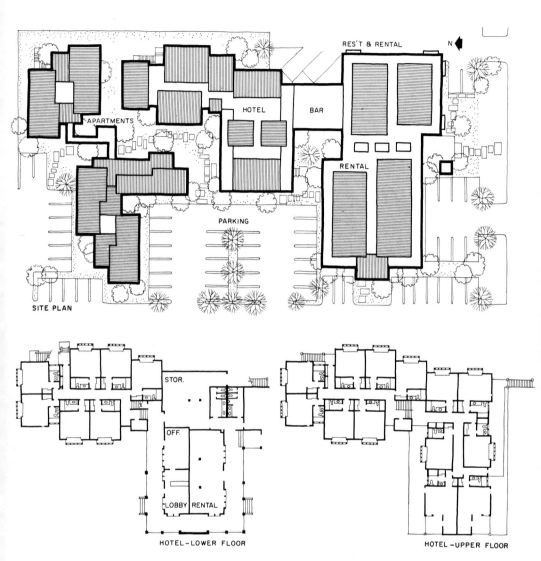

SITE PLAN

HOTEL—LOWER FLOOR

HOTEL—UPPER FLOOR

To make the Waimea Village Inn a contemporary version of the simple and very real buildings of the early ranch days of Hawaii, materials and details are simple. Rough cut redwood trim, railings, stairs and columns, and cedar shakes are treated with clear waterproofing; iron roofs are painted soft green; interiors are painted wallboard and rough redwood ceilings and trim.

A. Salbosa photos

Places to Stay

3

Resort hotels

on the water

EL CONQUISTADOR HOTEL

Punta Gorda, Puerto Rico
Jose de la Torre, Morris Lapidus and Associates

The Conquistador tells guests that they have made it. The architecture and siting are controlled to tell you why this hotel is expensive, how special you are, and therefore, why you are doing what you are doing at this price and loving it. There is a view from every room, sun deck, and snack bar. The guest is presented with an extravagant and sometimes dramatic series of spatial experiences—the drive through the golf course to the main entrance, a walk near the casino and major interior spaces to his room on the upper cliff, a tramway ride down the cliff to the lanai and pool portion of the hotel, which he has previously glimpsed from his room, or the continuation of that trip to the sea and man-made swimming lagoon far below. The architecture has been arranged to exploit the atmospheric possibilities of siting and view.

EL CONQUISTADOR HOTEL, Punta Gorda, Puerto Rico. Architect: *Jose de la Torre;* Hotel Consultants: *Morris Lapidus Associates—Alan H. Lapidus, associate-in-charge.*

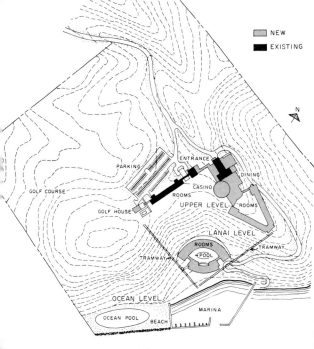

NEW
EXISTING

The site plan (above) shows the total El Conquistador complex, including a portion of the golf course, with the most recent portion of the hotel (completed in 1967) shaded in gray. It is located on a point of land about 36 miles from San Juan, with a sweeping view of the Caribbean. The lanai level (photos, left and right) of the hotel sits about halfway down a steeply sloping ridge of land from the major portion of the hotel, which houses the shops and lounges, dining rooms, casino and convention hall, and suites of rooms. The lanai level is reached via a rail car from the upper portion of the hotel, and this same rail car continues down to the sea-level facilities: a beach, an ocean pool, and a marina. The hotel will eventually have three separate rail lines linking its three levels of facilities. The section through the lanai level (below) shows the two floors of ocean front rooms curving around the central swimming pool, plus the dining and deck facilities nearest the ocean. The curving roof of the rooms, plus the white stucco finish on the exterior walls, echo earlier and indigenous Puerto Rican architecture.

Alexandre Georges photos

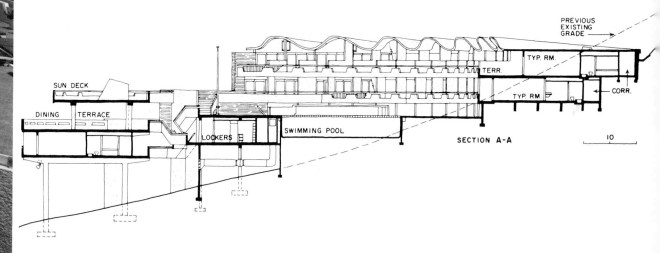

SECTION A-A

LANAI LEVEL

TYPICAL ROOMS

POOL

POOL DECK

OPEN

SUN DECK

DINING TERR. BELOW

20

The dining deck of the Conquistador's restaurant at the lanai level (left) enjoys a sweeping view of the sea, and is rather simply appointed to take advantage of this view. The outdoor bar adjacent to this restaurant exhibits this same comparatively restrained decor with plain white stuccoed walls and a simple awning—again emphasizing the siting and the view. Within spaces without a view, however, as in the upper level dining room shown below, right, allusive forms and artifacts abound, scrambling for attention and giving various messages, some of them redundant. The primary associations which the room attempts to imply are sumptuousness, wealth, aristocratic comfort. This will work for many people, appear vulgar to a few, and the use of eclectic forms—indeed, the whole methodology of the appeal—may offend the trained eye. More modern and rational in its associations is the underside of a portion of the upper level hotel wing (right), with its exhibition of primary forms, simple surfaces, and expression of structure.

MARTINIQUE HILTON

Martinique, French West Indies
Charles Rameau, Warner Burns Toan Lunde

N

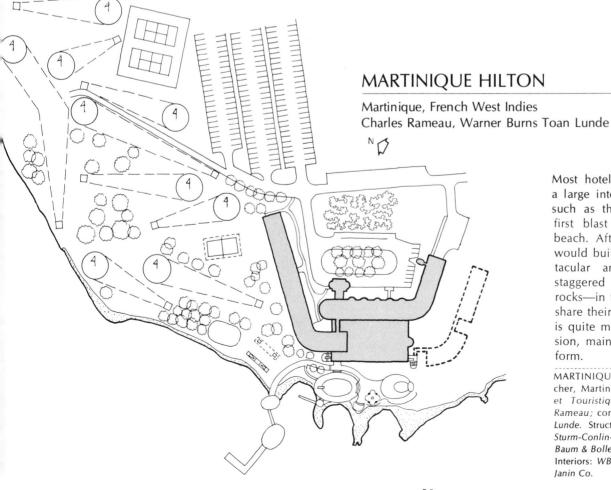

Most hotel developers about to construct a large international facility on a cliff site such as this Hilton for Martinque would first blast the rocks to create a sandy beach. After thus violating the site, they would build what they considered a spectacular and luxurious edifice—possibly staggered down what remained of the rocks—in the hope that the tourists would share their tastes. Happily this hotel, which is quite modest in its architectural expression, maintains the continuity of the land form.

MARTINIQUE HILTON, "Le Bateliere," Schoelcher, Martinique, F.W.I. Owner: *Societe-Hoteliere et Touristique Martiniquaise.* Architect: *Charles Rameau;* consulting architects: *Warner Burns Toan Lunde.* Structural engineers: *Severud-Perrone-Fischer-Sturm-Conlin-Bandel.* Mechanical engineers: *Jaros, Baum & Bolles.* Lighting consultants: *Wheel-Garon, Inc.* Interiors: *WBTL-Jacques Dunham.* General contractor: *Janin Co.*

50

As the air view and site plan indicate, the ocean side of the hotel is a beautifully planned series of spaces which include a pool jutting out over the rocks, terraces, a gazebo and steps leading down to the water. At the water level are a series of bridges and oval platforms which the architects call pods, which connect with a marina. The pods are for swimming, snorkeling and sun bathing. The two wings of the building surround a group of royal palms, the center of the courtyard of the original estate. A small golf course has been planned within the estate's botanical garden. Wherever possible, plant materials, rocks and water remain as the developers found them.

Louis Reens photos

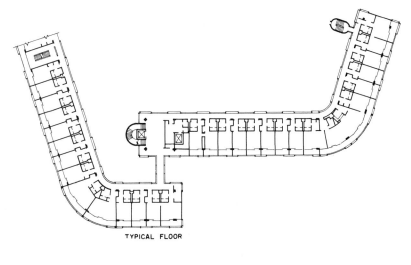

TYPICAL FLOOR

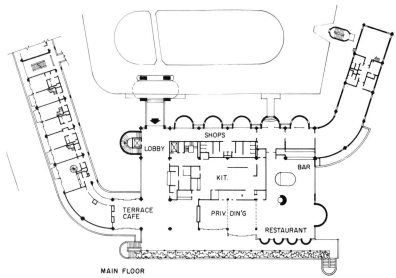

MAIN FLOOR

The royal palms and driveway from the original estate are shown at the right. Adjacent to the entrance, as the ground floor plan indicates, are a series of shops. enclosed within half circles. The dining terrace below overlooks the swimming pool and the ocean. As can be seen in the plan of a typical hotel room floor, all rooms are reached by a single-loaded corridor and have seaside terraces.

WAIOHAI RESORT HOTEL

Poipu Beach, Kauai, Hawaii
Vladimir Ossipoff

Lower jet fares to Hawaii and a tourist boom have created a demand for hotel facilities of all types, not only on the main island (Oahu) but on "neighbor" islands (Maui, Kauai and Hawaii) as well. Older hotels and resorts, like the Waiohai at Poipu Beach on the southern tip of Kauai, the "Garden Isle," have also felt the pressure of increasing business. Additions and alterations at the Waiohai so far have been carried out piecemeal, a program which interfered with neither the existing landscaping nor the relaxed atmosphere of the place.

WAIOHAI RESORT HOTEL, Poipu Beach, Kauai, Hawaii. Architect: *Vladimir Ossipoff*, F.A.I.A. Interior designer: *Marion Sox* for *Ansteth, Ltd.* Contractors: guest cottages, *Kauai Builders; T. Kure* and *T. Maeda;* service quarters and manager's cottage, *S. Honjiyo.*

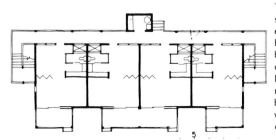

The new buildings are one- and two-story frame structures on concrete pedestals, with base walls of lava rock at building ends. Bleached redwood board-and-batten exterior walls, balconies for access to units, and wide lanais (or porches) for each unit are reminiscent of early Island architecture but sophisticated detailing and individual treatment mark the buildings as completely contemporary.

60

The Kona Hilton on the Kona coast of the "big island", Hawaii, is in the center of a resort area. Its 190 rooms are located on seven floors, and all have dramatic views along the coast, to the mountains or over the village of Kailua. The curving towers at each end enclose stairs, and derive their shape from local tradition. The hotel lobby is open, thanks to the warm, dry climate; a curving promenade leads from it to a group of shops.

Photos: Walton Tregaskis

Camera Hawaii

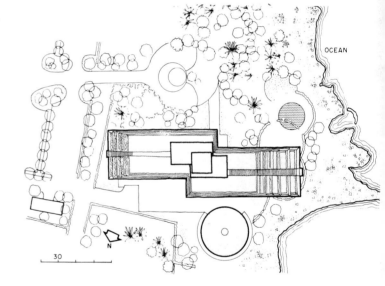

OCEAN

30   N

KONA HILTON HOTEL

Kona, Hawaii
Wimberly Whisenand Allison and Tong

The main problem in designing overseas resort hotels has been, in my experience, to convince the owners and operators that their hotels should fit the country in which they are built and that they should not simply reproduce (often badly) some stateside hotel. There are already too many of these—phenomenally successful, unfortunately, due partly to the tourism explosion, partly to the operators' international booking capability, and partly to the lack of other accommodations nearby.

But our experience in Hawaii and the Pacific countries has convinced us that hotels which are built of local materials, which fit into the landscape, and which identify with the country in which they are located, can be built for less money, and will command higher rates and greater occupancy.

The hotel in a foreign country must, of course, offer the same conveniences and modern amenities that these stateside hotels do, but the buildings do not need to look like stacks of gigantic shoe boxes. To convince the local owners of this is usually difficult and sometimes impossible. It is *sometimes*—but not always—possible to persuade international operators that this is also cheaper, but decisions are usually made at U.S. head offices and are based on unfamiliarity.

Relevance *and* prudence should favor the use of local materials and products. It does not seem logical, in a country where a farmer's house of brick and stone with plastered walls and tile roof costs three dollars a square foot, to build tourist hotels at $25 a square foot. Modern plumbing, electricity and air conditioning do not make that much difference in cost.

As hotels which combine modern conveniences, proper operation and local building practices become more common, increasing numbers of knowledgeable travelers will patronize them at luxury rates, leaving the expediently built stacked boxes to low-cost tour operators—and hotel buildings on foreign soil will again become architecture.

—George J. Wimberly, F.A.I.A.
Wimberly, Whisenand, Allison & Tong, Architects

KONA HILTON HOTEL, Kona, Hawaii. Architects: *Wimberly, Whisenand, Allison and Tong;* architectural consultant: *Joseph Rosenthal;* structural engineers: *John E. Mackel and Associates;* mechanical engineer: *United Air Conditioning Corp.;* plumbing engineers: *H.D.H. Mechanical Designers, Inc.;* electrical engineer: *Michael J. Garris and Associates;* landscape consultants: *Makihi Nursery;* builders: *Munro, Burns and Jackson Brothers.*

TAHARA'A INTERCONTINENTAL

Papeete, Tahiti
Wimberly Whisenand Allison and Tong

The Hotel Tahara'a Intercontinental is located about seven miles from Papeete, in Tahiti, and like the Conquistador has been designed to emphasize its site. Approaching by automobile, all that one sees of the hotel is the grouping of several long halls, with their sloping, textured wooden roofs, which together form the public facilities. These are attempts to blend by association into the indigenous architectural character of Tahiti. The 200 guest rooms are spread out below the ridge of the hill, to be as unobtrusive as possible within the landscape. Each tier of rooms has its plants and trellises on which the vegetation can grow, eventually making the terraces look very much like the hillside itself.

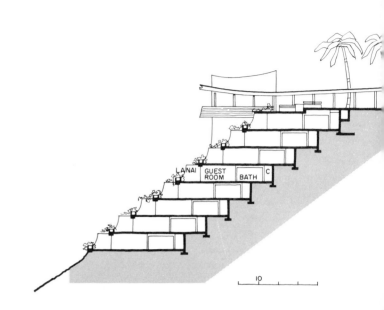

HOTEL TAHARA'A INTERCONTINENTAL, Papeete, Tahiti. Architects: *Wimberly, Whisenand, Allison & Tong, Ltd.* Structural engineer: *Richard Bradshaw, Inc.* Electrical engineer: *Douglas V. MacMahon, Ltd.* Interior design: *Neal A. Prince.* Contractor: *Swinerton & Walberg Company.*

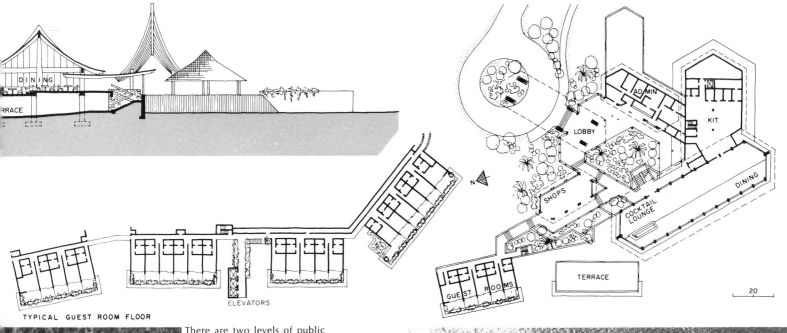

TYPICAL GUEST ROOM FLOOR

ELEVATORS

DINING

TERRACE

ADMIN

KIT.

LOBBY

SHOPS

COCKTAIL LOUNGE

DINING

TERRACE

GUEST ROOMS

N

20

There are two levels of public area above the guest rooms; the major interior space of the dining room and bar occupies most of one level with the pool, recreation area and night club below. A long covered ramp sweeps out from between the tiers of rooms to connect with the elevator tower serving the seven levels of terraces; as can be seen in the plan above, the lines of rooms are broken to conform to the direction of the hill as well as its slope. The Hotel Tahara'a was built almost entirely by native construction workers over a period of 18 months. A plant nursery was established on the site before construction began, so that immediate landscaping was available on completion. The hotel sits on seven acres of land at about 200 feet above sea level, sloping down to a black sand beach (right). The view from the site is directly across Matavaia Bay to the island of Moorea.

Erwin Christian photos

Wayne Soverns, Jr. photos

AMATHUS BEACH HOTEL

Limassol, Cyprus
The Architects Collaborative, Inc. and Colakides & Associates

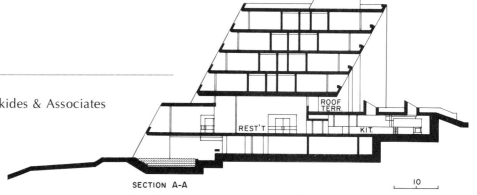

SECTION A-A

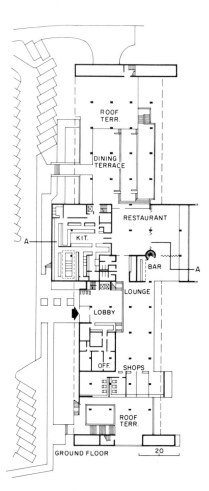

GROUND FLOOR

The Amathus Hotel is a strong form on a developing Cyprus beach. This resort and convention hotel is built of poured concrete and asserts its presence on a rugged coastline. At the same time, it recognizes its unique site by slanting (and thereby reducing) its visible bulk on the beach side, and by hiding two of its seven levels below grade on the entrance side (see section). An open feeling is given to the building by expressing the 220 guest rooms as a bridge over open or fully glazed public areas on the lower floors.

Associated architects TAC and Fotis Colakides & Associates agree that buildings for tourism must respond to local cultural and architectural traditions—but they do not see that this requires literal translation into a strictly indigenous building. In this case, where nearby high-rise buildings have already established an "international tone," the architects chose to produce a contemporary solution—and allow the natural site to provide the sense of place.

In keeping with the symmetrical plan, there are two entrances on either side of the central service block. One is for guests and leads to a lobby with an expansive view of the terraces and beach below. The other entrance leads to the extensive dining facilities, which have been placed on various levels to reduce the effect of a flat expanse of tables and provide views for more diners. A major portion of the dining area is completely open to the prevailing breezes. Rooms on the floors above are reached by double loaded corridors. Each has a balcony.

Because of proximity to an urban center of supply, the extensive storage areas found in more isolated hotels were not required; but certain areas do show marked differences from American practice. Among these are the kitchens—which are separated onto various levels for the various dining facilities. Amathus is the first of a planned chain.

AMATHUS BEACH HOTEL, Limassol, Cyprus. Owner: *Amathus Navigation Company Ltd.* Architects: *The Architects Collaborative Inc. and Colakides & Associates—principals-in-charge, Peter W. Morton (TAC), Fotis J. Colakides (Colakides).* Engineers: *Frank E. Basil* (structural/mechanical/electrical). General contractor: *Cybarco.*

TRAVELODGE MOTEL

Pacific Marina, Alameda, California
Campbell & Wong and Associates

This water-oriented motor hotel—or "boatel"—at a marina on the island of Alameda in San Francisco Bay is both destination and starting place for sports sailors. Sailors from other parts of the Bay Area dock at its piers after a day of sailing, dine at the adjacent restaurant (designed by the same architect), and spend the night or the weekend. Others keep their boats at the marina, drive to (and stay at) the boatel, using it as a base for weekend sailing. The buildings are designed to attract boatsmen rather than motorists, for the location is actually remote from any highway, but provision is made for parking cars of those who keep their boats at the marina. Simple, easily-maintained materials—wood frame, pressure-treated poles, resawn redwood siding, stained—make a virtue of their necessity: the buildings point up the value of design. Since the site is fill, piles were used, and the heavily reinforced concrete foundations were tied to the piles. Room sizes and spaces were not designed by the architects; the owners leased the buildings to a motel chain which required that its specifications be used.

TRAVELODGE MOTEL, Pacific Marina, Alameda, California. Architects: *Campbell & Wong and Associates.* Mechanical and electrical engineer: *Daniel Yanow.* General contractor: *Pacific Bridge Company.*

The three buildings were sited so they form an enclosed court both for privacy and to shield the pool area from wind, which is a problem in this locality. Not all of the units have terraces or decks; for those which do not have this amenity, protected individual sunning units are provided near the pool. The fence around the pool area permits a view through to the marina and boat moorage. The city of Oakland is in the distance.

Photos: *Morley Baer*

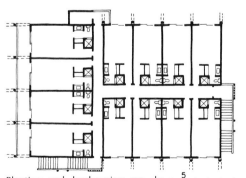

Planting and landscaping are designed for easy maintenance. At this end of the pool, a paved walk is between rooms and sunning areas which face toward the pool; at opposite end rooms open directly to the pool. Access to upper rooms in each of the units is by an open stairway with a simple redwood screen at the landing. The master site plan allows for additional units beside each of the present units.

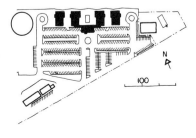

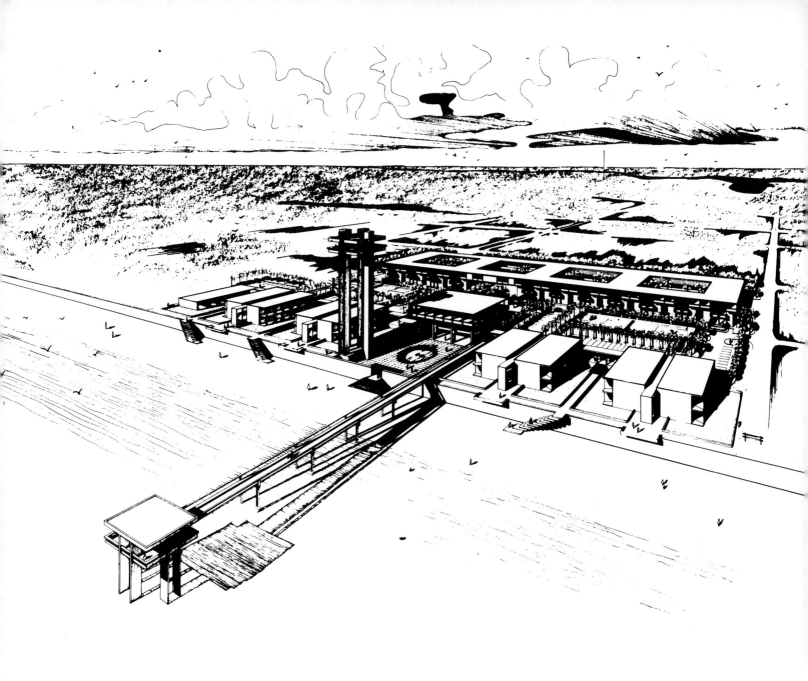

THE PLACE BY THE SEA

Atlantic Beach, Florida
William Morgan

THE PLACE BY THE SEA AT ATLANTIC BEACH, FLORIDA, IS a large resort development which will ultimately include motel units, cabanas, clubs and restaurants, a 600-foot pier extending into the Atlantic Ocean, and a 120-foot high tower with a bar at the top. Just completed is the first phase of its construction, 100 apartment units and two swimming pools. Over the next four years, the new buildings will replace buildings battered in storms. The completed apartment building is actually two buildings under one comprehensive roof. The apartment units are grouped around four landscaped courts, three of which offer protected outdoor space for sitting and swimming. The fourth court, open at ground level at both ends, is a through access to the beach. The well-ordered exterior design of the building derives directly from the interior space—and spatial quality is the essence of the architect's solution here. Of the apartment types, the most interesting are the two-bedroom units on the second floor where the living rooms are two stories in height, creating a "noble space," with a view through full-height glass panels.

THE PLACE BY THE SEA, Atlantic Beach, Florida. Architect: *William Morgan.* Consulting structural engineers: *Haley W. Kleister; Waitz and Frye.* General contractor: *Preston H. Haskell Company.*

At night the two-story living rooms are clearly expressed as strong elements of the exterior (top). By day (right) they emphasize the particular spatial quality of these units in contrast to the other two types. Access to beach is through court.

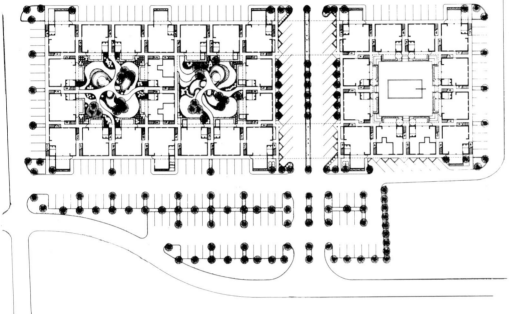

The continuous line of the comprehensive roof over the apartment structures is broken only by firewall projections which define centers of each court.

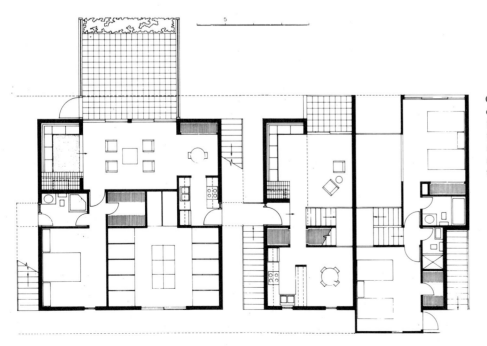

One- and three-bedroom units are on ground floor with two-bedroom two-story units above. Grouping these types (and a few four-bedroom penthouse units) determined much of exterior design, yet retained integrity of individual units.

Ascending the stair at one end of the two story living room provides changing views outward to ocean, inward to bedroom balcony, dining space below, and sheltered fireplace cove under balcony—a "controlled variety within an agreeable order." Entrance to two-story space is through low-ceilinged foyer.

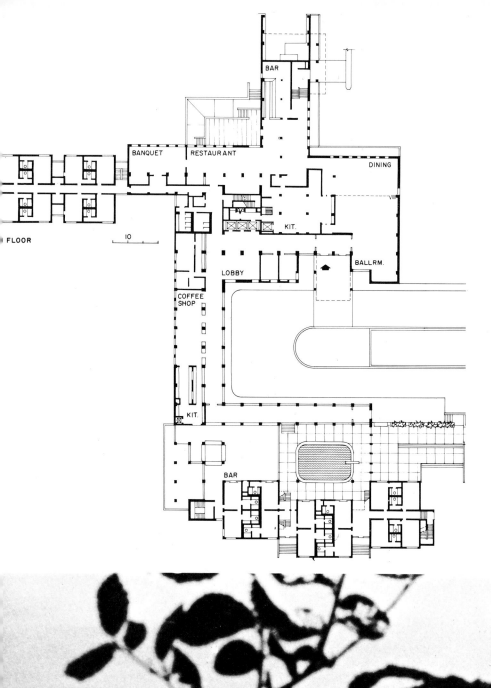

FLOOR   10

Labels on plan: BAR, BANQUET, RESTAURANT, DINING, KIT., LOBBY, BALLRM., COFFEE SHOP, KIT., BAR

SHERATON-ISLANDER INN

Newport, Rhode Island
Warner Burns Toan Lunde

This year-round inn on Goat Island in Nar-ragansett Bay is visible from Newport R.I., the great harbor, and the route over the Bay by way of a recently constructed bridge. The clients began by wanting a typical squared-off functional box in the tradition of chain hotels everywhere. The architects persuaded them that the visual prominence of the site was one of its great-est assets and that the hotel should have a form and shape to make the passing trav-eler wonder what it is. The result is a work of sculpture to be viewed from all angles. Its steeply pitched roofs are inspired by local shingle-style houses.

SHERATON-ISLANDER INN, Goat Island, Newport, R.I. Owner: *Island Development Corporation*. Architects: *Warner Burns Toan Lunde*. Mechanical and electrical engineers: *Francis Associates*. General contractor: *F. L. Collins & Son, Inc.*

Louis Reens photos

NINTH FLOOR

EIGHTH FLOOR

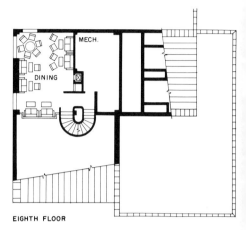

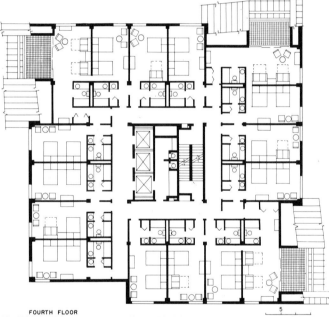

FOURTH FLOOR

5

Shown above is the 10-story inn's glass-enclosed swimming pool and at left the typical arrangement of rooms around the central elevator and stairway core. The most interesting feature of the hotel is its five-level cocktail lounge at the top of the building surrounding the elevator penthouse. Because this lounge is high, multi-level, and shallow, it offers a lighthouse-like viewing perimeter for those who like to look out over Narragansett Bay. The owners say that the lounge does an excellent business, especially during sailing race weeks. Four of the five levels and how they interconnect are shown at the right.

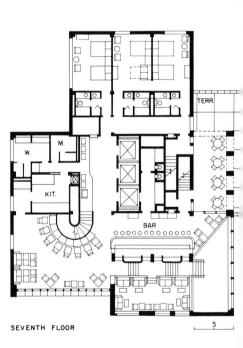

SEVENTH FLOOR

5

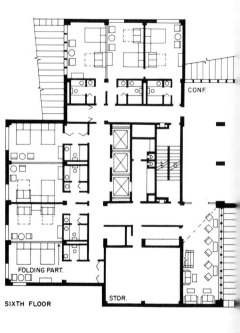

SIXTH FLOOR

The isometric (right) indicates that the cocktail lounge resembles the interior of a ship and people move through it by climbing steps as they would on a ship's bridge. The wood finishes, railings and light fixtures mildly suggest a nautical ambiance as can be seen in the photo above.

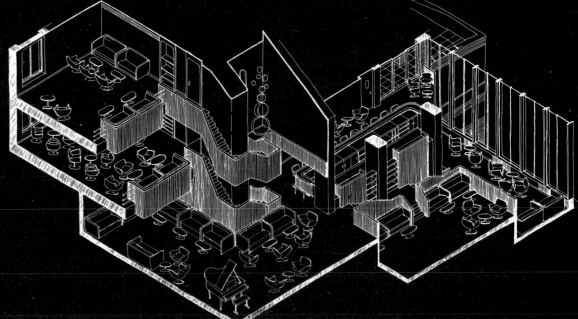

Places to stay

4

Resort hotels

in Snow country

PLAN LEGEND

A. 4-star hotel
B. 3-star hotel
C. 2-star hotel
D. 2-star apartment building
F. *Téléphérique* ski lift
G. Shops
H. Shops
I. Ski lift
J. 4-star apartment building
K. 3-star apartment building
L. Central heating plant
M. Bus station with roof-top
   rink convertible to tennis
N. Tourist office and school
P. All-purpose hall and cinema
Q. Shops and apartments
R. Church
S. Funicular and path
U. Mayor's office, post office,
   bank and medical center
V. Skating rink
X. Transient parking

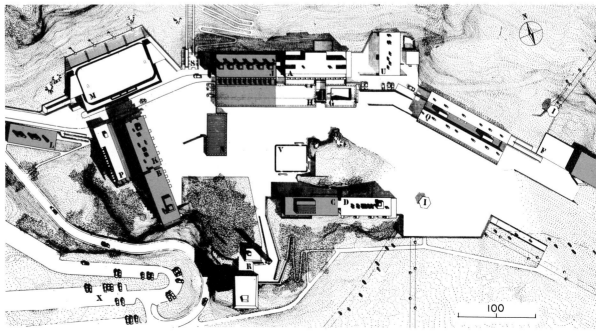

100

FLAINE SKI RESORT

near Chamonix, France
Marcel Breuer

Yves Guillemaut photos

The skiers descending to the valley in the photograph (left) were among the first down the hill last winter for the opening season at Flaine. It took nine years of work, and an undisclosed but huge amount of private investment capital to turn this remote and once isolated valley into a resort which now accommodates five hundred guests and will eventually have six to seven thousand visitors and one-and-one-half thousand employes. As yet far from finished, almost the entire town is being built of precast concrete parts. A specially constructed batching plant and concrete casting facility located in a neighboring river valley about 2½ miles below Flaine, where water, power, road and rail transport are available, operates the year round. The precast concrete parts and all other building materials are transported up to Flaine by a built-for-the-purpose freight-carrying *téléférique,* which will eventually be converted to visitor use.

This nine-year effort to make the valley habitable for skiers was inspired by its ideal terrain. The broad northern slopes of the mountains to the south of the valley retain the maximum amount of snow. The terraced southern slopes of the mountains to the north provide three sun-washed plateaus forming dramatic building sites. Breuer's prismatic facades, designed for sun and shadow, add brilliance to the skier's scene as he contemplates them from the mountain top or approaches them on his downhill run. The skiers, on their side of the valley, ascending the mountain face on ski lifts or zigzagging their way down, contribute beauty and liveliness to the views southward from the town. Another bonus of the terrain's exposure—snow-covered slopes behind the building reflect sunlight into those rooms which face north. Almost all of the buildings are on columns and some cantilever out over cliff edges.

The bus station and visitor parking areas are located to the west at the terminus of the new access road. By happy geographical coincidence the ski slopes are to the north, south and east and it has thus been possible to avoid dangerous conflict between automobiles and skiers and keep cars out of the town center. Automobiles serve the hotels and apartments by secondary dead end roads only. Space under many of the buildings is used for covered parking and access roads. All buildings will be heated by hot water produced in the central heating plant and distributed through a system of underground tunnels. The hot water heating system will not dirty the snow—thus giving Flaine an advantage over soot-covered rival resorts. Buildings shown in gray are complete.

RESORT TOWN OF FLAINE, Haute-Savoie, France.
Architects: Marcel Breuer and Robert F. Gatje.
Economic planners: B.E.R.U. (Bureau d'Etudes
et de Réalizations Urbaines).

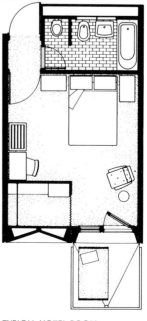

TYPICAL HOTEL ROOM

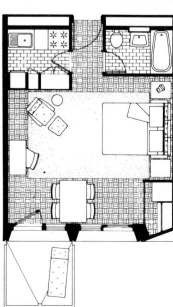

TYPICAL APARTMENT

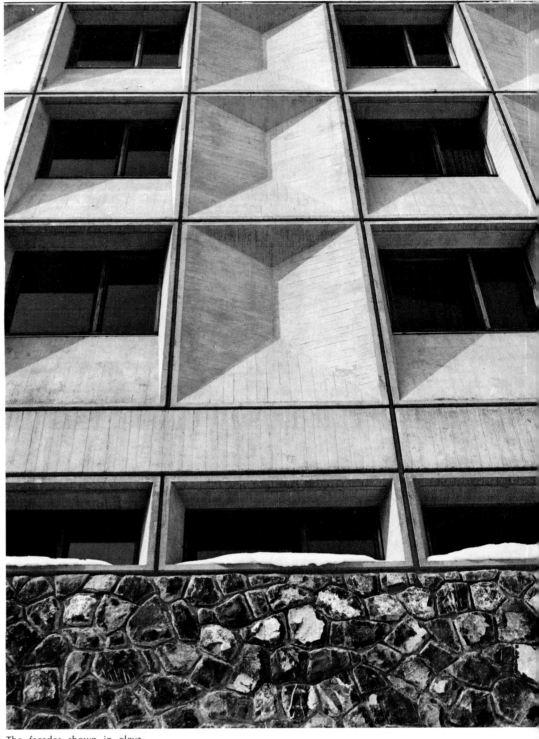

The facades shown in elevation and detail above and on the following two pages are composed of precast concrete panels with three-dimensional facets. Each type of panel has been designed to be load bearing, structural, and integrated and in scale with the module of space which it encloses. The panels form projections for sun protection and offer chases and hollows for pipes and ducts. They provide a depth of facade which has been characteristic of all Breuer's work in recent years. The elevation (above left) is of an adjoining hotel and apartment building with the tourist office and ski school in the foreground. The detail (above) shows a portion of the hotel facade. A typical fireplace is shown at left. Apartments are one-half module wider than hotel rooms.

Photos opposite and above by Lee English Biel

AVORIAZ SKI RESORT

Avoriaz, France
Atelier d'Architecture

This marvelous place is one of the few works of modern town planning which appears to be truly a part of its physical environment. Granted of course that the environment itself is spectacular and that the resort is a happy community of skiers, the successful ambiance of this village is chiefly the result of an unsurpassed architectural performance. Everywhere the profiles of the buildings echo the nearby rock formations or the fir trees. The silhouettes of the large groupings follow or are juxtaposed against the forms of the mountains. The forms are witty and capricious, but they function quite well and have an overall unity through consistency in structure and materials.

SKI RESORT, Avoriaz, France. Architects: *Atelier d'Architecture* — administrators: *Jacques Labro, Jean-Jacques Orzoni;* architects: *J. Hatala, P. Lombard, G. Rado-Orzoni, A. Wujeck;* collaborators: *P. Bahus, J. L. Brahem, Ngo Manh Duc, A. Lardière.*

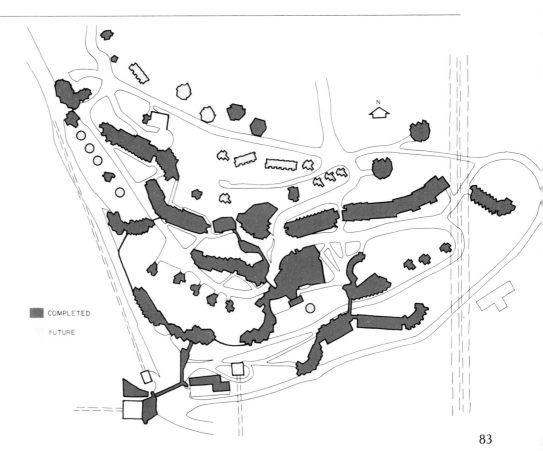

COMPLETED

FUTURE

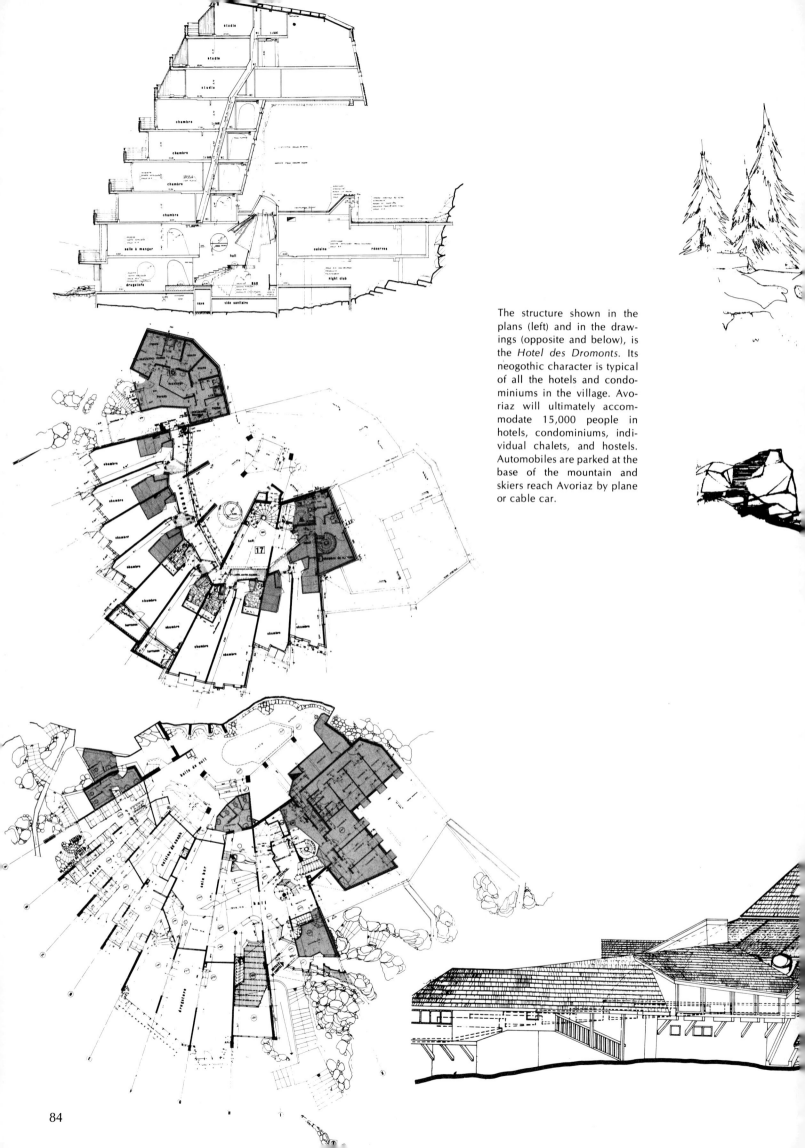

The structure shown in the plans (left) and in the drawings (opposite and below), is the *Hotel des Dromonts*. Its neogothic character is typical of all the hotels and condominiums in the village. Avoriaz will ultimately accommodate 15,000 people in hotels, condominiums, individual chalets, and hostels. Automobiles are parked at the base of the mountain and skiers reach Avoriaz by plane or cable car.

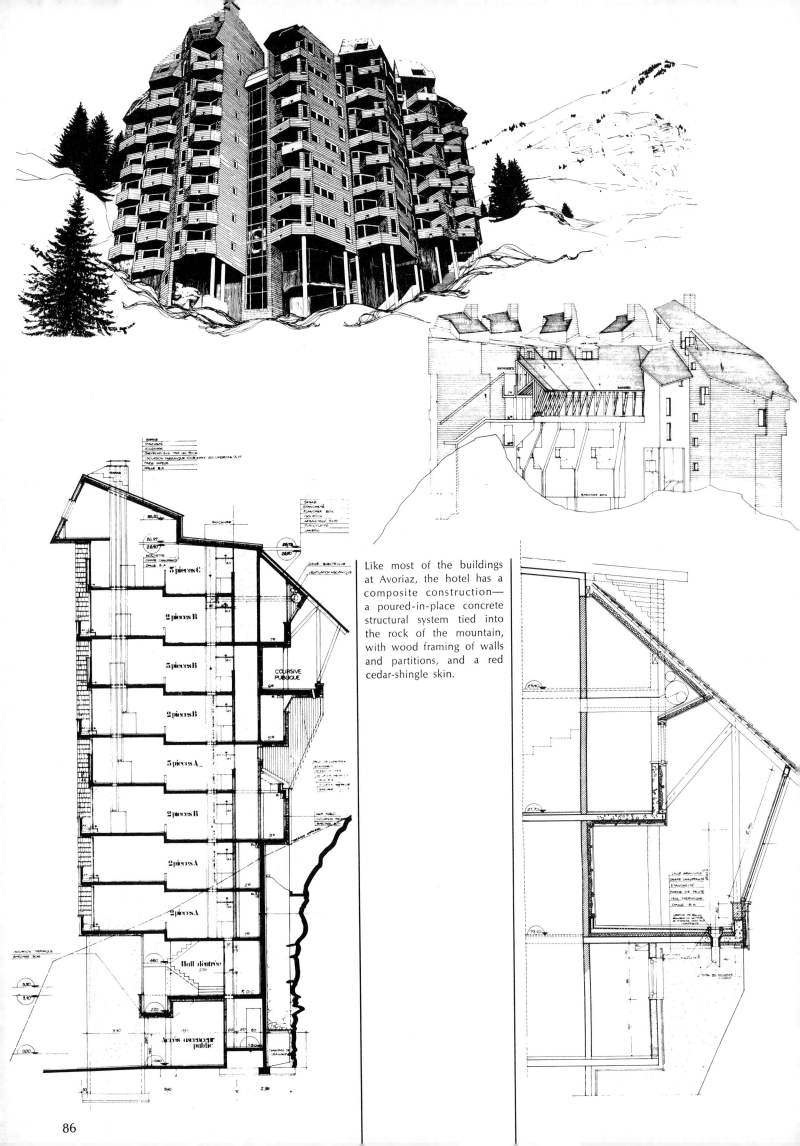

Like most of the buildings at Avoriaz, the hotel has a composite construction—a poured-in-place concrete structural system tied into the rock of the mountain, with wood framing of walls and partitions, and a red cedar-shingle skin.

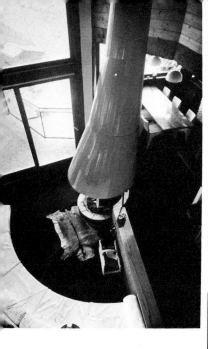

The restaurants and bars are playful and amusing and endlessly varied in shape and form, as can be seen in the photos on this page. Hotel and condominium suites (below) as well as chalet interiors (top) are equally fanciful and adroit.

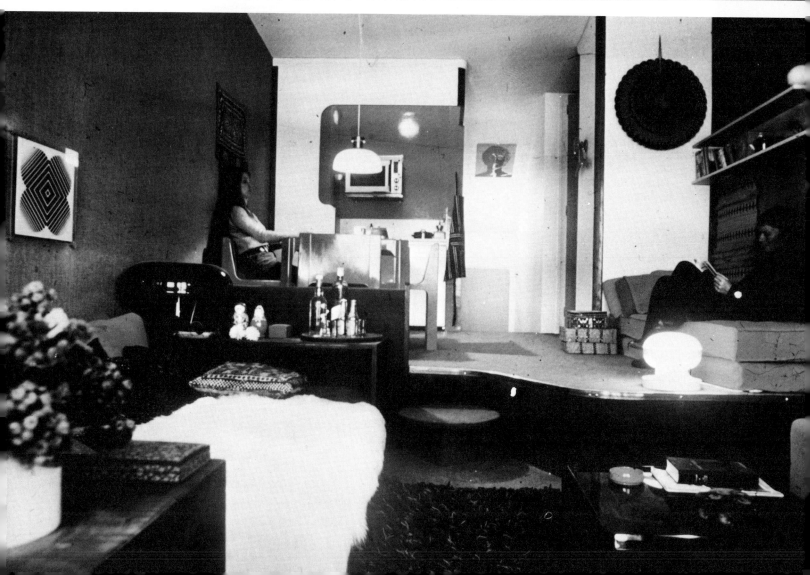

NORTHSTAR-AT-TAHOE

Tahoe, California
Eckbo Dean Austin and Williams, Bull Field Volkmann Stockwell

Northstar-at-Tahoe is a mountain resort community in California's Sierra Nevada, six miles north of Lake Tahoe, on the heavily forested slopes of 8600-foot Mount Pluto and 8100-foot Lookout Mountain. This is ski country—at least 20 other ski areas are within the immediate vicinity—but it is also summer vacation country, and it was inevitable that some kind of development would eventually take place on this land. Fortunately, the developing company—Trimont Land Company, a subsidiary of Fibreboard Corporation—recognized the property's natural beauty as its major asset. It set out, with a zeal and a thoroughness rare for land development projects, to devise a land use plan which would maintain the environmental and ecological—and the economic—values of their land. The forests that cover the mountainsides are not virgin preserves; they had, in fact, been logged for many years, but without devastation. Since 1946, when Fibreboard bought the property, logging had been carefully planned to maintain the landscape, minimize erosion and foster forest regeneration. Detailed studies made during this period of the ecology of sample forest plots—including tallies of trees by size and specie; extent of regeneration of vegetation; hazards like wind, lightning and fire; insect attacks, diseases and parasites; water and drainage—provided rich background data when development of 2500 of the company's acres was decided upon in 1966. From the beginning, Trimont set high goals and geared both thinking and processes to implementing them, with continuing scrutiny of plans to assure that the project would not veer from the original intentions. From site feasibility studies and land use proposals, it was clear that the best development potential was in outdoor recreation, and the best economic potential was in maintenance of a favorable environment for recreation. The company—and its outside consultants (Paul Zinke, forest environment; Eckbo, Dean, Austin & Williams, land planners; Bull Field Volkmann Stockwell, architects and town planners; Wilsey & Ham, engineers)—studied the effect on the environment of each kind of land use in the determination that Northstar should have a minimum ecological impact on the area. Site analysis by computer—of slope angles, exposure to sun and

James K.M. Cheng

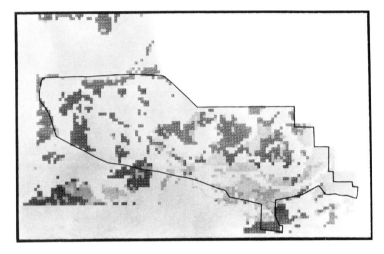

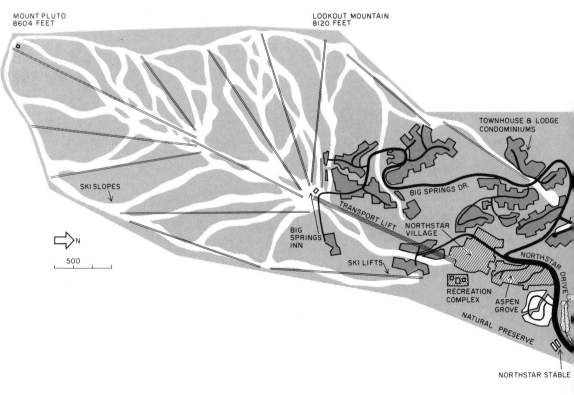

MOUNT PLUTO 8604 FEET

LOOKOUT MOUNTAIN 8120 FEET

SKI SLOPES

N

500

BIG SPRINGS INN

TRANSPORT LIFT

BIG SPRINGS DR.

TOWNHOUSE & LODGE CONDOMINIUMS

NORTHSTAR VILLAGE

SKI LIFTS

RECREATION COMPLEX

ASPEN GROVE

NATURAL PRESERVE

NORTHSTAR DRIVE

NORTHSTAR STABLE

The most striking feature of the Big Springs Day Lodge, part way up Mount Pluto, is its blue-enameled aluminum roof, designed to take care of snow problems through its forms. On one side it is so steep that snow can not build up on it; this is the "front," where people gather. On the other side the pitch allows snow to slide off to an area never used by people. Before ski trails were selected, studies of sun intensity for every month were made (computer printout, left).

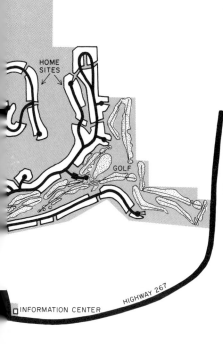

shadow (especially important on ski runs and trails), snow depths, tree species, plant variety, indigenous animals; in sum, of all possible aspects of the ecology—were developed into criteria for physical planning. Visual impact studies proved that buildings could be fitted into the environment without altering it and, indeed, so that they would be invisible from anywhere outside the property. Ski trails and runs can be seen only from the air. Even within the property, no more than three buildings can be seen at a time, and nowhere is an over-all view obtainable. The sense of seclusion belies the density of development (11 units per acre in the condominium area, 48.4 units per acre in the Village). "It is not quite true that no trees were cut down," points out architect Henrik Bull, "but it looks that way." Even eight-inch trees growing beside a doorway's location were saved.

One of the primary design goals was to create a completely pedestrian place and, with remarkable success, the architects have done this. Cars are parked away from the village and condominiums, and everyone walks (or takes one of the two minibuses which run through the area and also meet planes and Amtrak at Truckee, six miles away). Six hundred cars can be parked in a large lot just outside the village, laid out to follow the contours of the site, and well planted with trees that will eventually hide it.

Some 400 condominium units have been built, but the master plan provides for an eventual 3100 units and 585 houses by 1980, and a population of 13,000. Even then—if the original standards of design and planning are maintained—with only 359 of Northstar's 2,560 acres in development and well over 86 per cent of its land in open space, the character of the place is expected to be much as it is today. Since skiing is (and will be) limited to the capacity of lifts, slopes will never be crowded. Condominium owners (or their tenants) have priority over the public in use of the ski slopes, so the present 600-car parking lot outside the village will not be expanded, and parking for the future condominiums will be at their sites. Summer recreation facilities—for swimming and tennis—are under the trees outside the village center. An 18-hole golf course, part of the resort's open space, is in the individual house section.

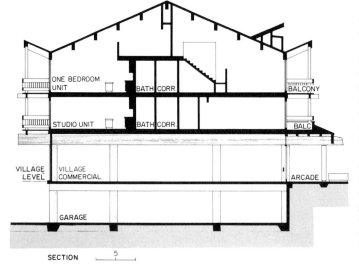

SECTION

Summer or winter, the Village is the center of activity for Northstar, the community's "downtown." Shops and restaurants are on the ground floor of the village buildings (one of these is completed and in use), with an arcade to shelter access to them. Above, European-style, are two floors of condominium units which double as hotel accommodations—studios on the second floor, studios with loft on the third. The grove of trees in the center of the village set the height limit for buildings in this area. Only foot traffic can enter the village; all cars must be parked outside. A ski lift and several trails start at the village. It is designed as a lively, intense place, defined by the buildings and semi-enclosed.

90

Tom Lippert

MALL

PHASE ONE

NORTHSTAR DRIVE

N

50

Designing for snow country

by Henrik Bull, FAIA
Bull Field Volkmann Stockwell,
Architects

It takes more than extra insulation and a larger furnace to design a good, tight building for snow country. The average architect, however, does just that, and even the sophisticated architect makes as grievous errors—using architectural clichés whose relevance to mountain climates is zero, and evidently expecting the weather to adapt to his design, instead of the other way around.

It is surprising how little common sense goes into design for snow country. Everyone knows that melting snow will slide on an inclined surface. But few people give any thought to where that snow will end up, and often it ends up over a doorway, a deck, or a path.

A good first rule for mountain areas is to pitch roofs away from where people are expected to be.

Ice dams, formed at eaves when heat from inside melts snow and sends it coursing down to the cold eave, where it freezes, eventually cause leaks inside or damage to the roof outside.

A good second rule in the mountains, therefore, is to design so ice dams can't form. This is accomplished either by using the European "cold roof"—two separate layers between which outside air flows, preventing heat transfer—or by introducing warm air into the eaves.

A good third rule in snow country is to design for a respectable snow load: at Northstar we used 240 pounds per square foot—far more than previous standards required. Flat roofs—as at Kirkwood (pages 94–95)—can be effective, and sometimes may even be preferable from an engineering standpoint.

NORTHSTAR-AT-TAHOE, California. Site feasibility, land planning: *Eckbo, Dean, Austin & Williams.* Architects: *Bull Field Volkmann Stockwell—Henrik Bull, partner-in-charge; Steven Y. Kodama, project architect; Robert D. Kendorf, construction administration.* Engineers: *Gilbert Forsberg Diekmann & Schmidt* (structural), *Dames & Moore* (soils), *Marion-Cerbatos & Tomasi* (mechanical/electrical). Consultants: *Mountain Marketing Services* (graphics), *The Len Koch Company* (cost), *Fred Schmidt & Associates* (kitchen). Contractor: *Murchison Construction Co.*

WALKWAYS
PINE OR FIR
GROVES

FIRST FLOOR

James K.M. Cheng photos

Northstar's almost completely wooded site presented the architects with a unique opportunity to relate buildings and environment. Condominium buildings, set among tall pines and firs, are all but hidden, and no building is seen in its entirety. Many are only glimpsed through stands of aspen and willow, specially designated for preservation as groves. For minimum disturbance to the terrain, buildings consisting of a varying number and type of units, depending on site conditions, are concentrated in clusters. Modular design of units makes adaptation to the site relatively simple. "We used four plans to create 20 different buildings," says Henrik Bull. "Units can be stacked vertically or linked horizontally as needed. The roofs don't belong to one unit only; we put three-story and two-story units right next to each other and the same roof slope serves both. It is complex in design but simple in construction." Roofs are designed to take a 240-pound snow load, a higher strength than formerly thought necessary, but required to take the very heavy snows of the Sierra. Entrances are located at right angles to pitch of roofs to preclude sliding snow and melting icicles from hitting people. Natural-finish, diagonally-cut cedar boards are used on exterior walls; heavy wood trim is stained brown. Roofs are blue aluminum.

Designing the ski resort base lodge

by Sherwood Stockwell
Bull Field Volkmann Stockwell,
architects

Kirkwood Meadows Lodge at Lake Kirkwood, California, initial building in an entirely new ski area, is a good example of what it takes to get a mountain destination resort into operation. At the moment, Kirkwood has only 60 units of housing, not enough to attract the volume of skiers (it would like 2500) to optimize the potential of the uphill ski facilities. There is always a chicken-and-egg dilemma in a resort of this kind: build the housing first and hope it will sell and thus support the ski area, or build the ski area in the hope that this will encourage others to build the housing. Kirkwood's developers favored the latter, and the two-story day lodge became Phase I of the new resort.

The lodge was designed and built in less than six months, and in operation, while construction of other new resorts was closed down for the winter.

It is a steel frame, single-roof structure supported by three-dimensional trusses tied to steel columns. The truss angles out from the building walls to the edge of the roof, and this sloping plane is glazed to provide a glareless, splendid view of the mountains. The roof is flat, designed for a snow load of 250 pounds per square foot. Melting snow drains off through pipes in warm interior walls so snow cannot slide onto people.

Restroom facilities (with twice as many fixtures for women as for men) are on the lower level.

Because the kitchen must serve a large number of people in a very brief period, we designed it for high efficiency and ample storage space, and located it on the upper level where it could serve both cafeteria and restaurant-bar. We used readily available materials and equipment, because in an out-of-the-way place, replacement can be a big problem. Equally important is the capability to change as the resort expands its operation.

KIRKWOOD MEADOWS LODGE, Lake Kirkwood, California. Architects: *Bull Field Volkmann Stockwell—Sherwood Stockwell, partner-in-charge; H.C. Bruce Jr., project architect.* Engineers: *Hirsch and Gray* (structural), *Marion-Cerbatos & Tomasi* (mechanical/electrical). Contractor: *Brunzell Construction Company.*

KIRKWOOD MEADOWS LODGE

Lake Kirkwood, California
Bull Field Volkmann Stockwell

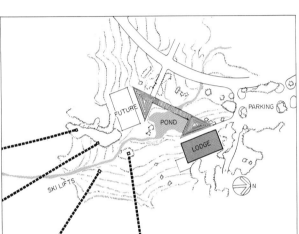

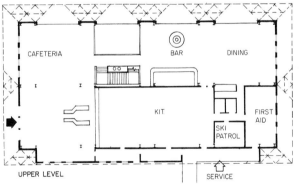

UPPER LEVEL

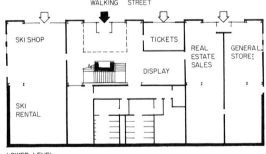

LOWER LEVEL

James K.M. Cheng photos

ELKHORN AT SUN VALLEY

Sun Valley, Idaho
Sasaki Walker and Associates, Killingsworth Brady
and Associates

Elkhorn Valley, a mile and a half south of Sun Valley and just over the saddle of Dollar Mountain, is a sunny, almost windless, completely treeless and —until 1972—untouched place in Idaho, known mostly to skiers and hikers. In 1972, Bill Janss, owner of the Sun Valley Corporation, joined with Johns-Manville Corporation in a plan to develop 2,950 acres of Elkhorn Valley as a new ski resort area to complement the resort at Sun Valley.

Fortunately, Janss and his co-developers were aware of the need to handle such an area with great care. Development at Sun Valley had extended that resort town to its furthest limits as a walking village, and further development would encroach on the character of the place, which, along with its splendid powder snow, had made it an internationally attractive area since 1936 when the Union Pacific Railroad began its development.

Site planners Sasaki, Walker & Associates were called in to master plan the new resort for phased development over a 10-year period. They studied every aspect of the valley's environment—climate, soil structure, geology and soil relationships, topography, vegetation—in order to know how to develop the land and at the same time maintain its natural relationships. A slope inventory was also made and—since the visual quality of the place was of great importance to its success—a visual analysis was made of the views and vistas of the site, from the site, and within the site. From this data, a physical and visual summary was made as the first step toward a conceptual plan for the valley.

To intrude upon the untouched grandeur of this open valley may have seemed a sacrilege, but its openness made it vulnerable and a sure target for development at some time. The decision to make of Elkhorn a human-scaled village within the vast scale of the valley and mountains at once brought it into the context of similar situations in the Alps. Indeed, there is a feeling of a Swiss mountain village in the location of Elkhorn in a valley below a lofty mountain. The man-made village seems tiny, drawn into itself, alone—especially in the snow. What makes it uniquely American and particularly Western American is its containment within, its circumscription by, a space vastly larger than itself and destined to remain so.

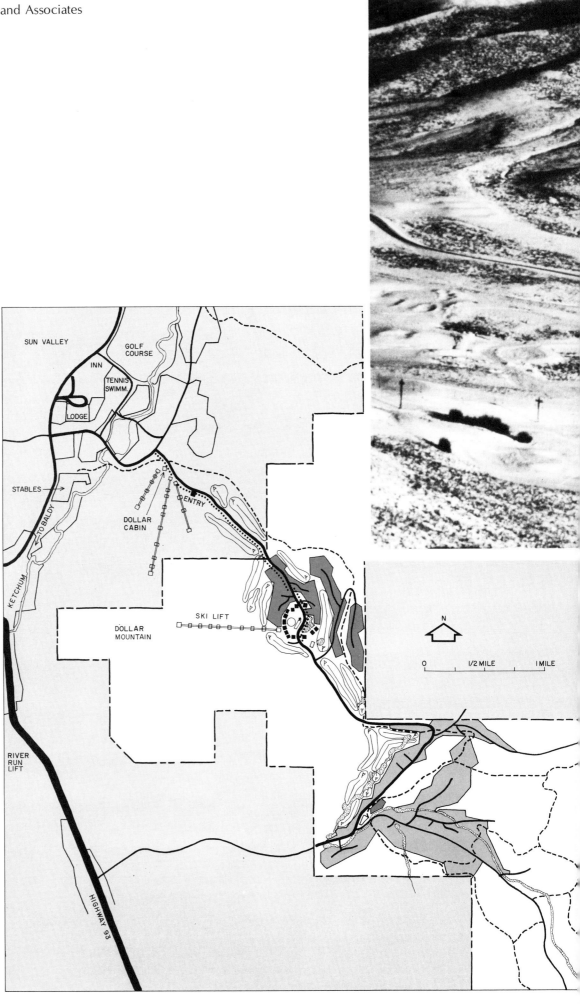

96

Steve Marks

Elkhorn's master plan was developed
by the land planners as part of the
over-all long-range plan for the city of
Sun Valley (left) of which it is a part,
so that the same standards—though
not the same architectural style—will
control development in each. The total
development plan for Elkhorn (right)
shows density of future condominium
development around village center.

CONDOMINIUMS

HOMESITES

PONDS & CREEKS

GOLF COURSE

EQUESTRIAN & HIKING

BIKE PATH

OPEN SPACE & RANCHES

VILLAGE CENTER

At Elkhorn, the view is up to the mountains, rather than, as more frequently happens in this country, from the mountain to a panorama of the valley.

Of the 2,950 acres of Elkhorn's site, only 300 will be covered by buildings. Approximately 400 will be paved and landscaped, and the remainder—75 per cent of the site—will be preserved as natural open space.

In the village center are community and commercial facilities, less extensive than a self sufficient village might require since Sun Valley's older and more extensive commercial development and its two large hotels are easily accessible by car or free bus service.

In developing an architectural expression for this new resort, Killingsworth, Brady & Associates, architects for both condominiums and commercial areas, studied mountain villages in various parts of Europe—not to borrow their forms but to analyze the characteristics which were common to all, and, using these basics, to devise a contemporary and individual style which would be distinct to Elkhorn. The pitched roofs, deep set windows and balconies, and stenciled patterns (in blue) catch the whimsical and the practical aspects of Alpine buildings but look little like them.

"Old villages," says Edward Killingsworth, "aren't precise and well-ordered; they just sort of happen." The analysis by Killingsworth and his associates netted good results: Elkhorn is no self-conscious putting-together of forms for a studied variation, but has a feeling of natural difference which comes from the siting of the groups of condominiums and from disciplined use of materials.

The valley's landmark is the village bell tower, a distinctive form which is the focal point of the village center, marking the location of the community hall. Nearby, and complementing the tower with its strong circular form, is the ice rink, used year-round. Ranged in a semi-circle about the rink is a terrace on which are located shops with condominiums above, and a hip-roofed restaurant building (bottom, right).

When it is completed in 1982, Elkhorn will look only slightly larger than it does now. More condominiums will be built around the village, but private residences and ranches (lots up to two and a half acres) will be located in the "finger valleys" off the big valley, preserving the unity of the village.

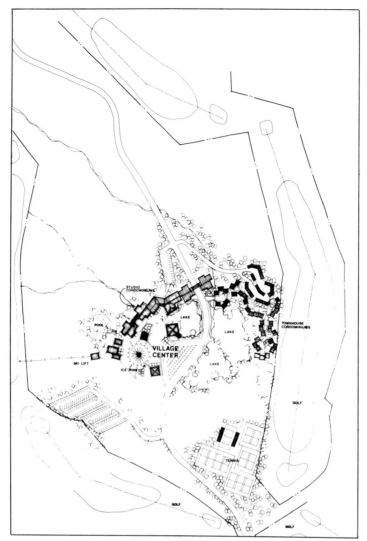

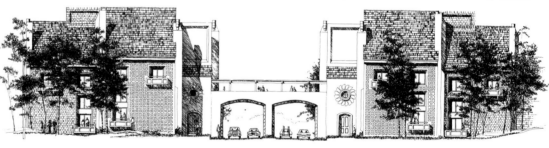

Lars Speyer

The village center concentrates community activity in a small area of shops, restaurants and recreational facilities, like the ice rink (top, across page). Although cars are not permitted in the center, ample parking is provided for visitors and skiers (the Dollar Mountain ski lift is just outside the center) on the periphery. The first phase development (plan, above, left) included the commercial area and village condominiums, Bonne Vie condominiums, the ice rink and some tennis courts. Actual buildings in the village show some changes from the early studies of architectural character, particularly in more formal proposals for Village entrance (above, center sketch), and in use of stencilling on the village buildings. The Bell Tower's strong form dominates the village center and is visible from all parts of the valley.

Designing a modern village with Alpine charm

By Edward A. Killingsworth, FAIA
Killingsworth, Brady & Associates

A new resort town, however small, deserves its own architectural character as much—perhaps more, because it is small and more easily seen—as any larger development. Sun Valley, in the next valley, had chosen years ago to use an eclectic, unspecific European approach for its buildings, but we determined that Elkhorn should be completely modern. We knew, however, that we wanted it to have as much charm as an Alpine village, so we studied European mountain villages and towns, establishing those basic elements that are so universally appealing to people.

Reduced to their basics, many villages—Swiss, Bavarian, Austrian, Italian: it makes little difference—are essentially identical. The towns have many common denominators, all of which contribute to an impression of inviting variety, carefully balanced by great discipline in the use of materials and details: a play of spaces; narrow curving streets, enticing the pedestrian, that spill out into squares; narrow slits between buildings through which shafts of light penetrate; a feeling of containment derived from tall buildings and restricted vistas. All contribute to a comfortable pedestrian scale and to the delight which spells success in any destination resort.

We determined to base our design for Elkhorn on these principles, but to develop only the subtlest resemblance to buildings of earlier periods so that a unique identity could develop for Elkhorn. We adopted and adapted the Tyrol's exterior surface stenciling using our own designs in a bolder contemporary way. (Stenciling proved economical and is easily maintained.) Deep wall recesses and double doors suggest but do not imitate old world details. Steep-pitched roofs became the strongest element in the village, marking it against the stark valley landscape as a place of unique and individual character.

In its initial development, Elkhorn is small, perhaps too small to have the scale needed to make an impact in the beautiful openness that surrounds it and is there forever. As it develops to its full size—1400 condominium units, 700 single-family houses and ranches—that scale will change.

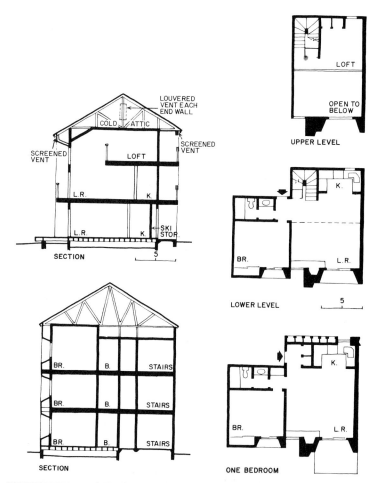

SECTION

SECTION

UPPER LEVEL

LOWER LEVEL

ONE BEDROOM

UPPER LEVEL

MIDDLE LEVEL

LOWER LEVEL

Elkhorn's master plan premises a total of 1400 condominium units (and an overall total of 2100 housing units, including ranches and single-family houses). There are three groups of condominiums: the Village Group (bottom, across page) is European-style, above shops and restaurants. The Bonne Vie (top, across page) is northeast of the Village, across the road from Sun Valley. Another group, Indian Springs (not shown) is northwest of the village. Bonne Vie units have garages as well as open parking; Indian Springs has open parking. Village units have parking on the periphery, near enough but well outside the actual village where no cars are permitted. Warm air is circulated under the pitched roofs of condominium buildings and to the eaves so that snow rarely builds up on them. Icicles do form, however, at roof edges and are removed with long poles (bottom left). Wood shingles, boards and plaster are used on condominium building exteriors.

Lars Speyer photos

Lars Speyer

Master planning land use in an unspoiled mountain valley

By Peter Walker
Sasaki, Walker & Associates
Planners and Landscape architects

The master plan for Elkhorn's development is based on the principle of open space and recreation as primary considerations. The same principle underlies the master plan, also prepared by us, for the city of Sun Valley, of which Elkhorn is a part. The two resorts, just a mile apart although in separate valleys, cannot be considered alone. The impact of one on its environment will inevitably affect the valley location of the other. Sun Valley, the older resort, is much more developed than Elkhorn, which, being newer, is the more fragile of the two. Over 75 per cent of Elkhorn Valley will be permanent open space; the other 25 per cent is in residential and resort use. The golf course which surrounds Elkhorn defines it and links it with the open valley and with the mountains that ring it.

In making the master plan for the city, we made a comprehensive study of future land uses, considering the economic and community goals of Elkhorn and Sun Valley as well as the environment itself. Now we have recommended continuing planning procedures for implementation by the city. As growth continues, transportation—whether by public bus or by car—will be increasingly evident and needs study as to appropriate controls so as to preserve the character of the area. Zoning, subdivision and architectural review and environmental controls are needed for each category of land use. Community facilities—for city hall, library, police, fire and public works services, schools, hospital, cultural activities—will be demanded in time. However much a resort may be a place apart at its beginning, and however limited its growth, it eventually takes on all the requirements of any other type of community. They will have to be provided, but they can be assets, in location and in architecture, if they are expected and planned for in advance of their need.

In planning for the future of these valleys, a sensitive stewardship of the land as a basic resource was, as it must be elsewhere too, our most important premise.

ELKHORN AT SUN VALLEY, Sun Valley, Idaho. Master planners: *Sasaki, Walker & Associates.* Architects: *Killingsworth, Brady & Associates.* Engineers: *Cornell, Howland, Hayes & Merryfield* (structural, Phase I and Village; soils, foundation, mechanical, electrical); *John Jacoby* (structural, Phase II). Consultants: *Barbara Elliot Interiors* (interiors), *William F. Mullen* (cost). Contractors: *Sato Construction Company; Wick Construction Co.*

Places to stay

5

Lodges that

invite Conferences

PLAYBOY RESORT HOTEL

Lake Geneva, Wisconsin
Robert L. Taege and Associates

The Playboy Club Resort is insistently rectilinear and hardedged in its individual forms, with bronze glass areas running from floor to ceiling, "office" style, and with its austere, undecorated right angles rigidly limited to two materials. In this sense the club is intellectualized, urbane, sophisticated; related to the city and suburban associations from which it springs. But in its siting, its landscaping, and particularly in its horizontality and jutting overhangs which hug the ground, the Playboy Club relates to the land, to the rural, attempting to speak of carefree pleasures in the country air. This is a valid combination of associations for this city-born club in this setting; but the combination is difficult to achieve, and is one of the chief successes of the architecture.

Playboy

Harr, Hedrich-Blessing photos

The resort is located in southern Wisconsin, on a large tract of land including a golf course, small lake, riding and tennis facilities, and a private airfield. The main lodge has 300 guest rooms in two symmetrical wings spreading out from the central public facilities, and each of these wings has three rectangular three-floor nodes with stair towers between them (floor plans and schematic, right). Exposed surfaces have been limited to two materials: redwood boarding along the roof edges and most balconies, and exposed aggregate concrete, usually poured-in-place. There is much use of retaining walls and planting terraces in the resort, so that the facade is everywhere jutting out or receding, with trees and shrubbery planted throughout the various levels. This, plus the large panes of glass, often butt-joined with mastic rather than set in mullions, breaks the massiveness of the architecture, making it transparent and open in places.

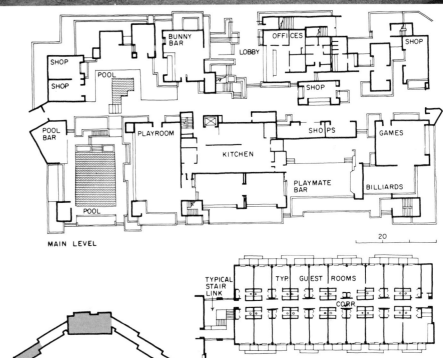

MAIN LEVEL

20

SCHEMATIC PLAN

TYPICAL 2ND & 3RD FLOOR

20

Playboy

KAH-NEE-TA LODGE

Warm Springs, Oregon
Wolff Zimmer Gunsul Frasca Ritter

Kah-Nee-Ta is the latest and largest development of the Confederated Tribes of Warm Springs Indians on their reservation in central Oregon. Funded in part by low-interest loans based on creation of new job opportunities in an underdeveloped area, the lodge is a major investment of the tribes. The clear air and brilliant year-round sunshine of the desert location make it an unfailing attraction to coastal residents used to much fog and rain. The handsome and sophisticated lodge with its 90 rooms, two restaurants and meeting rooms is important both for vacations and for small conferences and conventions. In the vast openness of this region, scale is difficult to determine, and a building needs to be both assertive and at the same time visually and ecologically unobtrusive. The architects for the lodge managed to achieve both objectives. The bold forms are, at a distance, part of the landscape; only on arrival in the court is their strength and boldness to be experienced. The rough wood exterior is painted earthy brown yellow so that the building fits into the landscape with complete composure. The triangular building protects the court from prevailing winds.

KAH-NEE-TA LODGE, Warm Springs, Oregon. Owners: *Confederated Tribes of the Warm Springs Reservation.* Architects: *Wolff Zimmer Gunsul Frasca Ritter—Brooks Gunsul,* partner-in-charge; *Robert Frasca,* partner-in-charge of design; *J. B. Garnett,* associate-in-charge; *Gary Larson,* associate in design. *Pietro Belluschi,* design consultant. Engineers: *Nortec, Inc.,* structural, mechanical and electrical; *Shannon & Wilson, Inc.,* foundation. Consultants: *Heinz Janders,* interior design; *Arvid Orbeck,* graphics. Landscape architect: *Robert Perron.* Contractor: *Lawson Construction, Inc.*

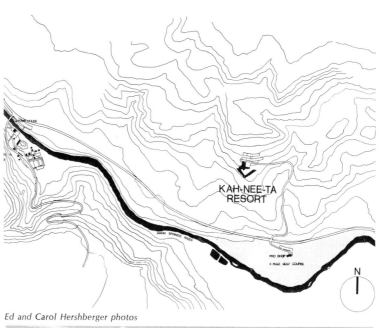

Ed and Carol Hershberger photos

Arrival point at the lodge is a landscaped parking court beside a covered walk that leads to the entrance (top, left). A few steps below and opening off the desk lobby is the lounge (below, right) with its massive fireplace and flying truss. From the lounge a corridor leads to the shop and the long open trestle (center, left) which is one access route to guest rooms; another route is through the pool terrace (top right). The Juniper Room (bottom, left), with an extensive view to the west, is for dining. Round concrete columns support the platform on which the wood frame and heavy timber structure rest. Exterior walls are stained resawn cedar, columns along guest wing balconies are treated peeler logs, and trim is painted orange and yellow. Throughout the lodge are Indian motifs designed by non-Indian artists, since the Warm Springs tribes did not develop an art of their own. The sculptured panels over the fireplace are by Spokane sculptor Harold Balasz.

1 Pool
2 Guest rooms
3 Lower dining
4 Employee dining
5 Mechanical
6 Fireplace lounge
7 Dining
8 Bar
9 Kitchen
10 Deliveries
11 First floor lobby
12 Administrative
13 Gift shop
14 Conference/banquet
15 Second floor lobby
16 Council room
17 Meeting

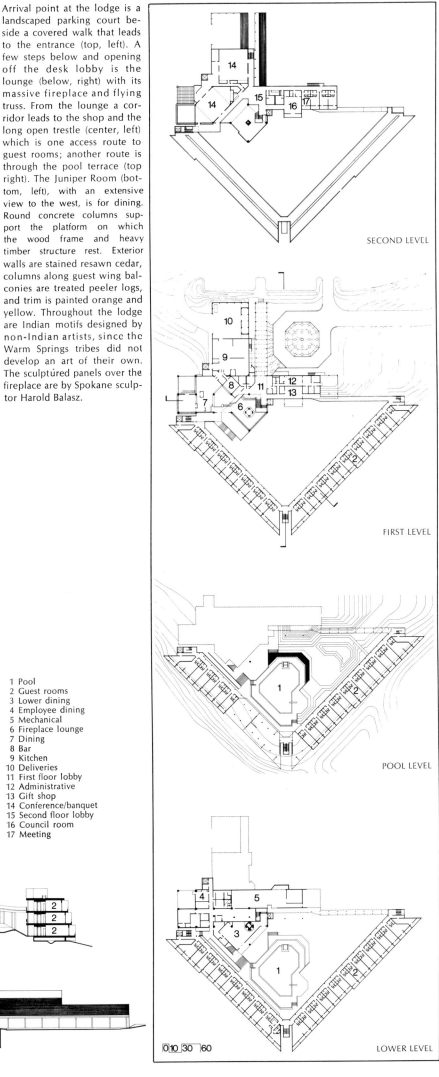

SECOND LEVEL

FIRST LEVEL

POOL LEVEL

LOWER LEVEL

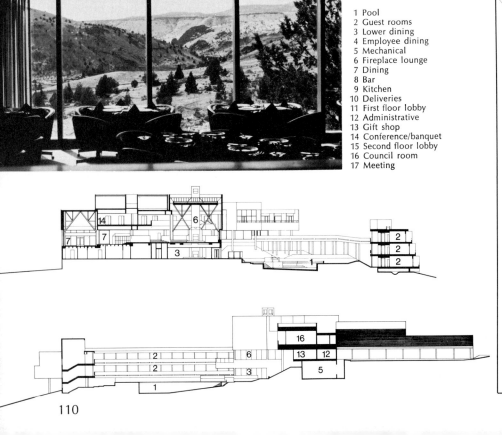

0 10 30 60

ASILOMAR HOTEL AND CONFERENCE GROUNDS

Pacific Grove, California
John Carl Warnecke and Associates

Conference and meeting facilities came first at Asilomar, established by the YWCA over 50 years ago; the hotel operation is recent, dating from the State of California's acquisition in 1956 of the buildings and grounds as a unique part of its chain of beaches and parks. But the early emphasis on conferences has continued to influence plans for Asilomar's growth. The most recent new buildings are three guest lodges and two meeting rooms designed, as were earlier additions and replacements, to fit into the beautiful natural environment with unaffected simplicity and to harmonize in scale and character with the first buildings on the site, for which the late Julia Morgan was the architect. Rooms in the guest lodges are designed to stimulate formal discussion and exchange of ideas: each accommodates four persons; furnishings permit day use as living rooms, and some units have fireplaces. The upper units have balconies, the lower units, decks; all look out to the Pacific Ocean. For larger group discussions and meetings, Triton (for 50 to 75 persons) and Nautilus (150 to 175 persons) are separate buildings equipped for lectures and talks or for lounging. These buildings are closely related by a paved terrace to the guest lodges in accordance with the master plan.

ASILOMAR HOTEL AND CONFERENCE GROUNDS, Pacific Grove, California. Architects: *John Carl Warnecke & Associates*. Structural engineer: *Stefan Medwadowski*. Mechanical engineers: *Eagleson Engineers*. Electrical engineers: *Edward S. Shinn & Associates*. Landscape architects: *John Carl Warnecke & Associates—Michael Painter*, partner in charge. Contractor: *Hampshire Construction Company*.

All photos: Joshua Freiwald

The master plan, drawn up in 1958 by the same firm of architects and periodically reviewed and updated, aims at using the site to its ultimate capacity without diminishing its natural and architectural beauty. Hence more small buildings rather than a few large buildings, for minimum disturbance to trees and site and for preservation of the original scale. Hence, too, important principle of including separate buildings for group meetings in each cluster of housing. Triton (left) and Nautilus (above) are the latest in such facilities. Nautilus, the larger of the two, can be divided by an airwall to provide greater flexibility of use.

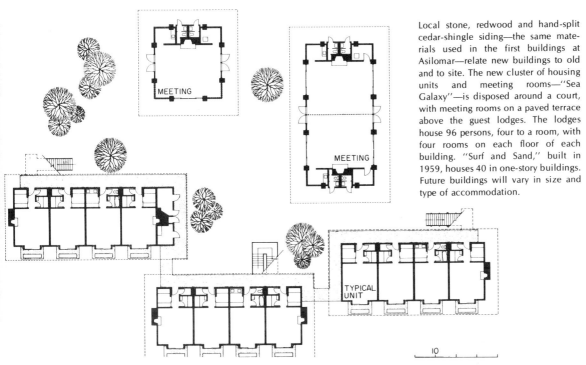

Local stone, redwood and hand-split cedar-shingle siding—the same materials used in the first buildings at Asilomar—relate new buildings to old and to site. The new cluster of housing units and meeting rooms—"Sea Galaxy"—is disposed around a court, with meeting rooms on a paved terrace above the guest lodges. The lodges house 96 persons, four to a room, with four rooms on each floor of each building. "Surf and Sand," built in 1959, houses 40 in one-story buildings. Future buildings will vary in size and type of accommodation.

MEETING

MEETING

TYPICAL UNIT

10

SUNRIVER LODGE

Bend, Oregon
George T. Rockrise and Associates

The architects of Sunriver Lodge combined exposed wood post-and-beam construction, pitched roofs and massive stone fireplaces to provide a warm, vernacular, "styleless" setting. The large roof planes of wood shingles radiate in fan-shaped sequence toward the land, with each change in elevation expressed with clerestory windows. Inside, the spaces intertwine on three floors with the framing often "free-standing" within them, so that the intricacy and informality of the exterior is repeated. Laminated round wood columns, paired laminated wood beams, wood purlins and wood decking are the basic structural ingredients. All wood in the project is rough or resawn, with a natural finish.

SUNRIVER LODGE, Bend, Oregon. Architects: *George T. Rockrise and Associates —James J. Amis, partner-in-charge; J. Matthew Myers,* project manager; *William F. Olin,* job captain. Structural engineers: *GFDS Engineers.* Mechanical/electrical engineers: *G. L. Gendler & Associates.* Landscape architects: *Royston, Hanamoto, Beck and Abey.* Interiors: *Heinz Janders.* Architects for condominium hotel units: *Church and Shiels.*

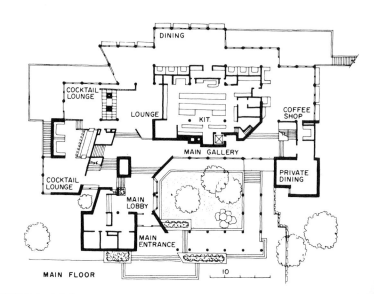

MAIN FLOOR

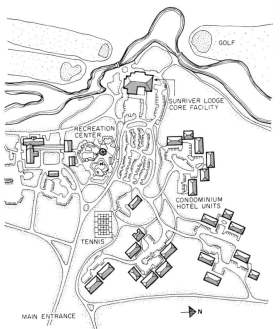

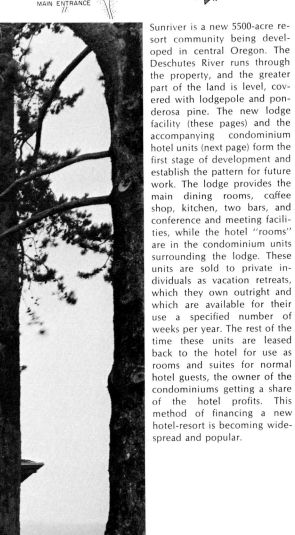

Sunriver is a new 5500-acre resort community being developed in central Oregon. The Deschutes River runs through the property, and the greater part of the land is level, covered with lodgepole and ponderosa pine. The new lodge facility (these pages) and the accompanying condominium hotel units (next page) form the first stage of development and establish the pattern for future work. The lodge provides the main dining rooms, coffee shop, kitchen, two bars, and conference and meeting facilities, while the hotel "rooms" are in the condominium units surrounding the lodge. These units are sold to private individuals as vacation retreats, which they own outright and which are available for their use a specified number of weeks per year. The rest of the time these units are leased back to the hotel for use as rooms and suites for normal hotel guests, the owner of the condominiums getting a share of the hotel profits. This method of financing a new hotel-resort is becoming widespread and popular.

Edmund Y. Lee photos

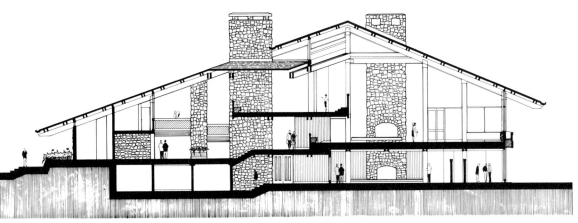

115

Above is one of the condominium units at Sunriver, with the lodge building in the background. At left is the main lounge space in the lodge, running through two floors, and below is an interior of one of the condominium units, which becomes a hotel room during most weeks of the year. Materials are similar in both the lodge and the condominiums.

SALISHAN LODGE

Gleneden Beach, Oregon
John Storrs

The Lodge at Salishan—a residential and recreational development on the coast of Oregon—looks, as its owners and their architect intended, "as if it had been dropped into the woods." The lodge buildings belong to the site in an easy, natural way, enhanced by the use of one material—wood, 1.5 million board feet of it, in various forms—in one color, throughout, detailed simply in the nature of the material. It is incredible that their actuality represents a total time lapse, from design contract to completion, of only 11 months.

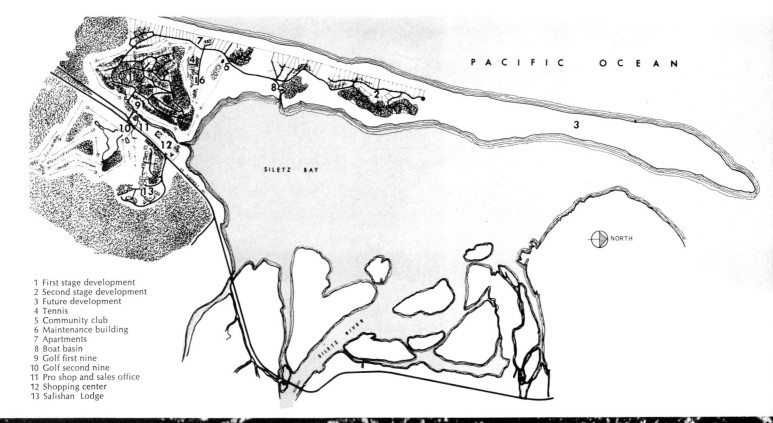

PACIFIC OCEAN

SILETZ BAY

SILETZ RIVER

NORTH

1 First stage development
2 Second stage development
3 Future development
4 Tennis
5 Community club
6 Maintenance building
7 Apartments
8 Boat basin
9 Golf first nine
10 Golf second nine
11 Pro shop and sales office
12 Shopping center
13 Salishan Lodge

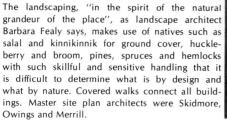

The landscaping, "in the spirit of the natural grandeur of the place", as landscape architect Barbara Fealy says, makes use of natives such as salal and kinnikinnik for ground cover, huckleberry and broom, pines, spruces and hemlocks with such skillful and sensitive handling that it is difficult to determine what is by design and what by nature. Covered walks connect all buildings. Master site plan architects were Skidmore, Owings and Merrill.

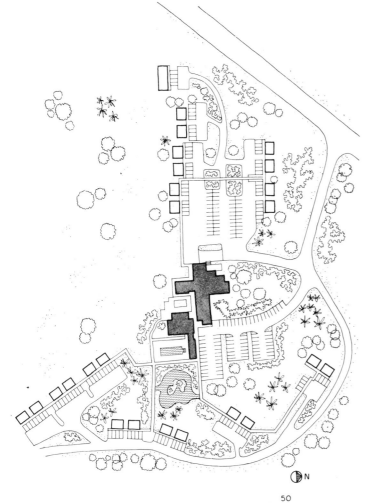

N

50

The Lodge

Salishan Lodge, part of a 600-acre ocean front development on the central Oregon coast, consists of 14 buildings: the main lodge building with the public rooms and convention facilities, 12 eight-unit guest room buildings and one four-unit apartment building. Six of these buildings flank the main building on rolling hills to the north and south; the rest form a formal court in front. As many of the existing trees as possible were saved, and these—spruces, firs, hemlocks and pines—tower over the low-pitched roofs of the guest units. In such a setting, wood is a highly appropriate material and, as used here, attains the rare combination of naturalness and sophistication. Exterior walls are rough sawn board-and-batten, the vertical lines complementing the trees around the buildings; balcony enclosures are faced with exterior plywood, also rough sawn; hemlock columns supporting the deck outside the bar are octagonal in shape; roofs are covered with cedar shakes. Some of the details were worked out on the spot with craftsmen on the job, some were craftsmen's inspirations, but everything is straightforward, honest, without pretense. "What we have tried to do," says John Storrs, the architect, "is to take this piece of ground and leave it the way it is, relative to nature. Nature and the presence of greenery and trees are neglected factors in resort planning, yet these are the very things that give a sense of relaxation. I don't know whether what we have done is an architecture of restraint or of boldness. Perhaps it is a combination of both."

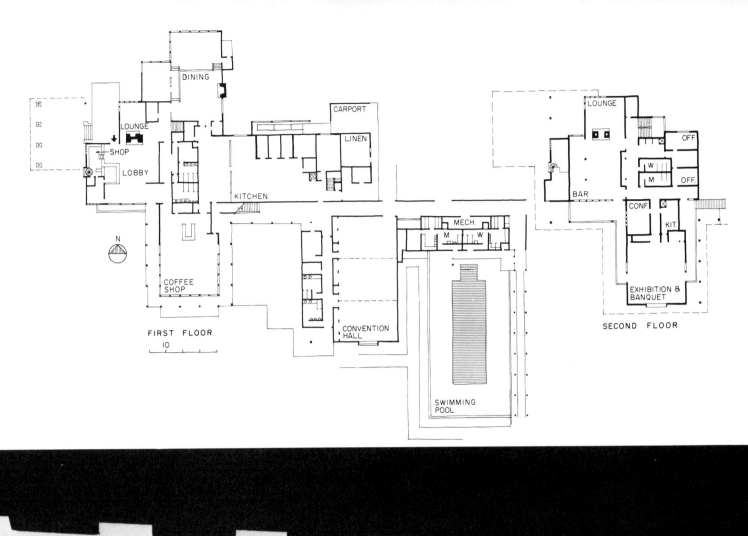

DINING

CARPORT

LINEN

LOUNGE

SHOP

LOBBY

KITCHEN

N

COFFEE
SHOP

MECH.

M   W

CONVENTION
HALL

SWIMMING
POOL

FIRST FLOOR

10

LOUNGE

BAR

CONF.

OFF.

W
M

OFF.

KIT.

EXHIBITION &
BANQUET

SECOND FLOOR

Art as an integral part of Salishan's design was a major premise of the architect. In addition to a collection of paintings and prints for display in the public areas of the Lodge, four major works of art by Northwest artists were commissioned as part of the building. Included among these are the mural screen behind the bar (left) by Eugene Bennett and the carved wood panels in the dining room by LeRoy Setziol. Globes on the bar chandelier are Japanese glass floats picked up on nearby beaches; other furnishings in the bar were designed by Henry Janders. The Lodge entrance is from the *porte cochère* (opposite page).

Public rooms

The public rooms—dining and banquet rooms, bar, and coffee shop—are in the main Lodge building, accessible to travelers along U.S. Highway 101 (which bisects the Salishan property just below the Lodge) and central to the guest units. Since the Lodge site is a promontory 70 feet above the highway, most rooms have superb views, over Siletz Bay to the ocean, over the golf course, or over the wooded Salishan development to the ocean. Large glass areas in all rooms take advantage of these views, and make the natural beauty of the surrounding area a part of the experience of each room. The three-level dining room looks out to the wooded entrance road and the bay and ocean beyond; the coffee shop overlooks the golf course, Salishan Lake and the mountains to the south; the bar looks both south across the golf coure and north to the ocean and the bay. The lobby's end wall opens to the golf course. Except for the lobby and the coffee shop where acoustical plaster is used for the ceiling, and the dining room where the upper walls are of plaster, the interiors are of wood—paneled, board and batten, tongue and groove. Two other public rooms on the second floor provide for special occasions: the board room, for small dinner parties or for meetings, and the gallery, designed for exhibitions, displays, meetings and movies as well as for banquets. Earth colors used in all rooms were chosen to complement the wood paneling and ceilings. A large meeting room for conventions adjoins the main Lodge building.

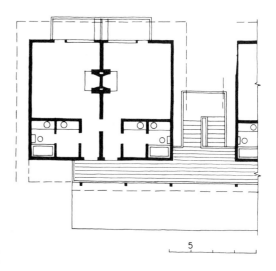

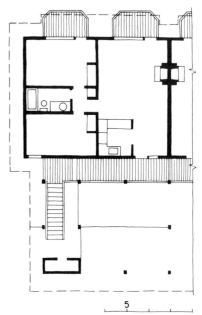

5

5

Guest rooms

The Lodge has 100 guest rooms in 13 separate two-story build-ings connected by covered walkways to the main building. Twelve of these contain eight units each; the thirteenth has four apartment units, each with two bedrooms. A central stairway divides each buildng; parking for each unit is provided in the carport which is part of each building. Individual balconies, with rails of weathering steel, and fireplaces in each unit are special features. Prefabrication reduced construction time for each building to seven weeks.

SALISHAN LODGE, Gleneden Beach, Oregon. Developers: *Salishan Properties, Inc.* Architect: *John Storrs.* Structural engineer: *James G. Pierson.* Mechanical engineer: *Keith Kruchek.* Electrical engineers: *Athay and Nonus.* Landscape architect: *Barbara V. Fealy.* Interiors: *Henry Janders, Dohrmann Company.* General contractor: *A. J. Bennett.*

PLANNING SUCCESSFUL RESORT HOTELS

by Alan H. Lapidus

A guest's image of any hotel is created not only by what he sees but by what he never sees—the "back of the house" service areas which make it all happen. Here Architect Alan H. Lapidus of Morris Lapidus Associates, Architects, offers some guidelines for the planning of those very important areas.

The resort hotel, like Janus, wears two faces. The paying customer sees only the "front of the house", and this must be all that he desires—a wish fulfillment, an ego builder, a status symbol, and the promise (and perhaps fulfillment) of great delight. The "front of the house" comprises every area that he will see: lobbies, dining spaces, rest rooms, bathers' passages, passenger elevators, hotel rooms, etc. These spaces must be handled and laid out with one thought in mind, the convenience and continued approbation of the guest.

But the "back of the house" is where all that makes this happen takes place. These are the areas of burnishing, butchering, baking; of boilers and many other functions. The guest never sees this but these unseen spaces will precisely determine his degree of contentment. These are the areas that will ultimately dictate whether the hotel will run at a profit or a loss.

Let us presuppose a hotel located in a thriving but not overdeveloped resort area, an architecture suitably superb—or suitably ghastly—to attract the clientele (either extreme will generally succeed; it is mediocrity that founders) and a competent top echelon management.

The "back of the house" must be laid out with two paramount objectives: control and efficiency. Control is crucial because pilfering is a real problem and improper design resulting in incomplete control can cripple or kill the operation. Take the case of a large chain that opened the first sizable hotel on a little Caribbean island several years ago. The building was finished, the employees had had several weeks of pre-opening training, but the hotel could not open on schedule: there simply was not enough of the new silverware left. Several changes in service area layout were made, the local constabulary called on employees at their homes and requested return of the "borrowed" flatware—and the situation was corrected. Liquor, meats, dry goods, linens and housekeeping supplies are all items that most people have need of in their homes; and maids, dishwashers, busboys, laundresses etc. are not the best compensated people in the labor market. The pilferage problem in hotel operation should never be underestimated.

The second objective is efficiency. Inefficiency results in two people doing a job that could be done by one person, thereby increasing the operating overhead of the hotel by the yearly salary of that person. It also results in the delay of or detriment to service to a guest. An employee who has to travel a maze of passages to accomplish his job is being paid for spending a lot of time walking. A poor layout results in lost time, effort, tempers and customers.

What is the flow diagram for a typical "back of the house"? First, the service entrance is located out of the view of the main entrance to the hotel but with direct access onto a road capable of handling truck traffic. It should have a loading dock—covered, to protect it from the weather. (Food, laundry and supplies will be off-loaded and stored on this dock and should not get rain-soaked while waiting to be checked in.)

All personnel will enter the hotel at this point. At least two small offices should be located here, for the steward (or receiving) and the timekeeper. Outside the steward's office is a floor scale to check the weights of the produce as it enters. If the food storage and preparation kitchens are located on a different level, a sidewalk lift or conveyor belts should be provided here. The timekeeper checks the employees in and out and makes certain that everyone stays honest. Immediately past the timekeeper, the employees should be separated into two different traffic flows: one for food service personnel, the other for everyone else. (It is advisable to provide separate locker facilities for these two types of personnel.) Once food service personnel enter their traffic flow they have no contact (with the obvious exception of waiters) with either guests or other house personnel. The reason is simply security. If there is any deep dark secret of successful hotel service design, it is a built-in security system. Uniform issue is related to the housekeeper, the housekeeper to the laundry room, and the laundry room to the soiled linen room; the soiled linen room, connected by vertical linen chute, to a service room on every typical floor; and every typical floor connected by service elevator(s) that open to the aforementioned service rooms and also to the service entrance, convenient to the scrutinizing gaze of the steward and the timekeeper.

For convenience, the trash chute from the typical floor service area is located next to the linen chute. The trash room must therefore be located next to the soiled linen room and, for ease of pick-up, near the service entrance. Depending on the size of the hotel and the frequency of trash pick-up, this room may be equipped with a trash compactor or some other such implement of destruction. The garbage room should be located somewhere near the trash room (ideally, opening directly onto the loading dock). It should be refrigerated and either have space for, or be in immediate proximity to, a can wash area with floor drain and hose bib.

The boiler room usually has a direct escape to the outside and, for ease of maintenance and repair, should be located near the service entrance. The boiler flue, extending to the top of the hotel tower, is usually located in the main vertical circulation core and its location, therefore, is important at the earliest stages of design. If there is enough height in the service floor to breach the flue horizontally, the problem is somewhat mitigated, but usually not without objections from the structural and mechanical engineers.

Telephone equipment, electrical and air-conditioning equipment rooms can be handled more flexibly than the other service areas, but their size and locations vary according to the size and location of the hotel.

The employees' cafeteria, generally a steam table-grill operation, should be located near the kitchen and as close to the employees' locker room as possible. Access should preclude passing through the food service area.

Before delving into the intricacies of the workings of the food service and laundry, let me comment on the services of the specialists who will actually lay out and design the equipment in these areas. They don't *really* need that much space. They will swear a mighty oath that they do, and will conjure up visions of irate chefs stalking off the premises and laundresses working overtime shifts, but they can really do with less. Believe me. However, before one can hope to cope with the specialist, it is necessary to understand how these spaces operate.

After comestibles have been weighed in, checked, and signed for, they are sent to either dry storage or liquor storage (a room with a big lock on it) or to one of the various cold holding rooms or boxes. If the hotel does its own butchering it is necessary to know what size cuts it buys (halves, quarters, etc.) and it may be necessary to provide ceiling rails to transport them. Meats, fish, dairy, bakery products, frozen foods etc. all require different cold facilities. Since these boxes require heavy insulation, slab sinkages will be required in these areas. If these are not provided, the floor of the box will have to be ramped—but the person who has to push a heavy cart up this ramp will curse the architect for all the days of his life. An alternate method, if the exact sizes will not be known until later, is to depress the entire slab and build up the rest of the floor with lightweight fill.

Any resort worthy of its credit cards will have one main restaurant, *at least* one specialty restaurant, a night club with a dinner show, and a bar where sandwiches and/or snacks will be available. It will also have that service—beloved of guest and hated by manager—room service. Most resort hotels these days also have convention facilities which entail feeding large numbers of people the same meal at the same time. If that meal turns out to be semi-congealed chicken-a-la-king the hotel has lost that convention group forever.

From kitchen storage, food goes to the prep kitchen to be prepared for final cooking in the main kitchen. The main kitchen actually consists of several kitchens (and must have a flue extending to the top of the building lest the guest get an odoriferous foretaste of his next meal). The specialty restaurant(s) and the main restaurant will have their own kitchens and their own chefs but these should all be located within the same general area. ("Kitchen" refers to a cooking line with its back storage tables, reach-in boxes, work areas etc.) The "common" areas that all of the kitchens can use are the dishwash, pot wash, salad set-ups and dessert set-up (waiters usually set up desserts such as ice cream, cakes, etc.). The dishwashing area should be located near the door of the kitchen so that the waiter or busboy can enter, drop off the dirty dishes, and get out again without walking through the cooking area. This is, however, a noisy area and it should be sound-baffled.

Cooking for banquets is usually done in the main kitchen and then brought to a banquet or "holding kitchen", equipped with banks of ovens where food is kept hot until served. De-

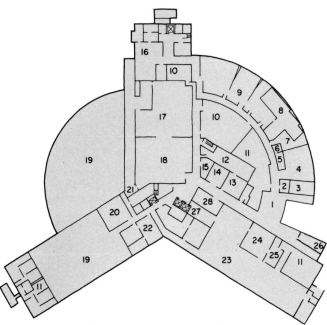

Service area for a large resort hotel—Paradise Island Hotel on Paradise Island, Bahamas (Morris Lapidus Associates, architects). 1. Loading dock. 2. Receiving steward. 3. Garbage, refrigerator and can wash. 4. Trash. 5 Purchasing agent. 6. Steward. 7. Liquor storage. 8. Cold boxes. 9. Prep kitchens. 10. Employees' cafeteria. 11. Toilets. 12. Lockers. 13. Lockers (upper echelon). 14. Transformer room. 15. Switch gear. 16. Bakery. 17. Mechanical equipment. 18. Boiler. 19. Storage. 20. Maintenance shop. 21. Locksmith. 22. Switch gear. 23. Laundry. 24. Housekeeper. 5. Uniform issue. 26. Timekeeper. 27. Soiled linen. 28. Trash collection.

pending on the size of the operation, this kitchen may also have its own dishwashing equipment. Other facilities include reach-in boxes, set-up areas, and storage areas. Hot and cold carts are another means of servicing a smaller banquet facility. Both methods require direct access between main kitchen and banquet area.

There is usually a service bar for alcoholic beverages in the general area of the kitchen. As the waiter leaves the kitchen he must pass a checker who verifies that what has been billed is being served and that only food that has been billed is walking out of the kitchen. The checker's station is always located immediately inside the door between kitchen and dining area. The head chef should have his office in the main kitchen area, in an office with enough glass to permit visual control over the kitchen operation. In addition, silver storage and burnishing room must be under his visual control.

Room service should work from the main kitchen area, with direct access to the service elevator. It has its own checker and it may have its own "kitchen" usually consisting of a generous amount of grill. (Breakfast is the most popular room service meal.) Storage and setting up room service carts—these take up considerable space—must be provided.

It is evident from this cursory survey that all the food facilities of the hotel, from the coffee shop to Old Watashi's Polynesian Luau Room, must feed directly from the main kitchen without going through tortuous service corridors or across public areas. With this flow line, food can be requisitioned from storage to the kitchen and go through just one control.

The laundry size will depend upon such diverse factors as the number of people who will use the pool or water facilities (beach towels); whether tablecloths are used for lunch and breakfast; whether there is a health club (towels again); and how many employees there are (uniforms). The main concerns in allocating space for this facility are the enormous amount of ventilation required, the large headroom required over items such as a ten roll ironer, and the fact that circulation within the laundry is by means of large heavy carts. (*No ramps here; avoid columns in the aisles.*)

The principal items in a laundry are the washers, extractors, dryers, ironers, sorting rooms and the folding areas. There must also be linen and uniform storage, a sewing area, a dry cleaning area and a spot cleaning area. The housekeeper's office is

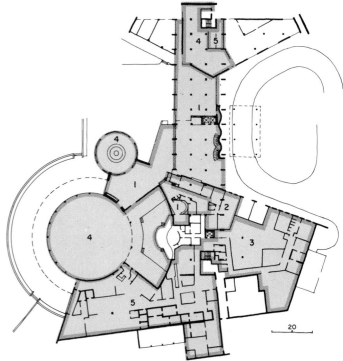

Main floor of the Jamaica Hilton Hotel (Morris Lapidus Associates, architects), Jamaica, B.W.I. 1. Public area. 2. Administration. 3. Support personnel. 4. Restaurant (or cocktail bar). 5. Kitchen.

always located in this area and, like the head chef, she should be situated so as to maintain visual control.

There are other areas in the back of the house, repair shops, locksmith, administration, miscellaneous storage and so forth but the items set forth above are the prime space determinants. They must be set up in a certain pattern and that pattern will set the plan for the front of the house.

When a guest enters the hotel lobby (and there should never be confusion as to where the entrance is) he should be overwhelmed by a feeling of serenity—*or* enchantment, *or* revulsion —but *never* confusion. The registration desk and the elevators should be immediately apparent. The registration area should consist of the front desk, behind which is a clerk, behind whom is the key and mail rack, behind which are various administrative spaces. At one end of the desk (and partitioned off from the rest of it) is the cashier and next to this is the valuables room, a separate room where the guest is given a safe deposit box. After filling his box with jewelry, cash or other valuables, the guest hands the box to the cashier who locks it away.

The main administrative area usually backs up to the desk but the type and amount of space for this depends solely on the management. The telephone board is located here. The restaurants, bars and other *divertissements* should be either visible from or well indicated in the lobby area.

If the hotel has a casino, local regulations will determine how visible or accessible it may be. In Las Vegas the idea is to force *all* circulation through the casino whereas in Puerto Rico the casino is only open during certain hours and there are strict regulations as to how obvious the gaming may be. Nonetheless, the ironclad relationship here is that the casino entrance should be immediately opposite the night club entrance. The psychology is simple. After being entertained by the stars of stage and screen, the patron walks out of the night club and practically falls into the casino. He thereupon sees the glitter of the wheel, hears the click of the dice, remembers how Bond did it in Casino Royale and immediately blows the egg money.

A bathers' passage should be provided from the elevators to the pool or beach. This is so that clothed dry guests do not have to associate with half-naked, wet and oily guests. In designing the pool deck do not forget the little nicety of making sure that a large shadow does not fall across it. Most pool decks containing the shadow of the hotel at 2:00 P.M. have pools with the architects at the bottom. Since the main occupation at any pool deck is sunning rather than swimming, a generous area must be allocated for chaises. These are large and it is a good idea to overestimate space for them. If at all possible the pool should be oriented so that the diving board does not face the afternoon sun. A bar and snack bar for the pool deck should be provided and access to the coffee shop should be from the pool deck as well as from the public spaces of the hotel.

The typical floors of a hotel are strictly a matter of budget and esthetics. The module for the floor set up (and thus for the building) is based on the fact that a maid can make up 12 to 14 rooms per day. (It is inadvisable operationally to have a maid make up six rooms on one floor and five on another.) A normal double-loaded hotel tower is at least 60 feet wide (minimums are 17 feet clear living space from outside window to bathroom wall, 10 feet for bathroom and closets, 6 feet for a hall). A typical floor should have a number of interconnecting rooms (soundproof connecting doors) and some rooms that by size, configuration and furniture can be combined into suites of various sizes. However, for the most efficient hotel design every room should have a fully equipped bathroom so it may be rented as a separate room. A room furnished as a living room should have convertible beds instead of couches. Thus every room is a "key." (In hotel parlance rentable rooms are called "keys" and a two-room suite where the rooms cannot be rented separately is only one "key".)

The service area on the typical floor is located near the vertical circulation core (service elevator, dirty linen and trash chutes). The service area also contains space for storage of the service carts (one per maid), a slop sink and storage for clean linens, towels and supplies. Walls of rooms that adjoin the elevator core should be sound proofed.

And now that I have lovingly laid out the principles of practical hotel layout let me stress that all generalizations, including this one, are false. Depending upon the terrain, the view, the solar orientation and the size of the property many of these guidelines may have to be stretched.

At the Conquistador Hotel on the eastern tip of Puerto Rico, the program was to enlarge an existing 90-room hotel with minimal facilities by adding 300 more rooms and full public facilities, including convention ball rooms and a casino. The site was a steep mountain with no available flat areas but an incredible view. A high rise building was deemed inappropriate and the operation of the existing hotel could not be interrupted during construction. The solution was to break most of the rules. A large portion of the hotel, including the pool and pool deck, 70 hotel rooms, a bar, kitchen and outdoor dining, was located in a fold of the terrain halfway down the mountain. The only way to reach this complex is by an aerial tram and a cable railway. This means that all foods, linens and supplies have to be brought down this way and garbage, trash, etc. have to be removed this way. The total number of employees per guest is high and operational problems are legion. However, these considerations are secondary because of the unique layout which attracts guests at premium rates, thus insuring a successful operation. Which is, after all, what it is all about.

Rules are for the ideal. If you can take advantage of a special situation or create spatial excitement by bending or breaking these rules, do so. Just be aware of the consequences, and be sure the owner concurs the result will be worth it.

Part Two
Places to eat,

Restaurants and bars have always been
stage sets—whether places to see and
be seen or romantic hiding places.
But only fairly recently, with some few
notable exceptions, have they been
deliberately *designed* as stage sets.
Not only convenience and functional
comfort, but a setting which provides
a sense of occasion—whether it's
"fast food" with the kids or New Year's
Eve at a nightclub—are increasingly
required for any establishment to
compete effectively in the increasingly
competitive world of restaurants, bars
and clubs.

drink enjoy!

Places to eat, drink, enjoy!

1
Restaurants

& Bars

RESTAURANT

Toronto Squash Club
Neish, Owen, Rowland & Roy

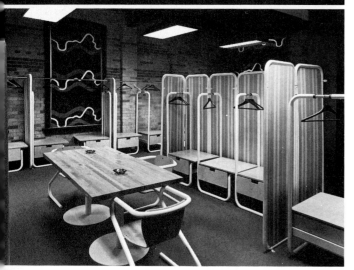

The owner of two four-story brick buildings and an adjoining vacant lot commissioned the architects to design a squash club using the existing structures for lounge, locker and restaurant space, then integrating these with a new building containing squash courts constructed on the vacant lot.

The main entry is at the first floor of the new structure and gives access to the 400-seat viewing gallery that overlooks two exhibition courts which are fitted with large, back-wall viewing panels. There are two additional floors of courts on levels 2 and 3 above and these include 15 American singles courts, one English singles court (dimensionally different) and one doubles court. Connected to these playing facilities, but occupying renovated space in the existing structures, are a restaurant (with separate entrance), lockers, lounge spaces and other support facilities (see plans).

The program was unusual and its requirement for blending old and new into a coherent unity was a challenge the architects gladly assumed. The result is an interior that is not only functionally efficient but visibly unified—this in spite of the disparate elements the architects began with and in spite of the radically different requirements placed on each kind of space by the program itself. The interiors, though not glamorous, achieve an even level of design concern throughout and seem to convey quite clearly that fun and physical exertion are elements that can be contained and given suitable design expression.

TORONTO SQUASH CLUB, Toronto, Canada. Architects: *Neish, Owen, Rowland & Roy—William J. Neish, partner-in-charge; Peter Manson-Smith, project designer.* Contractor: *Camston Ltd.*

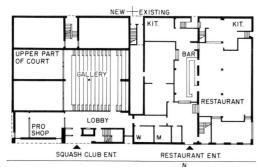

FIRST FLOOR

SECOND FLOOR

Panda Associates photos

NOODLES RESTAURANT

Toronto
C. Blakeway Millar

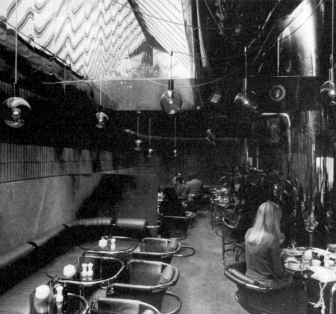

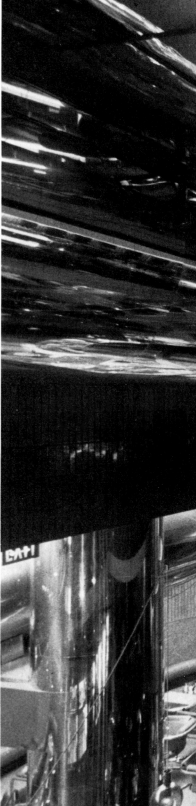

Noodles Restaurant, in midtown Toronto, is a shimmering space that awakens dulled senses and excites the imagination. Stainless steel cladding on columns and ductwork reflect fractured images back to the viewer and a mirrored ceiling, hung on a T grid, compounds the visual perplexity. Downstairs, a cook prepares food at a stainless steel servery right in the midst of diners who sit at individual tables or at long banquettes. The carpet is a bright orange and is turned up at the wall to meet a finish of handmade Canadian tile. Concealed fluorescent lighting, marking the junction of wall and hung ceiling, washes the tile in soft, colored light that changes in both intensity and character at different times of day. Additional lighting is provided by pendant globes over the tables downstairs. Chairs and banquette upholstery is brown leather, legs and arm rests are chrome-plated.

The richness of detail and finish combined with imaginative lighting make Noodles a favorite with a luncheon clientele that includes many advertising executives who work in the area. Open from noon until the early morning hours, the restaurant offers an atmosphere of easy elegance that enchants diners and urges them to linger.

NOODLES RESTAURANT, Toronto, Canada. Architect and interior designer: *C. Blakeway Millar-Robert Taylor, project manager.* Contractor: *J. Faion.*

AMERICAN RESTAURANT

Kansas City
Warren Platner Associates

Few architects work more elegantly in interior design than Warren Platner, and his American Restaurant, in Kansas City, mingles opulence with elements of fantasy to create his most striking and theatrical dining space to date. The restaurant is a glass-walled penthouse atop a building by Edward Larrabee Barnes and overlooks Crown Center. The dining space is spatially expressed as a group of three dining pavilions and a fourth that houses a reception area and services. The pavilions are articulated by changes in floor level and by decorative ceiling canopies in floral forms that also conceal a myriad of clear-filament lamps that provide a low but pleasant level of illumination for dining. Some tables are lighted directly by brass domes and others by theater lights set in the ceiling that wash diners (photo, bottom left) in a scatter pattern reminiscent of falling petals. Similar fixtures throw sprays of light against the oak window shutters.

Upholstery colors in the banquette and alcove seating are red, pink and indigo. Painted plaster wall surfaces are ivory cream, and the carpet is a bronze gold. The level of detail throughout is exquisite.

Some readers may find the whole space overworked—too rich for their particular tastes—but Platner set out to create a pleasure dome and this he has done with enormous skill. The American Restaurant is a place of enchantment, a place where routine concerns can be suspended, where the frictions and abrasions of day-to-day living can be momentarily soothed in an atmosphere of fine food and fantasy.

AMERICAN RESTAURANT, Kansas City, Missouri. Architects: *Warren Platner Associates—David Connell, project architect; Jill Mitchell, graphics; Allan Stadler, construction documents; Lee Ahlstrom, furnishings.* Contractor: *Eldridge & Sons Construction Company, Inc.*

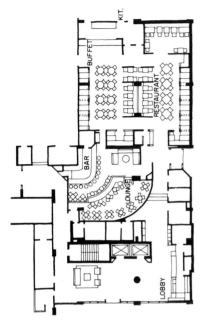

The owners of this Kansas City motor inn commissioned the Urban Architects to renovate the inn's main dining and entertaining areas. The first challenge was to accomplish the renovation with as little interruption to normal hotel service as possible. Second, and more difficult, the architects had to plan the space so that it could be bright and cheerful in the morning when it serves as a coffee shop and more relaxed and intimate in the evening for quiet dining. The architects attacked this problem directly and simply. They selected reflective finish surfaces and then provided variable lighting levels carefully keyed to these surfaces. By adjusting the lighting levels, finish surfaces—as well as dinner- and glass-ware—either sparkle or become subdued. Mirrors, mounted on the side walls over the booths, contribute to this process and also serve to extend the space visually.

Colors are generally dark and restrained: rich brown leather for seating, brown and black for carpeting, black laminate on table tops. The generous application of light wood trim, occasional panels of red felt and a warm reflective character keep this elegant space from ever becoming overly somber.

DOWNTOWNER MOTOR INN, Kansas City, Missouri. Owner: *Downtowner Corporation.* Architects: *Urban Architects (Stephen Abend, partner-in-charge).* Mechanical engineers: *Smith & Boucher.* Contractor: *Jenkins & Blaine Construction Company.*

DOWNTOWNER MOTOR INN

Kansas City, Missouri
Urban Architects

Paul Kivett photos

Alexandre Georges photos

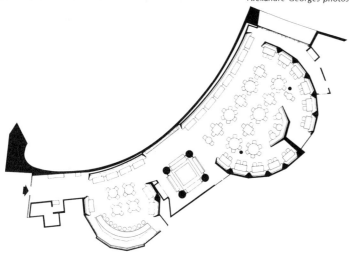

LE MONDE RESTAURANT

TWA Terminal, JFK Airport, New York City
Warren Platner with Kevin Roche and John Dinkeloo

Fine food and drink are the things here and the visual character is made of these elements, their preparation, and the furnishings and fittings necessary to properly enjoy them.

The vocabulary of materials is simple: clear glass and mirrors, polished stainless steel, natural leather, and myriad custom-designed lighting fixtures set in a plaster ceiling. Carpets are dark red. Deeply-absorbing wool tapestries, designed by the architect in collaboration with Sheila Hicks, flank the back bar (photo, right). The space and its forms flow together into near fantasy compounded of softly fractured images and reflected detail (photo, top of page). TWA wanted a warm, rich, intimate ambiance for dining and drinking. They got it with little more than the necessary functional elements splendidly conceived and elegantly detailed. Mechanical engineers: *Jaros, Baum & Bolles;* contractor: *Hennigan Construction Co.*

The restaurant won an award in Record Interiors of 1971.

BOSTON MADISON SQUARE GARDEN CLUB

Keith Kroeger and Leonard Perfido

Bill Matts photos

Two problems faced architects Keith Kroeger and Leonard Perfido when they were commissioned to redesign the Boston Madison Square Garden Club at the Boston Garden Arena. First, they had to solve the functional problems involved in more than doubling the size of the original club into space formerly occupied by Arena offices and a concessions commissary. Secondly, and more important, they had to retain the flavor of the club, a gathering place for members attending events at the Boston Arena for more than forty years. Materials and furnishings were chosen carefully. The ash boards and chair frames are lightly stained to accent the grain. The chairs, banquettes and the bar arm rest are upholstered in stretch vinyl. Natural linen covers the wall panels and green wool carpeting continues up the front of the bar (right). Engineers: *LeMessurier and Associates,* structural; *Reardon and Turner,* mechanical. Contractor: *Turner Construction Co.*

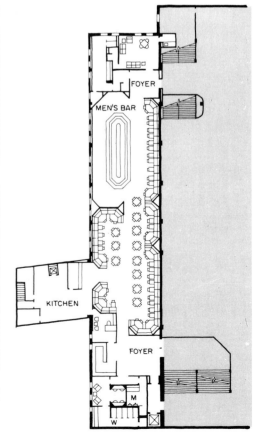

142

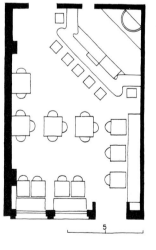

Robert C. Lautman photos

5

CLYDES BAR

Washington, D.C.
Hugh Newell Jacobsen

Space-expanding techniques with mirrors and beautiful craftsmanship give a sense of unusual ease and quality to this addition by Hugh Jacobsen to Clydes Bar in Georgetown. All woods are a lustrous, clear white oak: oak strips for the hung ceiling covering the air-conditioning ducts; lacquered oak flooring for the walls; an oak laminate for banquettes, tables and bar. To contrast with all this wood, all floors are surfaced with a white, unglazed ceramic tile. The chairs are also oak and covered with black plastic. The comfortable bar stools were fabricated from brass-plated tractor seats; this metal is echoed in a mirror-finished brass gutter to the bar, and in all hardware. Great spaciousness and sparkle are added to this monochromatic scheme by extremely effective lighting and a knowing use of mirrors. To visually extend the height of the walls, mirror was laminated to the existing ceiling around the perimeter of the room; the bar and banquettes are visually extended by floor-to-ceiling mirror strips. With the careful, handsome detailing and execution of everything in the bar, Jacobsen has clearly met his design objectives: "Clydes Bar opened in 1966 with dark-stained, beaded-siding walls of pine, bentwood chairs, Tiffany lamps and low camp. It was a howling success. I was retained to add more room in the building next door. Under the premise that any camp is too much, my objective was to use traditional materials in a new way, but to keep the pub saloon-like atmosphere that had proved so successful." The contractor for the project was Edwin Davis.

Eizaburo Hara

CAESAR'S PALACE

Tokyo, Japan
Paolo Riani

In the midst of Tokyo's ebullient Akasaka district, young Italian
architect Paolo Riani has designed a paradoxical contemporary counterpart
of a tea house. To gain attention in the brilliantly lighted
jumble of architecture dominating this night-life center, Riani has
created a stark cube of rough concrete (the forms were reversed to enhance
the texture), punctuated by a recessed entrance wall of undulating,
shiny brass. Reflections of surrounding lights, people and cars form
its "decoration." As in others of his projects, Riani makes
these idioms, combined with peek-a-boo levels on the interior, a lively
trademark of his designs. Caesar's Palace combines coffee shops, restaurants,
music bars and a dancing place, with a mélange of the owner's Italian antiques.

The various levels of Caesar's Palace are stylistically unified, but are arranged to provide a variety of spaces and services: *intime* to open, coffee or a drink to full meals, musical soloists to a full stage performance. Reflections, vistas and softly dramatic lighting vastly increase the visual spaciousness of what is really a very small building (see plans overleaf). The incorporation of a variety of Italian antiques, Roman to eighteenth century, was handled with verve, sophistication, and in some cases a dollop of wit—as with a large gilded "Portantina," with its mass of baroque scrolls, set into a lighted glass box as a perch for a guitar player.

Apart from the discrete graphics, the first hint of the club's "Roman" overtones is at the entrance, where a pair of eighteenth century baroque door panels have been enclosed in a double glass box, pivoted in the middle, to form the front door (left photo).

The rest of owner Makoto Matsuyama's collection of busts, carvings, statues, columns and furniture is displayed throughout the premises with equal discretion and ingenuity. The overall effect of the interiors is one of warm and festive color, glitter, and somewhat astonishing vistas up, down and through the relatively limited spaces. Floor levels were designed as a series of four open platforms, two below ground and two above; where specific operational functions (kitchen, performers' dressing rooms, toilets, stairs, etc.) required separation from the public spaces, they were enclosed by gilded curvilinear walls juxtaposed as free form elements on the open floor plans. All other partitions are temporary and may be changed at will. Fittings and furnishings were designed with a limited palette of materials: concrete, metal, leather, carpeting, and tiles on the first and second floor. All use elementary geometric forms as a design theme, many of which have been "transmuted" into Roman motifs—curves are "apses," cylinder tables are "column fragments," circles, squares and stripes are "echoes of the murals and mosaics of Pompeii." However much this may be intellectualizing, it is certainly a current of freshness for a club with an identity built on a "motif." Junko Enomoto, who designed the interiors with Paolo Riani, comments that it is "my belief that modern design is based on strength, simplicity, and clarity—as it was during the Roman period."

Riani adds, ". . . despite my sincere efforts, the final solution may only elicit the visitor's comment that 'It's just a place like all the others.' But perhaps for some people, the spatial and environmental experience will evoke a happy occasion which deepens and broadens their dimensions of life. If such is the case, my architecture will have fulfilled its function." For the people of Tokyo, who are prone to meet outside their family-oriented homes, Caesar's Palace does, indeed, provide a well designed "happy place."

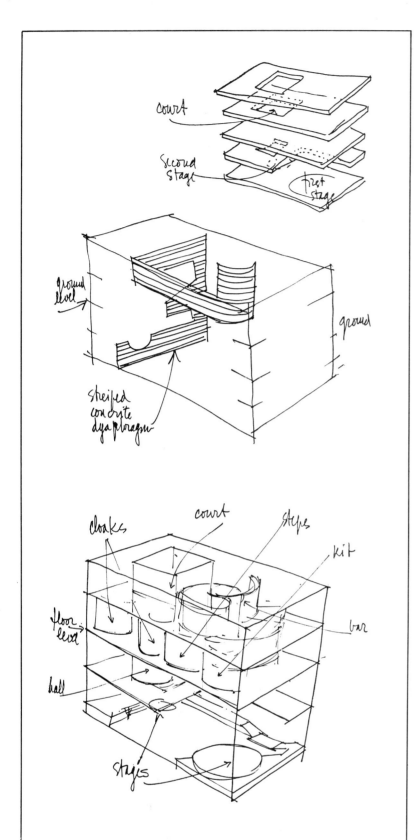

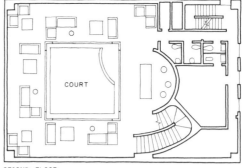

SECOND FLOOR

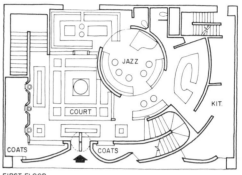

FIRST FLOOR

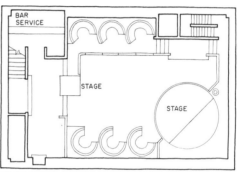

SECOND BASEMENT

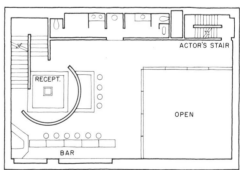

FIRST BASEMENT

Riani's spatial organization of four levels within an almost windowless concrete box (left) is clearly seen in his original conceptual sketches (above left). Each level is pierced with a "court" to vastly expand the vistas—but as can be seen in the photos on the preceding pages, glass partitions help with acoustical isolation if several performers are entertaining on different levels. Two of the floors are below ground—which, Riani says, "makes the best earthquake design."

CAESAR'S PALACE, Tokyo. Owner: *Makoto Matsuyama.* Architect: *Paolo Riani.* Interiors: *Junko Enomoto.* Contractor: *Kyoritsu Kenchiku.*

MID GAD VALLEY RESTAURANT

Alta Canyon, Utah
Enteleki Architecture, Planning, Research

The bridge-like structure of this restaurant in the mountains near Salt Lake City makes feasible its location on so isolated a site at the midpoint of a ski trail system. The heavy glue-laminated timber trusses, designed for the severe conditions at the site (winds up to 125 mph, snow loads of 125 psf, possible earthquakes, and a limited, 16-week, building season) and the six concrete piers which support them take all stresses. The infill panels are of glass, permitting superb views of the mountains and of the village of Snowbird below.

Raising the building on stilts makes it independent of the heavy snowfalls and minimizes snow removal. Snow on the flat roof is blown off by winds from the south. In a severe winter, the building was erected expeditiously.

MID GAD VALLEY RESTAURANT, Alta Canyon, Utah. Architects: *Enteleki Architecture, Planning, Research— Franklin T. Ferguson, partner-in-charge.* Engineers: *Edmund Allen* (structural/foundation); *Bridgers & Paxton Consulting Engineers, Inc.* (mechanical); *Nielson Engineering* (electrical). General contractor: *Cannon Construction Company.*

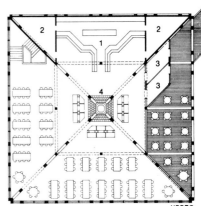

Upper floor:
1. Kitchen
2. Storage
3. Vestibule
4. Fireplace
5. Future bridge

UPPER FLOOR

Lower floor:
1. Women's restroom
2. Men's restroom
3. Mechanical
4. Receiving and storage
5. Lower entrance

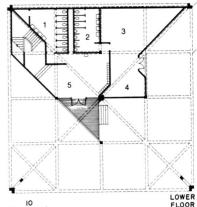

LOWER FLOOR

10

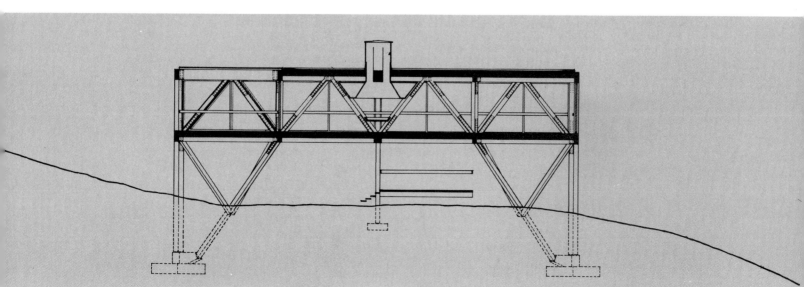

PHASES RESTAURANT

Bernardston, Massachusetts
Drummey Rosane Anderson

Phases Restaurant is a paradox: a sophisticated dining environment on a rural site in the Berkshire Hills, which looks out over an old orchard to a panoramic view east, south and west. An entrance gallery-lounge-bar element runs through the building as a slate-paved street, with a skylighted courtyard at the center. At a level four feet higher, and separated by a low parapet wall, are two dining rooms which can be separated by low modular panels (designed to double as waiters' stations) to provide private dining space. For further flexibility, the courtyard can be stripped of its furnishings to permit it to be used as a theater.

PHASES, Bernardston, Massachusetts. Architects: *Drummey Rosane Anderson—principal-in-charge, David W. Anderson; project architect, William V. Gillen; design architect, Jack L. Frazier.* Designers and planners: *Ferguson Sorrentino Design Incorporated.* Engineers: *Patrick J. Menehan* (structural); *Robert W. Hall, Inc.* (mechanical/electrical). Consultants: *Ferguson Sorrentino Design Incorporated* (graphics); *Stuart Levin* (restaurant). Contractor: *Vincent & Williams, Inc.*

Vincent D'Addario photos except as noted

Photo opposite: Wayne Soverns

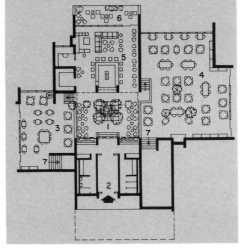

1. Courtyard
2. Entrance
3. East dining room
4. West dining room
5. Bar and lounge
6. Outdoor lounge
7. Kitchen

BOREL RESTAURANT

San Mateo, California
Robinson and Mills

The site for this restaurant is the highest point in an office park, some 30 miles south of San Francisco. The rough texture of cedar shake roof and side walls, and the triangular form of the building set it off from the nearby concrete-framed office buildings, and give it the desirable identity such a business requires. The triangular section also provides interior space of exceptional height—40 feet—in the dining areas. The entrance from the parking area is at the mezzanine level, where bar and lounge are located, and from which a dramatic stairway leads down to dining and cafe rooms. A diversity of woods—Douglas fir glue-laminated beams and columns, left exposed, paneling of stained fir and redwood, and decking of hemlock—is used for interior surfaces.

BOREL RESTAURANT, Peninsula Office Park, San Mateo, California. Architects: *Robinson and Mills.* Engineers: *Richard R. Bradshaw Engineers, Inc.* (structural). Consultants: *William Klein Engineers* (lighting); *Lee & Praszker* (soils); *Reis & Manwaring* (graphics); *Donald Campbell* (laser artist). Contractor: *WEBcor Builders, Inc.*

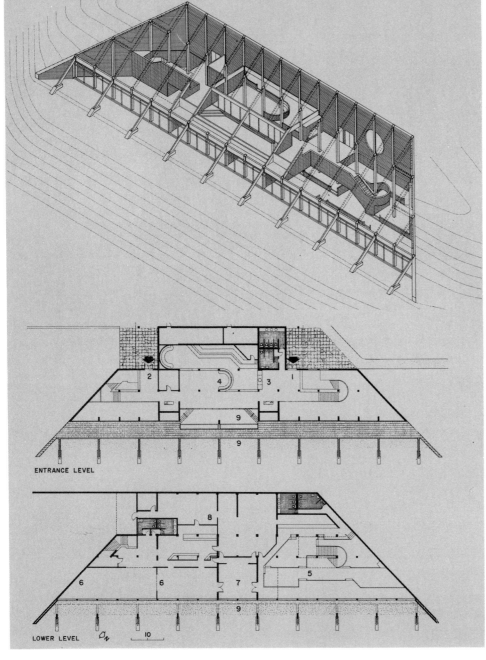

ENTRANCE LEVEL

LOWER LEVEL

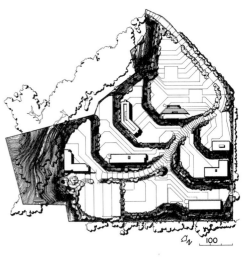

1. Dining entrance
2. Coffee shop entrance
3. Waiting area
4. Bar and lounge
5. Dining room
6. Coffee shop
7. Banquet room
8. Kitchen
9. Outdoor terrace

Robert Brandeis photos

Places to eat, drink, enjoy!
2

Clubs

JACARANDA COUNTRY CLUB

Plantation, Florida
Donald Singer

Encouraging their client, the Gulfstream Land &
Development Corporation, to depart from the local tradition
of "ship's wheel and stuffed sailfish" design motif,
architect Donald Singer and interior designer
Terry Rowe have created a private country club that is
thoughtfully planned, elegantly appointed and well suited
to function as the recreational focus on an
850-acre, planned residential community on Florida's
fast-growing Atlantic coast.

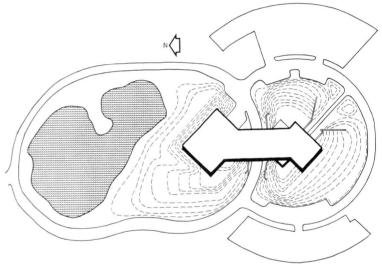

Alexandre Georges photos

Singer's decision to polarize the club's recreational and social functions led to the binuclear solution shown in the plans on the opposite page. The dining room, cocktail lounge and kitchen facilities are grouped together to form a social area that flows gently around its own service core. The golf shop, locker rooms and cart storage area form a second, quite separate, nucleus. The two sections are linked at the upper level by a bridge that spans the access road and provides, in the swale below, a natural point of arrival. Golfers alight from their cars under the bridge and proceed up to the locker rooms while their cars are parked and their golf bags transferred to carts. The procedure is reversed at the end of play.

Singer sought to achieve a feeling of repose and harmony with the surrounding landscape by keeping the building mass low and stringing the destination points out horizontally for maximum "stretch." This elongation and emphasis on horizontal movement, says Singer, "makes the user aware of his role in a pageant he himself is creating." The two man-made hillocks are visual shock absorbers that cushion the impact between building and site while strongly reinforcing the duality of the scheme.

The elevations are handled with appealing simplicity in concrete and glass. Because there is so much design interest at grade in the form of level changes and retaining walls, the roof line is smooth and continuous, broken only as the building turns on its site. Concrete bearing walls have been lightly sandblasted to remove stains and tie holes have been packed with lead

The materials used consistently
throughout the interiors are wool
carpet, concrete, aluminum and glass.
Other materials find occasional use:
the lounge tables, bar top and
waitress station are black granite;
the reception area and bridge deck
are finished in river gravel.
The whole building is air conditioned
using a multi-zone, air-to-air system.

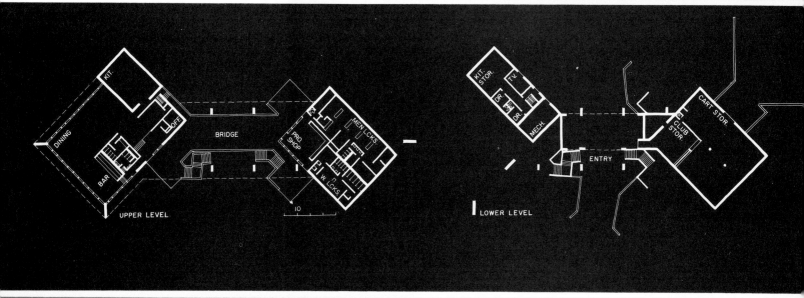

UPPER LEVEL

LOWER LEVEL

wool. The roof structure, although originally designed as a waffle slab, is framed in steel.

The interiors, although more stylish and self-conscious, reflect the same consistency in material and detail. Singer and Rowe, collaborating for the first time, have produced a sequence of elegant spaces, heightened by careful lighting and enriched by powerful color accents. The dining room and the cocktail lounge (see page 159) are inviting and intimate—their scale made easily manageable by fitting them around an internal service core. The locker rooms (photo below) treated as low grade space in so many clubs, at Jacaranda are detailed, textured, appointed and furnished with really meticulous care. Thoughtful lighting, much of it recessed or concealed, imparts a lyrical warmth to the interiors and, at night,

bathes the building's perimeter, and its principal approaches, in a luminous medley of powerful, form-revealing highlights (see photo page 159).

If the design intention had simply been to create a handsome structure that unmistakably conveyed an aura of suburban elegance and ease, then the designer's task would have been easier. For, although the Jacaranda Club expresses these qualities in abundance, it also generates in its users an important sense of community focus and purposeful play.

JACARANDA COUNTRY CLUB, Plantation, Florida. *Architect:* Donald Singer. Engineers: *Gaston DeZarraga* (structural), *Luis Aguirre* (mechanical). Interior design: *Terry Rowe Associates, Inc. in collaboration with Donald Singer.* Contractor: *Caldwell Scott Construction Company.*

The club manager's office (photo left) continues the theme of concrete wall and speckled carpet. In the dressing rooms (photo below), custom lockers were molded in gray fiberglass. The molding process was reversed so that the locker's exterior surface is rough textured while the inside is smooth and white. Plastic laminate, chrome, and mirror glass are used as contrast to the concrete walls.

Main entrance and lobby are on the lower level, with stairs leading directly to the main dining room and its bar. From the deck surrounding the dining room, there is a 360-degree view over the countryside and to Montauk Bay. The berm on which the building sits is simple and appropriately landscaped with easily maintained juniper; salt spray from the ocean necessitated a very limited palette of plant materials.

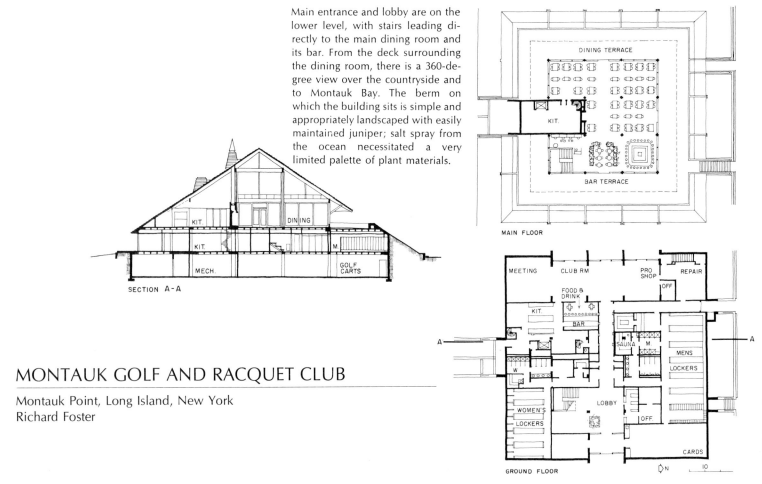

SECTION A-A

DINING TERRACE

KIT.

BAR TERRACE

MAIN FLOOR

MEETING | CLUB RM | PRO SHOP | REPAIR

FOOD & DRINK

KIT.

OFF

BAR

SAUNA | M.

MENS LOCKERS

W

WOMEN'S LOCKERS

LOBBY

OFF

CARDS

GROUND FLOOR

MONTAUK GOLF AND RACQUET CLUB

Montauk Point, Long Island, New York
Richard Foster

1. Kitchen
2. Dancing
3. Dining
4. Bar
5. Terrace
6. Refreshment
7. Future bath house & locker rooms
8. Pro shop

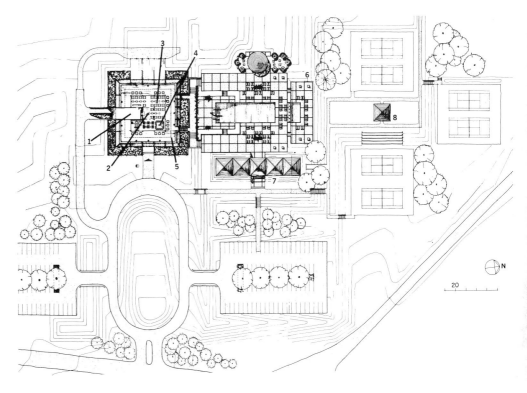

Rising from a windswept sand dune site, the pyramidal form of the Montauk Golf and Racquet Club is a landmark in the surrounding area. The strong lines of the roof—which emphasize the slope of the dune hill (highest in the area) on which the building sits, and recall indigenous farm buildings of the locality—are a happy design solution for function and for sensitivity to the environment. The building divides vertically by function, with the utility areas on the ground level and entertainment areas on the upper level, from which there is a 360-degree view of Montauk Bay and Suffolk County. The pyramidal roof lends its inverse form to the dining room and bar on the upper level, and overhangs a part of the surrounding terrace. All materials are simple and reflect indigenous uses: decks and lower floor are of ironspot brick pavers, walls are rough sawn red cedar and plank, exposed concrete faces are sandblasted or hand hammered, and the roof is covered with hand split cedar shakes. The building and its recreational facilities are designed for a membership of 500 families.

MONTAUK GOLF AND RACQUET CLUB, Montauk Point, Long Island, New York. Architect: *Richard Foster.* Developer: *Montauk Improvement, Inc.* Structural engineer: *Zoldos Meagher.* Mechanical and electrical engineers: *Harold Rosen Associates.* Interiors: *Luss/Kaplan And Associates.* Contractor: *Tandy and Allen.*

The dining room's high ceiling gives it exceptional spaciousness. Ceiling is red cedar plank, oiled; columns and rafters are fir. Location of the entertainment facilities on the upper level takes advantage of the sweeping view of the surrounding area; glass walls and low parapet around the terrace permit a clear view. Tables and chairs are of oak; carpet is green. Ground level bar (right) serves card, club and meeting rooms on that level. Stairway (above right) leads from main dining room to lobby on lower floor (above); rail is leather over foam rubber. The Olympic-sized swimming pool and the tennis courts are reached by steps from this level.

PALMETTO DUNES CLUBHOUSE

Hilton Head, South Carolina
Copelin and Lee

This central clubhouse for two full golf courses was built within a new resort development. The main upper structure, 28 feet high, is a series of trusses cut out and varied to receive light and to modulate the space beneath. Below the shingle roof and slung between the round columns that support the trusses are all the "functioning" elements of the building—locker rooms, storage areas, and kitchen facilities— all designed for future expansion. These lower elements are solid, of beige stucco, while the large truss structure containing the pro shop, lobby, and restaurant is completely glazed both between the columns and at the triangulated gable ends. Beyond the glass, with long vistas of the golf courses, are the terraces and benches to accommodate those people waiting to play. Engineers were Dolton & Dunne (mechanical/electrical) and Donald Butterfield (structural). Contractor was G. E. Moore, Inc.

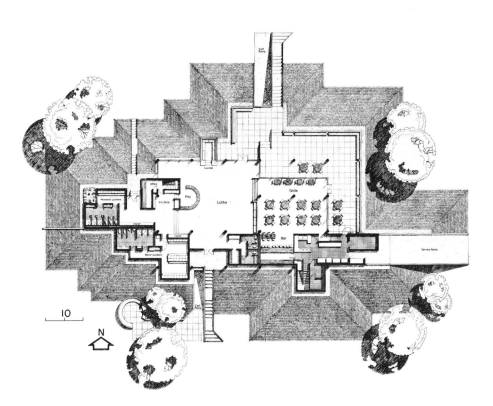

Joseph W. Molitor photos

This club—being developed by two entrepreneurs who have built several outdoor and indoor tennis facilities in recent years—is being completed in two stages. The first stage, already in use: 12 clay courts facing the first floor of a proposed two-story building. The completed section has complete locker room facilities, the pro shop, and a snack bar sheltered under a broad slatted-wood roof.

The second stage, shown in the rendering below, will add the second floor, which will include a cafe-bar, lounge, and offices, surrounded by a broad deck. Further proposed for the 26-acre site is a swimming pool, a series of four-plex units (sketch, lower right), and a few single-family houses.

The idea of building in stages is often inevitable for this type of building, where budgets are so often a problem. What is essential is—as in this case—a well-thought-out design that is at least nearly as functional and attractive incomplete as it will be when completed.

THE TENNIS CLUB AT EAST HAMPTON, East Hampton, Long Island, New York. Architect: *George Nemeny—associates, Richard Henderson and Debora Reiser.* Contractor and owner: *Bernard Jacobsen and Joseph Fishbach.*

THE TENNIS CLUB OF EAST HAMPTON

Long Island, New York
George Nemeny

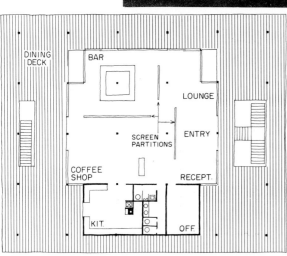

SECOND FLOOR

Detailing of the first-stage structure is simple, yet disciplined and full of visual interest. Folding partitions open the building's facilities (shown at right, the pro shop and snack bar) to the broad bluestone terrace. Slatted roof will become the deck of the second floor.

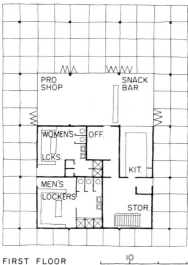

FIRST FLOOR   10

Housing units to be spotted through the wooded site have same simple, flat-roofed design. Each of units in typical four-plex will open through sliding glass doors to an individual and quite private terrace.

TYPICAL COTTAGE   5

MILL VALLEY TENNIS CLUB

Mill Valley, California
John Louis Field

Although it has no actual resemblance to a Victorian building, this new clubhouse for the Mill Valley Tennis Club is designed to continue the tradition of the club's turn-of-the-century building which had to be torn down to make way for the new structure. The unusual roof and the pavilion-like veranda reflect this tradition and the social nature of the building's use, and the roof form makes a pleasant focus for residents of the hillsides above and around the clubhouse. The restricted site determined the location of the building between the tennis courts and the road, and the curved ends of the building fit it to the site with a minimum of crowding. A requirement of the program was that the activities of tennis players and swimmers be completely separate; hence the provision of locker rooms for tennis players and separate changing rooms for swimmers, with separate access for each to lounge and bar. The high-ceilinged lounge receives light from both sides and from a skylight at the ridge. For large parties, the veranda offers extra space as it is heated by gas units. Office and caretaker's apartment are upstairs.

MILL VALLEY TENNIS CLUB, Mill Valley, California. Architect: *John Louis Field.* Structural engineers: *Pregnoff and Matheu.* Contractor: *Page Construction Company.*

Jeremiah Bragstad

Karl Riek

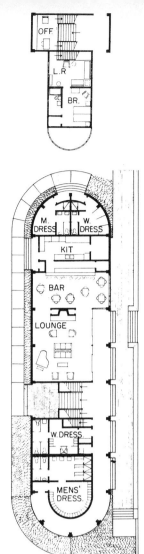

Roof and shingle-covered wall (or screen, to use the architect's word) do not meet; instead, a band of glass encircles the building just under the eave line, admitting light to the lounge where it would otherwise have none, and making of the lounge a singularly light space. A skylight at the ridge, which runs the length of the building, amplifies this effect. Laminated wood bents carry the roof deck which uses laminated 2 x 4's on edge along the straight portion of the roof, and bent laminated 1 x 4's at the curved end sections. The screen has arched openings toward the tennis courts but is left solid toward the road except for main entrance and service doors.

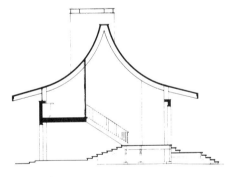

Kark Riek

Part Three

From neighborhood centers to national parks,
community facilities for recreation have come
to play an ever more significant part
in the leisure activities of Americans of
all ages. And the use of such facilities
has come to be ever more a *part* of daily life
rather than a *departure* from it. The lunch-
hour or after-work swim or tennis game, the
family bowling, skiing or boating outing have
become quite ordinary aspects of contemporary
life; and more and more facilities are being
designed to accommodate them.

Places to play

Places to play

1

Community

recreation facilities

ROXBURY BRANCH, YMCA

Boston, Massachusetts
The Architects Collaborative

Strong and monolithic, with a finish and with forms that are more often seen in much bigger buildings, this relatively small (26,140-square-foot) YMCA was designed as much more than a community center. As the first structure to rise in a major Boston renewal program, it brought freshness and color to what was an old and blighted area. In the kind of place where impermanence is common, the building's strong shapes and finishes suggest commitment. Yet there is nothing of the fortress about the design. Indeed, sculpture and art "integral with the very stuff of the building" (see photos) add a nonfunctional value too seldom realized in tight-budget settings like this where it is most needed.

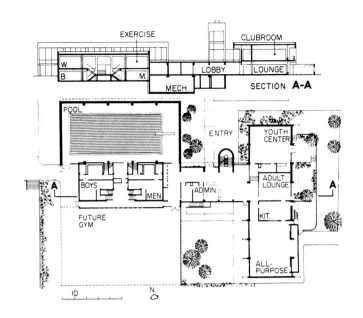

On the street side, the reinforced concrete structure is essentially closed on the pedestrian level; but the second level and the rooms open to the interior courts have large glass areas. Both plastic-coated and random vertical-board forms were used to vary the texture of the unfinished concrete.

Bold and massive curve of the stairtower dominates the entrance courtyard. Behind, on the entrance wall, is a relief sculpture by Harris Barron. Free-standing sculpture is planned for the rear patio and as a focal point for the playfields.

ROXBURY BRANCH YMCA, Boston. Architects: *The Architects Collaborative—Norman C. Fletcher,* principal in charge, *Howard Elkus,* job captain, design, *Arthur Hacking,* job captain, construction. Structural consultants: *Sousa & True.* Mechanical consultants: *Fitzemeyer & Tocci.* Electrical consultants: *Vern Norman Associates.* General contractor: *George B. H. Macomber Co.* Sculpture and mural: *Harris Barron and Ros Barron.*

Photographs: Louis Reens

The interiors are spare, but get color and texture from the forming of the concrete, the use of red oak paneling, and—in the teenage meeting room—a strong, bright mural painting covering one entire wall (photo, lower right). The interior includes a large multi-purpose room, above, which opens to the open rear courtyard; an adult lounge; the pool, which has hot-air inlets around the entire periphery to minimize condensation; locker units in a split-level arrangement to maximize control and minimize changes in level between the lockers and the pool; three club rooms, and an arts and crafts center; a darkroom; a kitchen and a hi-fi listening room which, for both practical reasons (acoustical privacy) and symbolic reasons is located at the head of the stairtower. A gymnasium is planned for the future. Building and site work cost $611,741. Total cost per square foot: $25.32.

177

CLINTON YOUTH AND FAMILY CENTER

New York City
James Stewart Polshek
Walfredo Toscanini

Van Brody photos

At least one building among the deteriorating tenement facades of West 54th Street in Manhattan is bright and inviting—as city life and its institutions can be. It is the Clinton Youth and Family Center, once the Seventh District Police Court building. The painted metal doors, windows and new intake pipes for air conditioning make vigorous images for the future, and have at the same time been fitted within the orderly stonework of the past; they seem to say that we need not insist on historically accurate restorations to provide a necessary feeling of continuity with our roots, nor do we need to level old architecture to make cities better. The Youth and Family Center is operated by the YMCA of Greater New York and the Rotary Club of New York, and the majority of the renovation costs were paid for by the Astor Foundation, which has funded several other building projects of notable worth in declining New York neighborhoods. James Stewart Polshek and Walfredo Toscanini were the architects. A fine, old building has been "added" to New York, and similar buildings, sound of body but needing a fresh new spirit, could be added in many of our cities.

Inside, the old six-story structure built at the beginning of this century has been transformed by brightly painted walls, movable/storable furniture, and plenty of irreverent writing on the walls. The surprisingly appropriate flowing spaces house noisy children and under-financed neighborhood health programs as well as they once housed the solemn, not-too-happy processes of criminal justice. By removing several full-height brick walls erected during previous remodelings, the vaulted solemnity of the old main entrance lobby (top, right) was reclaimed. But elsewhere on the ground floor, in the new lounge and the entrance foyer to the elevators (right and following page), color rather than space has been added. The old wall planes, moldings and right angles have been properly violated by paint in diagonal stripes and overlapping circles, yet the sense of old architecture conserved still remains. This large ground floor space is a kind of "mixing valve" where all of the diverse groups coming in and out of the center each day are brought together.

The center can be understood as having its large-group "mixer" spaces—including the gymnasium—on the lower floors, the park in back, and the progressively smaller and more private-use spaces on the upper floors. The central staircase that connects them all is a finely scaled circular shaft (see isometric, following page) filled with open wrought iron lattice work and skylighted at the top. The center of the shaft used to be occupied by an elevator—the only one in the original court—that unfortunately had to be removed. The old main courtroom is now the gymnasium, with a new maple floor and with bouncing balls and the arc of their travel painted boldly on the brick walls. The coffered ceiling of the courtroom provided excellent recesses for new lighting fixtures, and a classical portico that was a feature of the courtroom has been allowed to remain, now framing a basketball backboard. A second, low-ceilinged courtroom occupied what is now the fourth and fifth floors, but there was no need for a second large space. So, it has been divided into seminar rooms and offices (see isometric again) and most of the new partitions on this floor are surfaced with hardboard and left unpainted. These fourth and fifth floors have wall-to-wall carpeting throughout, and they are—not surprisingly—among the most popular for smaller meetings and games.

The renovation commission was received by the architects in 1968, and the project was complete in 1970; it took one year to prepare contract documents and about 18 months for construction. The original contract called for about $400,000 in work, but the cost of the project rose to almost $1 million through change-order additions during construction, as the fund-raising drives became more successful and additional money became available for additional work.

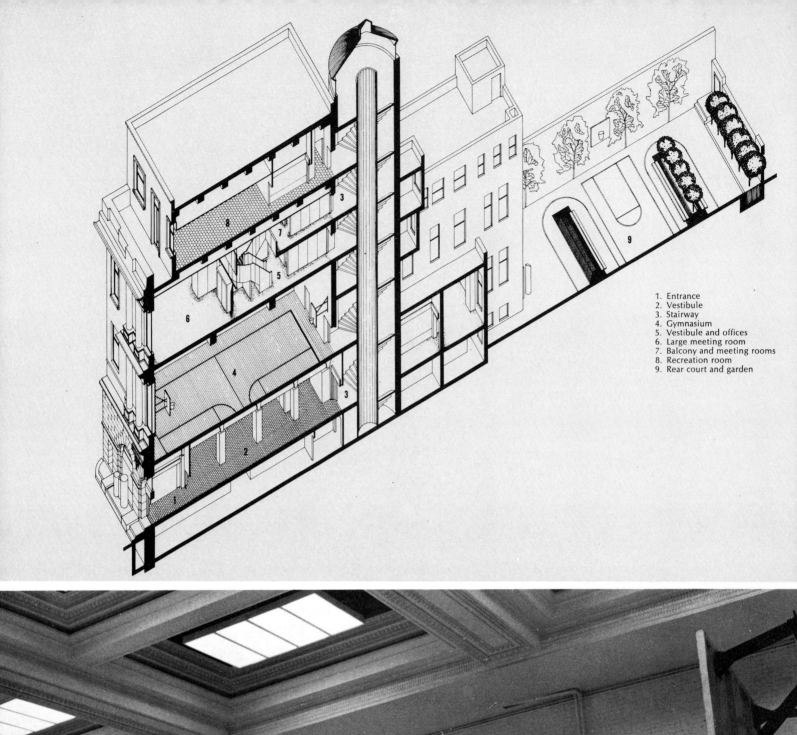

1. Entrance
2. Vestibule
3. Stairway
4. Gymnasium
5. Vestibule and offices
6. Large meeting room
7. Balcony and meeting rooms
8. Recreation room
9. Rear court and garden

The large meeting room on the fourth floor (below) exhibits the graphic skill and color that makes the center as a whole so successful. The three dimensionality of the windows is painted on, not real, but it is almost better this way. The stair to the fifth floor mezzanine (below) shows how the unpainted hardboard is used in conjunction with the red carpet, to achieve a remarkable feeling of richness with inexpensive, wear-resistant surfaces. The rear garden (photo right) was once the site of one of the most decrepit jails in Manhattan, torn down in the course of this remodeling at a cost of $90,000. Now the trees are beginning to grow there, to complement the painted trees on the walls.

CLINTON YOUTH AND FAMILY CENTER, New York City. Architects: *James Stewart Polshek and Associates*, and *Walfredo Toscanini—J.S. Polshek*, project architect. Graphic design: *James Stewart Polshek and Associates—David Bliss*, project designer. Mechanical and electrical engineers: *Benjamin & Zicherman Associates*. General contractor: *Dember Construction Corp.*

Stan Menscher photo

JEWISH COMMUNITY CENTER

Portland, Oregon
Wolff Zimmer Gunsul Frasca

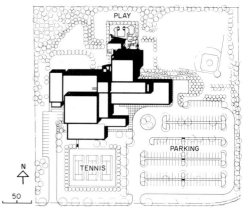

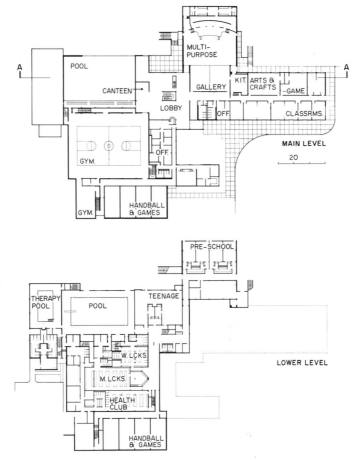

A center for social, cultural and athletic activities is an important part of the program of a Jewish community. Sometimes such a center is part of a religious building complex, but it need not be so connected. The Portland (Oregon) Jewish Community Center is not part of a complex, but is instead located in a suburban part of the city, on a 10-acre tract surrounded by residences. apartments and a tree nursery. From this location it serves the whole Jewish community of Portland, and because of a long tradition of opening its swimming pool for therapy to any handicapped persons, it also serves others of the city as well as its own membership. The new building includes both a regulation-sized pool for general use and a smaller pool with separate entrance and lockers especially for therapy patients.

Since the building serves a full range of age groups, the program for the new building required provision of both specific areas for each group's activity and places of general assembly where all could come together for events of interest. As the plans show, a wide variety of special places, from pre-school to teenage to senior rooms, are provided in ways that preclude conflicts in use.

The building is two stories high, with the main entrance on the upper level (at grade because of a sloping site). Secondary entrances, serving the therapy pool and the preschool, are on the lower level. The lobby, off the main entrance, is central to all principal activity areas, and has direct spectator access to the gym, pool and multi-purpose room, all of which, because of the grade change, are at somewhat lower levels. The open balcony above the lobby (page 184) is a small reading room.

With a stringently limited budget, the provision of such a diversity of spaces was no simple accomplishment. To achieve both the kind of building that the clients wanted and the economy necessary, the architects devised a vernacular for the building based on the use of optimum (and different, but compatible) structural, mechanical and material systems. Reinforced concrete is used for foundations, floors, and columns. Where exterior walls appear as extensions of the foundations, they are of concrete, board-formed; where they are otherwise supported, they are of prepainted steel panels. The roof structure is wood frame.

PORTLAND JEWISH COMMUNITY CENTER, Portland, Oregon. Architects: *Wolff Zimmer Gunsul Frasca—Robert Frasca, partner-in-charge; Prescott Coleman, project architect; Wallace Roeder, job captain; John Williams, interior design.* Engineers: *Nortec Engineers, Inc.* (structural, mechanical, electrical). Landscape architect: *Robert Perrin.* Contractor: *Minden Construction Company.*

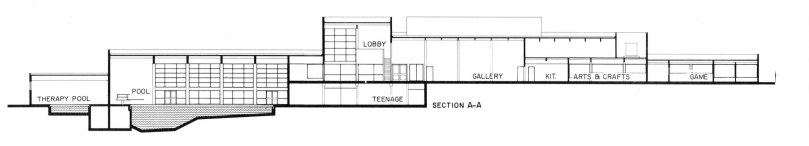

THERAPY POOL · POOL · LOBBY · TEENAGE · GALLERY · KIT. · ARTS & CRAFTS · GAME

SECTION A-A

The multi-purpose room (left, top), is a place of general assembly, used for events of interest to the whole community. The lobby (left) is a dramatic place, by day and at night, with its two-story concrete columns which support, midway, balcony spaces. The large pool (top photo) is regulation size and is used by the membership. A smaller pool, with separate entrance and its own lockers, is used by therapy patients from all parts of Portland, a long-time tradition of the Jewish community of the city.

Cochise Visitor Center's primary function is to attract highway travelers along Interstate 10 near Willcox, and introduce them to the area and its history. It is also an asset to the people of Willcox and Cochise County, and a strong landmark. The walls are stuccoed, the roof is wood-shingled, and the building plan is organized around a 40-foot-square courtyard.

COCHISE VISITOR CENTER

Willcox, Arizona
Dinsmore, Kulseth and Riggs/Architecture One, Ltd.

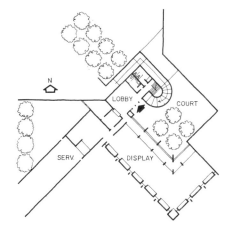

DRAKE'S BEACH FACILITIES BUILDING

Point Reyes National Seashore, California
Worley K. Wong, John Carden Campbell

This visitor facilities building is the first such to be built in the new Point Reyes National Seashore, some 30 miles northwest of San Francisco, for which funds have just been authorized to complete acquisition of private lands within its overall boundaries. The building, housing ranger's office, dressing rooms, garage and dining facilities, is for year-round use, in weather which varies from dense fog to warm bright sun, with winds which range from light to uncomfortably strong. The four uses of the building determined the plan and provided the desirable addition of a protected court for wind-free lounging and for interpretive talks by rangers. The slant of the roofs aids in reducing the amount of wind that reaches the court. The building is of wood construction, and stands on piles 30 and 40 feet long. Pilings are used throughout the building itself, treated with weathering oil. Like the other materials used, including the copper roof, they were selected because they required minimum maintenance.

DRAKE'S BEACH FACILITIES BUILDING, Point Reyes National Seashore, California. Architects: *Worley K. Wong* of *Wong & Brocchini & Associates* and *John Carden Campbell* of *Campbell & Rocchia & Associates.* Structural engineers: *Eric Elsesser & Associates.*

Joshua Freiwald photos

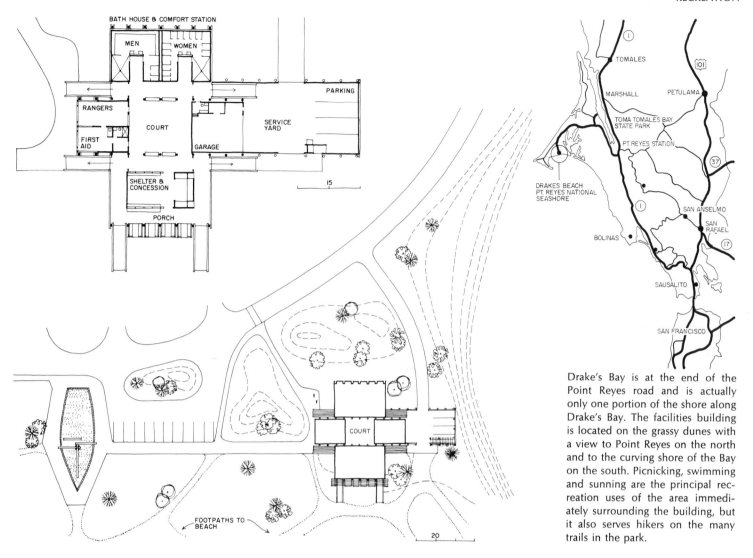

BATH HOUSE & COMFORT STATION

MEN | WOMEN

PARKING

RANGERS

COURT

SERVICE YARD

FIRST AID

GARAGE

SHELTER & CONCESSION

PORCH

15

COURT

FOOTPATHS TO BEACH

20

TOMALES

MARSHALL

PETULAMA

TOMA TOMALES BAY STATE PARK

PT.REYES STATION

DRAKES BEACH PT. REYES NATIONAL SEASHORE

SAN ANSELMO

SAN RAFAEL

BOLINAS

SAUSALITO

SAN FRANCISCO

Drake's Bay is at the end of the Point Reyes road and is actually only one portion of the shore along Drake's Bay. The facilities building is located on the grassy dunes with a view to Point Reyes on the north and to the curving shore of the Bay on the south. Picnicking, swimming and sunning are the principal recreation uses of the area immediately surrounding the building, but it also serves hikers on the many trails in the park.

More than just a pool, although that was what the program called for, this lively outdoor recreation center is the focal point—and largest open space—for a crowded ghetto neighborhood. "The People's Pool" is the name given it by the people of the neighborhood, but its formal name locates it in a high-density area of Brooklyn, Bedford Stuyvesant. Despite a small site—three-quarters of a city block—this center provides a competition-sized pool, a diving pool, spectator seats along one side, dressing rooms and lockers and, for smaller athletes, a wading pool with fountain and imaginatively equipped play areas. The means for getting so much onto the site and at the same time maintaining exceptional openness—more welcome in Bedford Stuyvesant than in most city districts—was the architect's decision to sink the bathhouse facilities one half level below grade in order to use their rooftop as a playground for small children. Broad steps, which double as places to sit and form an amphitheater for various kinds of neighborhood performances, make the transition between the rooftop playground and the main deck. Protrusions of mechanical equipment are put to use as part of the play equipment: ventilating fans are inside a pyramid for slides, and vent stacks would never be recognized in the maze of plumbing pipes which are interlocked to make a jungle gym. To be as vandalproof as possible, play equipment is built of concrete, painted cast iron pipe, or cargo nets. The wading pool (left, center) is connected to the upper level of the playground by a flight of steps which is also a water cascade, and by two water slides.

The structure is poured-in-place concrete throughout, with various textures at different points. All of the pools are of aluminum, and the fountain spray sculpture is also aluminum. Light poles are of weathering steel with narrow-beam targeting luminaires. The total cost of the center was $4,413,278.

BEDFORD STUYVESANT COMMUNITY POOL, Brooklyn, New York, Architects: *Morris Lapidus Associates—Morris Lapidus, Alan Lapidus, John Bowstead, designers*. Engineers: *Ralph Dell'Abate, James McCosker and Associates*, (structural); *Herman Scherr Associates* (mechanical); *Meyers & Locker* (electrical). Lighting consultant: *Abe Feder*. General contractor: *Tern Construction*.

BEDFORD STUYVESANT COMMUNITY POOL

Brooklyn, New York
Morris Lapidus Associates

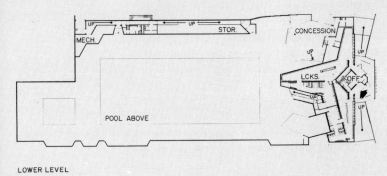

LOWER LEVEL

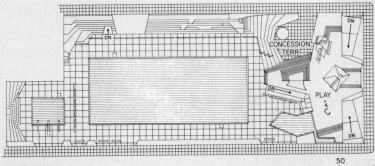

UPPER LEVEL

50

Sandy Nixon

COAL STREET POOL

Wilkes-Barre, Pennsylvania
The Allen Organization, Bohlin and Powell

Coal Street Park derives its name from a former colliery on the 36-acre site which once separated two economically diverse neighborhoods and is now intended to become a meeting ground of recreational activities. The project was backed by the State Department of Community Affairs, the Federal Model Cities program, other Federal agencies, and the owners, the City of Wilkes-Barre, Pennsylvania. The latter commissioned The Allen Organization as park and recreational planners, who in turn hired the firm of Bohlin and Powell as architects. When construction of the first facility—the pool—began, the terrain consisted of coal refuse.

The initial problem that confronted the architects was the lack of funding provision for enclosed pools in an area where an exposed facility could be effective for only three months of each year. There was a clear requirement for a solution that would provide more than a sometime use and still be affordable and conform to Federal guidelines. An inflatable structure was the answer here, and the limitations of time, cost and gaining approvals required an uncomplicated product which had been tested by standardized manufacture. The available choices could have posed visual and functional problems, but Bohlin and Powell have been innovative in their imaginative adaptation of a commercial object to fit the context of its use.

Mark Cohen

Ace Hoffman

In giving this project a First Honor Award in 1973, the Pennsylvania Society of Architects' jury commented: "Carefully wrought composition in the 'mecho-mod' style. Sensitive land planning and approaches. Designed with a refreshing abandon for simple pleasures." Others besides Peter Bohlin were mystified by the exact meaning of "mecho-mod" and whether or not the refreshing abandon might be better applied to the mood of the users rather than to the design process, but the comments do sum up the results fairly accurately.

The linear plan of the permanent structure fulfills two purposes. The first is to direct public traffic in a required progression of access ramp, central lobby, separated dressing rooms and pool, while housing the necessary dressing rooms, offices, pool filtration and air handling equipment, maintenance spaces and air-supported-structure storage. The open spaces beside the ramp contain picnic tables covered with bright yellow canvas awnings, and the "stretching" of the building achieved by the spaces' location have the visual advantage of providing a larger and more easily identified setting for Coal Street Pool and a hard-edged counterpoint to the rounded shape of the "aquadome" when it is in place. The second reason for the linearity of this concrete frame and exposed stone-aggregate block building is to relate it to a 800-foot-long walkway which will connect the other facilities of playing fields, children's covered play areas (under construction in the photo right) and an ice skating rink planned for the Park. The eventual plan for the Park can be seen on page 195. The playful configuration of the round air-induction pipes (photo, opposite at top) which provide the air-support for the canvas structure when it is in place (below), is determined by basic functional requirements. But the architects have not been afraid to take full advantage of the sculptural possibilities by contrasting angular and rounded bends and by painting the sheet metal black on the outside and bright red on the inside. The most economical and tamper-proof location for the air-heaters and blowers was the roof of the permanent building, and the inflatable's manufacturer recommended that the forced air be introduced via the pipes at the bottom of their structure where construction was the strongest and the material least likely to tear. The large size of the ducts was determined by a desire for minimum velocity and thus low draft and noise levels.

Ace Hoffman

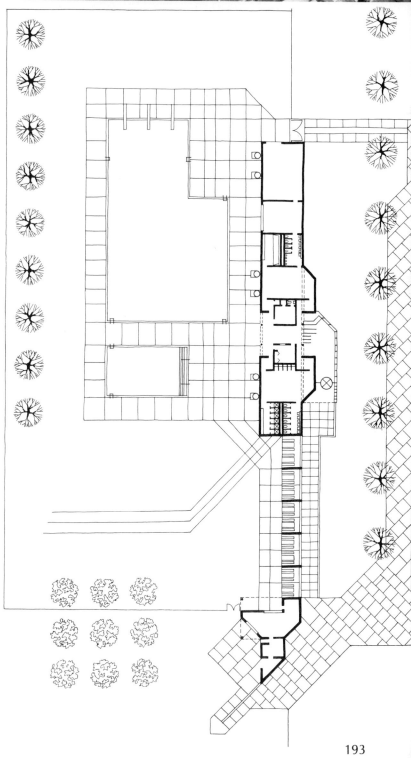

There are two "ready-made" structures at the Coal Street Pool. The lobby's glass enclosure (bottom, page 192) is ordered from a manufacturer's catalog and shares the inflatable's theoretical advantages of testing by previous use, predictable costs and speedy erection. But the architects do not see prefabricated buildings as the answer to all problems, and state that the advantages are not always as real as could be supposed. In the case of the inflatable aquadome, the largest disadvantage may be increased long-term costs which have to be weighed against a first construction cost that is far less than that for a permanent structure. The cost of the fabric enclosure was $38,000 to which $24,000 was added for footings, extra heating, air blowers and a storage room bringing the total to $62,000 for the 20,000-square-foot space. The estimated saving over the cost of a permanent enclosure was $218,000. The premium for operating expenses, including added heat, extra help in putting up and taking down the structure and 10-year replacement costs, was estimated to be $11,500 annually or $460,000 over a 40-year-life expectancy for the facility, and it is reasonably certain that these costs will rise. However, an answer to the apparently greater long-term costs here might be found in the interest value of the monies initially saved. For example, $218,000 multiplied by 8 per cent and 40 years would total $697,000 leaving a large margin for cost inflation. The above calculations do not take into account the advantages of having the option of an open pool in the summer with only one facility, the appropriately festive atmosphere created by the aquadome or the increased number of posible users when the enclosure is removed. The architects estimate that about 500 people can use the pool at one time in the winter while 2,000 can enjoy the full facilities in the summer. An earth berm has been successful in deflecting the wind during periods of cooler weather when the dome is down. The playful atmosphere is carried into the permanent structure by skylights in the dressing rooms and supergraphics by Mrs. Bohlin.

THE WILKES-BARRE AQUADOME, Wilkes-Barre, Pennsylvania. Owner: *The City of Wilkes-Barre*. Park and recreation planners: *The Allen Organization*. Architects: *Bohlin and Powell—Ronald W. Huntsinger, project architect, Peter Bohlin, partner-in-charge*. Engineers: *Vincent B. Szykman, Inc.* (structural); *Paul H. Yeomans, Inc.* (mechanical/electrical). Landscape architects: *Kennedy and Brown*. Graphics: *Annie Bohlin*. General contractor: *Charles A. Malpass Sons*.

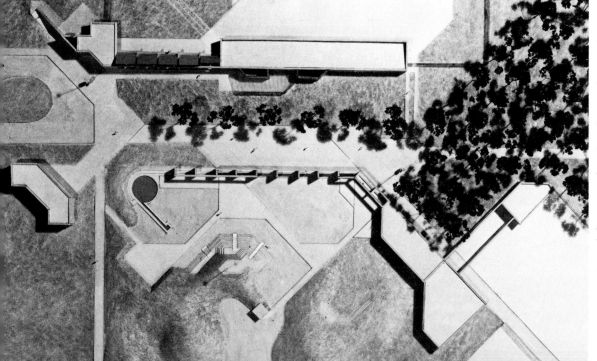

One of the most interesting visual experiences produced by the aquadome occurs twice a year during the inflation and deflation process (left, top). Forced air is introduced through the visible-round ends of the large pipe-ducts seen without the fabric in place (lower photo, above), and adding a playful atmosphere for the many children using the facility. The open picnic spaces (top) are shielded from the summer sun by bright-yellow awnings and overlook the entrance ramp along which they are located. The pool's permanent ancillary-facilities building is located at the top of the Coal Street Park's masterplan (left) and forms an edge to the Park's central walkway between it and the covered-children's-play arcade bordering athletic fields and playgrounds at the bottom of the plan. A future skating rink is planned in the lower right hand corner.

195

Places to play
2

Camps

This soaring timber dining hall is part of Camp Louise, a 186-acre Girl Scout camp which nestles into a wooded valley in northeastern Pennsylvania. It is the latest addition to a master plan (page 202) which Bohlin and Powell, the architects, have been implementing since 1967.

All of the ten buildings now completed share visual similarities, from a tiny director's cabin, page 203, to the largest one, shown here. But the dining hall carries the idiom beyond the pleasant and the useful to a poetic expression of the community spirit of the camp. Each day as the 250 campers and leaders gather for meals, the quality of light, which changes significantly from morning to night, will remind them of their kinship with nature. Light gently manipulated by primary colors, is thus the building's only ornament Vaguely reminiscent of Aalto's pre-war proposals for athletic buildings in Helsinki, the south elevation (left) thrusts toward the sun in a series of richly-faceted forms, all generated by the same section.

The columns, built up of five 3x12s, and the beams, five 3x14s, neatly accept pairs of 3x10 diagonal braces. Special steel column bases tie them to the foundations. From the roof deck, standard incandescent RLM fixtures hang, their feed-wires looped gracefully from boxes integrated into the beams. The plywood flaps have two parts; the larger, outer one is fixed while the inner one can be closed.

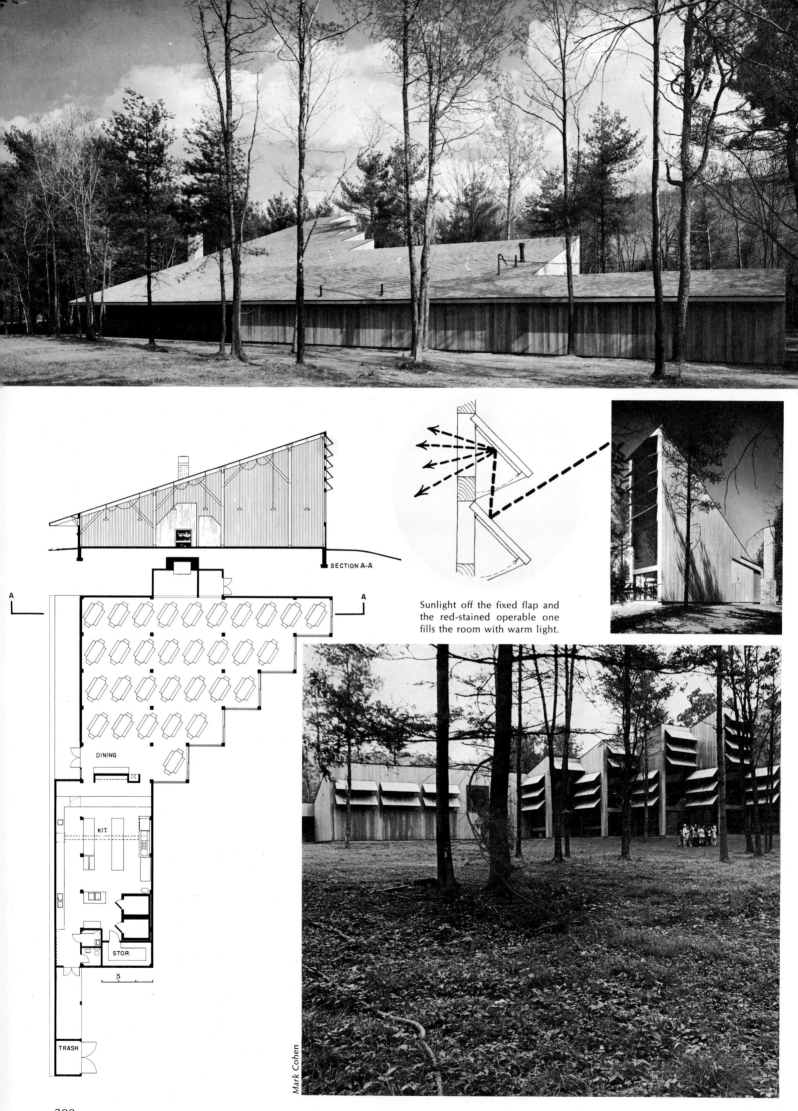

SECTION A-A

DINING

KIT.

STOR.

TRASH

5

Sunlight off the fixed flap and the red-stained operable one fills the room with warm light.

Mark Cohen

Mark Cohen

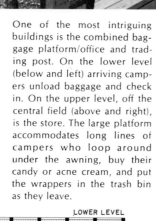

One of the most intriguing buildings is the combined baggage platform/office and trading post. On the lower level (below and left) arriving campers unload baggage and check in. On the upper level, off the central field (above and right), is the store. The large platform accommodates long lines of campers who loop around under the awning, buy their candy or acne cream, and put the wrappers in the trash bin as they leave.

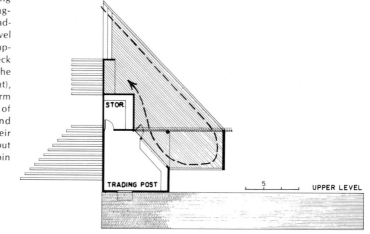

STOR.

OFFICE

BAGGAGE PLATFORM

LOWER LEVEL

STOR.

TRADING POST

5

UPPER LEVEL

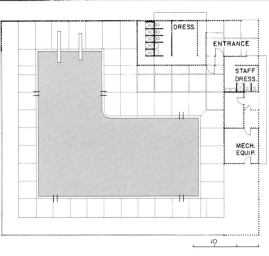

The site plan of Camp Louise, one of two operated by the Penn's Woods Girl Scout Council, does not derive its strength from the buildings Bohlin and Powell have designed—but rather the buildings are sympathetic reinforcement of the natural qualities. The dining hall, for instance, turns its tall facade to the sun, a long low one to the central field of the camp on which it is built. Thus, the field itself and its relation to existing hedgerows of adjacent state game lands dominates.

But most camps are like that, aren't they? They have simple buildings that tend to disappear into the trees. The thing that differentiates the work at Camp Louise is that while the new buildings relate humbly to nature, they do it with a flair and cleverness that makes them sophisticated indeed. As in the dining hall, bright colors and elements such as industrial windows and light fixtures are combined with old-fashioned structural details and careful circulation planning to produce unique and stylish results. The swimming pool (above), for instance, has cement-asbestos sheets on the inside faces of the studs. This provides an easily maintained surface in the changing rooms and a lively shadow pattern on the exterior.

CAMP LOUISE, Columbia County, Pennsylvania. Architects: Bohlin and Powell—Peter Q. Bohlin, partner-in-charge; Donald E. Maxwell, project architect. Engineers: Vincent B. Szykman, Inc. (structural); Martin and Fladd (mechanical). General contractor: Strausser Construction, Inc.

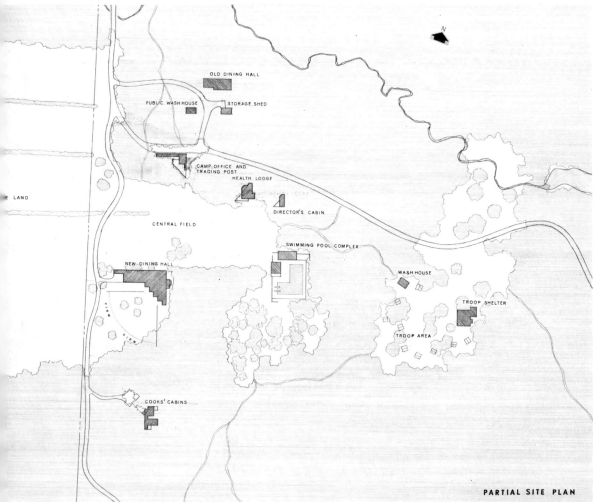

PARTIAL SITE PLAN

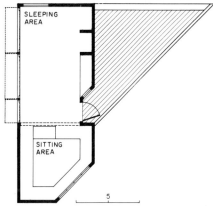

SLEEPING
AREA

SITTING
AREA

5

The director's cabin (above) and the health lodge are two adjacent buildings on the trail through the camp. They have been given similar facade treatment for that reason: industrial-type steel fenestration set into angled walls facing west. The pine grove protects them from heat build-up and casts lacy shadows on the walls each afternoon. Both have shed roofs which slope toward the central field. The health lodge, in which every camper is given a physical check-up, has a porch for those waiting.

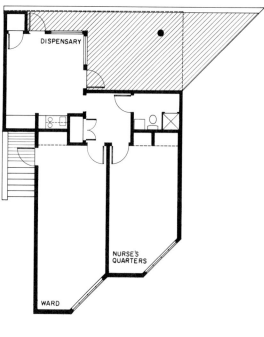

DISPENSARY

NURSE'S
QUARTERS

WARD

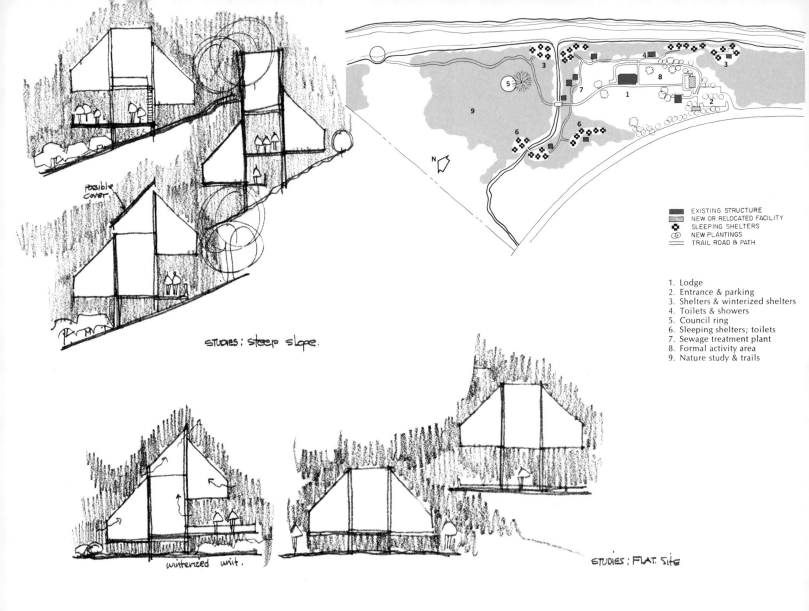

STUDIES: steep slope.

possible cover

winterized unit.

STUDIES: FLAT site

EXISTING STRUCTURE
NEW OR RELOCATED FACILITY
SLEEPING SHELTERS
NEW PLANTINGS
TRAIL ROAD & PATH

1. Lodge
2. Entrance & parking
3. Shelters & winterized shelters
4. Toilets & showers
5. Council ring
6. Sleeping shelters; toilets
7. Sewage treatment plant
8. Formal activity area
9. Nature study & trails

Robert Lindsay photos

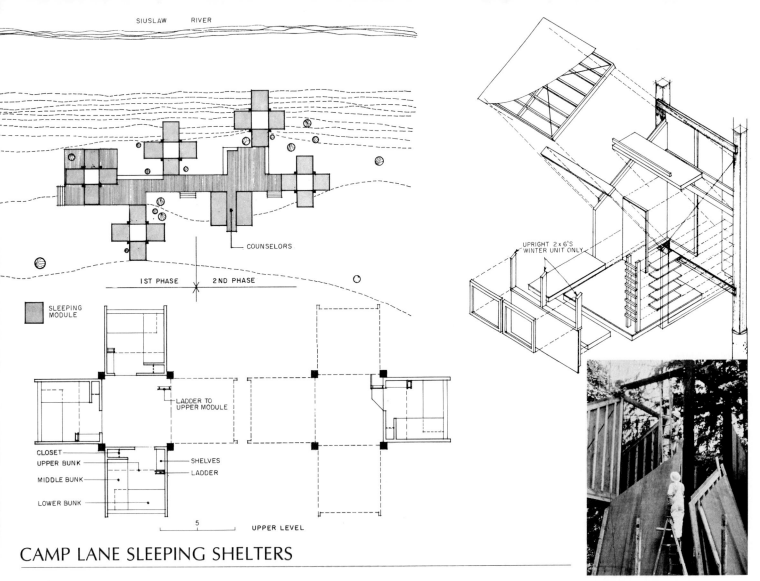

SIUSLAW RIVER

COUNSELORS

1ST PHASE   2ND PHASE

SLEEPING
MODULE

LADDER TO
UPPER MODULE

CLOSET
UPPER BUNK
MIDDLE BUNK
LOWER BUNK

SHELVES
LADDER

5   UPPER LEVEL

UPRIGHT 2 x 6'S
WINTER UNIT ONLY

CAMP LANE SLEEPING SHELTERS

Mapleton, Oregon
Unthank Seder and Poticha

County owned and administered, Camp Lane is used by organizations for conferences, programs and camping, with especial emphasis on young people's and children's groups. The architects were asked to prepare a master site plan to incorporate new shelters (some winterized) into an existing camp, for an eventual 150 persons. The 15-acre site is small for such a density; shelters are located on the edge of open activity spaces. Decks and elevated areas double as conference and play areas. Each unit is self-contained: furnishings are built in, simple and rugged. Because the camp is in such constant use, new construction has to be done fast and in brief periods. A prefabricated panel system permits rapid erection: a basic unit can be erected in slightly less than an hour, a group of 12 finished in one month. Units are grouped in clusters of four, with three persons to a unit. More units will be added as budget permits. The forms, bright colors, siting among trees, and interplay of decks were designed to be "different from home" and "fun" for all users, but particularly for children.

SLEEPING SHELTERS, CAMP LANE, (Phases 1 & 2), near Mapleton, Oregon. Architects: *Unthank, Seder & Poticha.* Contractor: *Lane County Parks Department (Phase I), Howard Nelson (Phase II).*

AIRPARK LODGE, REELFOOT LAKE STATE PARK

Tiptonville, Tennessee
Gassner/Nathan/Browne

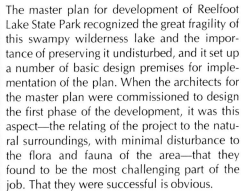

The master plan for development of Reelfoot Lake State Park recognized the great fragility of this swampy wilderness lake and the importance of preserving it undisturbed, and it set up a number of basic design premises for implementation of the plan. When the architects for the master plan were commissioned to design the first phase of the development, it was this aspect—the relating of the project to the natural surroundings, with minimal disturbance to the flora and fauna of the area—that they found to be the most challenging part of the job. That they were successful is obvious.

Reelfoot Lake was formed in 1811-12 as a result of the great New Madrid Earthquake which caused the Mississippi River to flood extensively on either side of its channel. After the river resumed its natural course, what had been a vast sunken cypress forest remained flooded, and became Reelfoot Lake. Located in the northwest corner of Tennessee, the lake has an area of some 18,000 acres at normal level. Although it has been for many years a paradise for hunters and fishermen, much of it is still wilderness. Making it possible for many people to enjoy the very special beauty of this unique place was the goal of the state's master plan. Airpark Lodge—so called from the existing airstrip for fly-in campers—and the development around it is the first step toward the implementing of this goal.

The swampy nature of the site made the use of piers particularly appropriate, since they could extend through the swamp without disturbing either trees or water plants and would allow the development to spread out, minimizing its impact and at the same time maximizing the visitor's experience of the place.

The Lodge complex consists of several buildings set on pilings over the water and connected to the main pier by short walks. At the entrance to the pier is the park office with a supply shop and a boat rental dock adjacent. Beyond the office, astride the pier, is the restaurant/lounge building with decks for outdoor dining, and farther along are clusters of motel units among the trees, each of the 20 units with a balcony for fishing or for looking at this almost-wilderness. At the lake end of the 600-foot pier is a public fishing deck. The interiors and the engaging graphics, bold against simple rough sawn cypress boards, were designed by the architects.

AIRPARK LODGE, REELFOOT LAKE STATE PARK, Tiptonville, Tennessee. Architects: *Gassner/Nathan/Browne*. Engineers: *Wooten, Smith & Weiss* (structural); *Pickering Engineering* (foundation, soils, mechanical/electrical). General contractor: *McAdoo Contractors, Inc.*

The very pleasant motel units are an important part of the changed image of Reelfoot Park, making it attractive to families as well as to sportsmen, as is provision of restaurant/ lounge (left top and center) for day and overnight visitors. Public fishing deck terminates the 600-foot-long main pier.

MOTEL CLUSTER

LOUNGE AND RESTAURANT

10

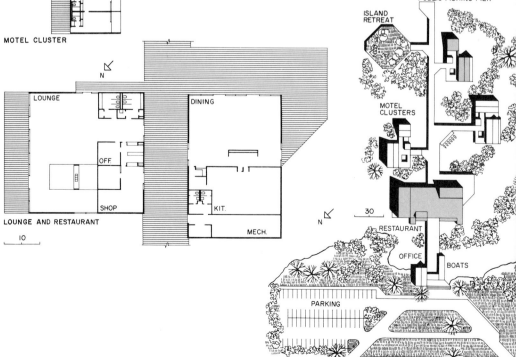

1. Future camp
2. Picnic area
3. Camp circle
4. Bus parking
5. Future model farm
6. Pond
7. Ski and sled run
8. Nature trail
9. Natural amphitheater
10. Open for vista
11. Knoll

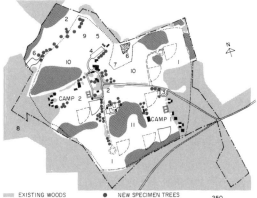

EXISTING WOODS ▦ NEW MASS PLANTINGS ● NEW SPECIMEN TREES ⋯ BRIDLE PATH   250

MILLDALE CAMPS

Reisterstown, Maryland
RTKL, Inc.

The Milldale Camps of the Jewish Community Center are located on a 155-acre site northwest of Baltimore, and serve a variety of purposes: city children get a taste of the country, adults and families use the camps year round for weekend outings and older people use an old farmhouse (existing on the property) for their activities. The site is kept as natural as possible, with the buildings—simple and modest wood structures with steep hipped roofs—unassertedly placed on the hillside, with the knoll kept open. Each of the basic units is 20 feet square; some with open, railed sides are used for shelters; others with red cedar walls are utility buildings. There are 20 such structures in each camp, and the camps, on the edge of the forest around the open hill, are almost concealed in spring and summer when the trees are in leaf. Each camp also has a large open pavilion located up the slope. In the open meadow are two swimming pools with minimal dressing shelters. Camps are far enough apart for their programs, simultaneously involving some 1000 young people, to be under way simultaneously without conflict.

MILLDALE CAMPS, Reisterstown, Maryland. Owner: *Jewish Community Center of Baltimore.* Architects: *RTKL Inc.—Charles E. Lamb, partner-in-charge; Paul T. Heineman, project captain.* Contractor: *Ira C. Rigger, Inc.*

Places to play
3
Parks, Plazas,

Playgrounds

INWOOD HILL PARK NATURE TRAILS

New York City
Richard G. Stein and Associates

Walking for pleasure is—and will be, say recreation experts—one of this country's most popular recreation activities. But pleasant places to walk are few in number, especially in urban areas. The new nature trails at Inwood Hill Park are rare exceptions to the insensitivity of walks in city parks. This old park—a unique remnant of Manhattan's original natural state, historic in connotation, wild in much of its extensive acreage—is surrounded by the densely populated streets of New York City, and is easily accessible to city dwellers. The three new trails have been developed with exceptional sensitivity to the natural qualities of these environments. Restraint and subtlety of design keep man-made intrusion at a minimum but at the same time introduce new ways of heightening the outdoor experience: the concrete "information prism" with rocks and plant materials cast into its acrylic plastic top; sitting terraces and resting places using simple forms in informal groupings.

INWOOD HILL PARK NATURE TRAILS, New York City. Client: *New York City Parks, Recreation and Cultural Affairs Administration—August Heckscher, Administrator; Elliot Willensky, Deputy Administrator for Development; Roy Neuberger, Director of Conservation.* Architects: *Richard G. Stein & Associates—Diane Serber, associate-in-charge.* Contractor: *Whitler Construction Company.*

Many new plantings were specified along the trails: on River Cove, blueberry, bayberry, mountain laurel and hemlock; on Rock Face, ferns, iris, narcissus, dogwoods; on Woodland Summit, flowering trees, hyacinths, mountain laurel, narcissus, daffodils, viburnum. Plant materials were selected (with suggestions from City horticulturists) to enhance existing plant materials with seasonal color and variations of texture.

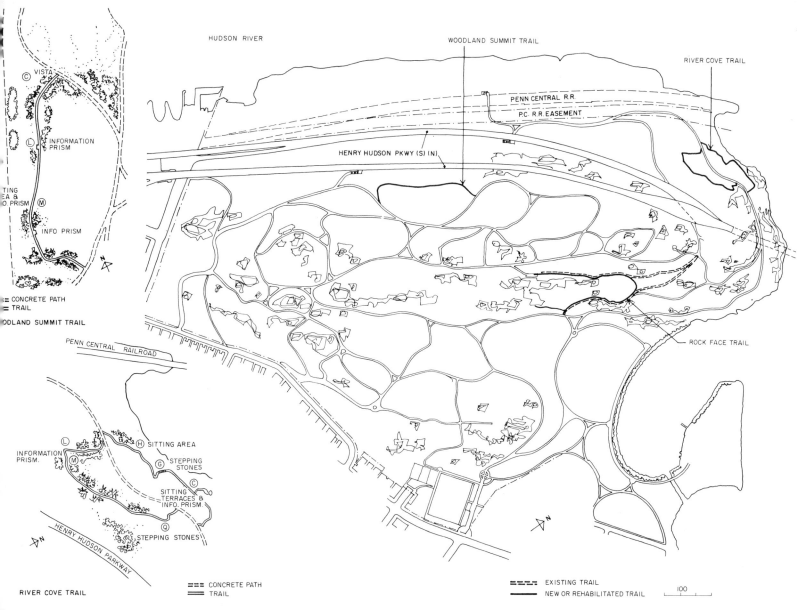

VISTA

C

L INFORMATION PRISM

TING
EA &
O. PRISM

M

INFO PRISM

N

≡≡ CONCRETE PATH
═══ TRAIL

ODLAND SUMMIT TRAIL

HUDSON RIVER

WOODLAND SUMMIT TRAIL

RIVER COVE TRAIL

PENN CENTRAL R.R.

P.C. R.R. EASEMENT

HENRY HUDSON PKWY (S) (N)

ROCK FACE TRAIL

N

PENN CENTRAL RAILROAD

INFORMATION PRISM.

L

M

H SITTING AREA

G STEPPING STONES

C SITTING TERRACES & INFO. PRISM

Q STEPPING STONES

N

HENRY HUDSON PARKWAY

RIVER COVE TRAIL

≡≡ CONCRETE PATH
═══ TRAIL

═·═·═ EXISTING TRAIL
────── NEW OR REHABILITATED TRAIL

100

Red Maple

Acer rubrum

Diane Serber photos

214

DESIGNING THE URBAN LANDSCAPE

New concepts of urban open space developed in projects by M. Paul Friedberg and Associates

If the phrase "urban landscape" is developing a contemporary meaning, the work of landscape architect and planner M. Paul Friedberg is contributing significantly to its evolution. In a wide range of projects, Mr. Friedberg has been creating, with his innovative concepts of space and use of materials, new images which suggest the infinite possibilities of open space for human use and enjoyment. He has reintroduced a well-scaled spatial complexity to the urban scene by means of intricately related multi-level planes connected by steps, amphitheater seats, chutes, glides, waterfalls or banks of trees. He uses familiar landscape materials —stone setts, gravel, pebbles and ground cover; commonplace landscape objects — benches, bollards, drinking fountains, light fixtures; and customary structures and focal points—trellises, fountains, pools and water, in delightful new ways. Friedberg's work shows that he understands the diverse needs of city people. Assessed as a whole it responds to the requirements of citizens of all ages, economic levels and ethnic groups.

This collection of his current work includes two unique projects—a small private playground for the children of one family (page 220) and a privately-owned portable video carnival (page 218) designed to be moved from one vacant lot to another and open to the public for a small admission fee. Under construction is the Harlem River Bronx State Park (page 216) which incorporates a housing development as well as generous public recreational facilities within its boundaries. His work so far has encompassed the design of combined public and private space for public use; of public space for total public use illustrated here by Ward's Island Park (page 220); of new developer-built total communities with a network of public open space as in the proposed Watertown East Development for Watertown, Massachusetts (left); and of private space for public use in the park and visitor center on the site of a Con Ed nuclear power plant at Indian Point on the Hudson (below).

There should be more work done to Friedberg's standard, by more designers given the chance, through more public and private funds being spent on the urban landscape.

East Development

rk and Visitor Center

215

A 22-acre park designed to contain 1,000 units of housing

In the future we will have fewer urban parks designed exclusively for recreational use. New concepts of urban landscape architecture call for the integration of park and recreational facilities within an interrelated system of residential, educational, commercial and cultural buildings.

The $12 million Harlem River Bronx State Park, the first phase of which is now in construction, was designed by M. Paul Friedberg and Associates for the State Park Commission for the City of New York. Programed for 3500 active users plus spectators, it will become the neighborhood community center for the residents of Harlem River Park Housing designed by Davis, Brody & Associates for the Urban Development Corporation.

The skillfully interwoven linear open space fabric will include a school, shops, railroad station, teenage center, amphitheater, gyms, pools, athletic fields, day care center, marina, exhibition spaces and eating facilities. Located in the Bronx on the abandoned and derelict industrial site shown in the lower photo, the new park will become a link in the chain of existing or proposed waterfront parks. The plan shows the proposed development for the entire 65-acre riverfront parcel extending from Marble Hill and Kingsbridge Road on the north to a point south of Highbridge. Development will be focused upon the four so-called activity nodes indicated. The Harlem River Bronx State Park falls within the Morris Heights node and is the first element in this proposed linear open space system to be developed. Land acquisition was funded by New York State, assisted by a grant from the Federal Bureau of Outdoor Recreation.

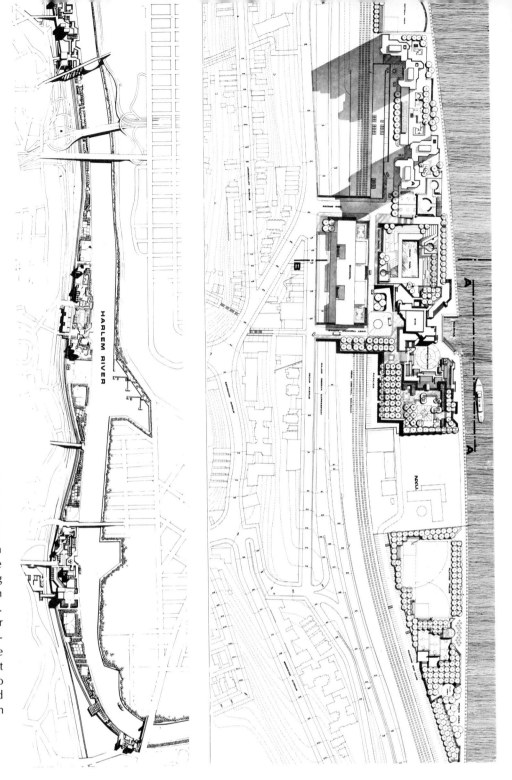

A privately developed park for New York City workers in the Wall Street district

By the end of 1972 Lower Manhattan will have an elegant new public plaza, approximately one-third of which has been built upon existing city park land and a closed-off public street, with the remainder made available for public use by a private developer. The major cost of developing the entire plaza is being born by the developer—the Uris Buildings Corporation—in conjunction with their construction of two speculative office buildings which adjoin the plaza.

M. Paul Friedberg and Associates have designed this plaza in a new manner which reflects the fact that office workers during the working day have different recreational needs than they do at other times in other places. It is essentially a place for Wall Street pedestrians to rest and have lunch. To this end the plaza will be uncluttered and serene in striking contrast to the active, crowded streets of the district. At the upper level will be a cluster of large honey-locust trees which form a canopy of shade. No other trees are used and this simple consistency is matched by the use of a brown iron spot brick on all surfaces—plaza floor, walls, stairs and kiosks.

The only accents will be the vertical cylinders which serve as ventilating stacks. These will be surfaced in stainless steel. The plaza will have backlighted waterfalls, fountains and quiet pools.

It is hoped that a portion of the lobby floor of one of the two office buildings can be leased to a restaurant so that the lower plaza may be used for outdoor dining. One of the two circular kiosks may become a food concession.

A modular and mobile money making urban park for video watchers

Small circuses, carnivals and amusement concessions still visit our neighborhoods and towns, set up tents and mechanical rides on available lots, do business for a few days or a week or two and then pack up and move on. M. Paul Friedberg and Associates in collaboration with Jay K. Hoffman Presentations have devised a contemporary carnival based upon video projection. Designed to be moved from one vacant neighborhood lot to another the video park, for which admission would be charged, would consist of projection equipment, collapsible screens, a video tape library and a restaurant. The latter would have monitors which would televise to the diners inside the events going on in the park outside.

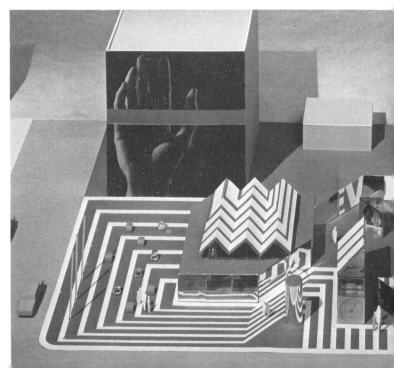

218

Louis Checkman photos

Abstract forms for children's play stir their imaginations and challenge their bodies

This is a private playground for the children of one family built on a causeway between their house, designed by Ulrich Franzen, and the mainland. Multiples of this design are, of course, adaptable to many kinds of playgrounds, public and quasi-public as well as private, on many different kinds of sites.

The causeway is narrow and sandy, flanked on one side by a road and on the other by a rip-rap bulkhead. The problem was to design a playground to fit into this area which would reflect the character of the marine landscape, while not conflicting with the bold design of the residence. To accomplish this, M. Paul Friedberg and Associates used a commercially available precut timber play unit system consisting of 12 in. by 12 in. timbers of varying lengths.

This play unit system effectively challenges a child's physical capabilities, teaching him how high he can go, how strong he is and how strong he can be. He learns how long he can balance and hang and how much physical effort he can endure.

As Friedberg describes it, the units have been assembled "to create a silhouette of verticals which would penetrate the skyplane and mark the event—yet not block the view. "A series of interconnected stepping column mounds, vertical climbing units and raised horizontal elements satisfy the play requirements.

The owners have pronounced it an extremely successful play environment and the configuration—now weathered by salt spray—appears to belong in the landscape. When the children grow up the assembled play units will remain, elevated by the passage of time into a work of art.

Ron Green photos

A portion of Ward's Island designed as a park for the Harlem community

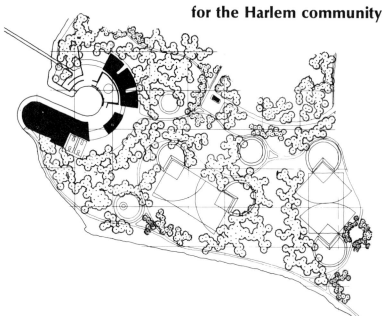

Ward's Island Park is connected to Harlem by means of the existing foot bridge shown in the rendering by M. Paul Friedberg and Associates indicating their scheme for the improvement of this portion of the island. At present this area, which can only be reached on foot, is idyllically uncrowded. On weekends a few Harlem ball clubs use the playing fields, bicyclists meander on neglected footpaths, and families picnic along the water's edge. The views of Manhattan are dramatic from many points along the shore. Friedberg proposes an urban plaza, near the end of the bridge, to act as a magnet to bring more people to the park. The park's value as a place of almost pastoral contrast to the teeming streets of Harlem will disappear, but in Friedberg's hands new urban values will emerge.

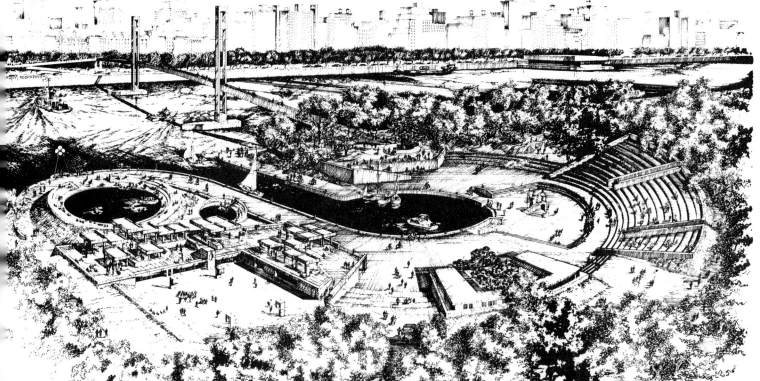

Place's to play 4

The 50th State:

«Test for the Landscape of Tourism»

Hawaii's problem is success: can it further expand tourism and also preserve its natural beauty?

When one-and-a-quarter million people converge on a place, they are bound to cause it to change. The mere need of providing housing for them—overnight or longer—will do things to a place. Add to that their need for a reasonable amount of activities, and the whole problem is vastly compounded. For 1.2-million people—the number who have visited Hawaii this year, more visitors than there are residents—will have a broad range of tastes. For some the remote sandy shore, shaded by coco palms and keawe trees, is enough; for others, it's instant boredom.

Hawaii is a multi-island state whose fabled beauty could become a near-fatal attraction. Because its beauty is confined to no one island—and not even to one spot on an island—the whole state qualifies as a resort area. The whole state thus is subject to the very considerable pressures of tourism. For tourism is big business in Hawaii. Its dollar volume is second only to government (defense) spending, and is far ahead of the Islands' traditional industries, sugar and pineapples. The pressures it exerts come from all its components: the airlines, which say flatly that they "can't sell a seat without a bed" (at the destination point); the hotels, which want full occupancy; the developers and financiers, who want as quick a return on their investments as possible; and all the service agencies essential to satisfying the tourist. Pressure comes, too, from the associations which promote tourism.

These pressures have meant that where environmental decisions were concerned, preference has gone to the proposal or solution which best answered the demands of tourism. Since the only jet airport until a year ago was at Honolulu, the greatest pressure—and the greatest economic advantage—was in Waikiki, the resort district of Honolulu. As a result, tall hotels replaced small hotels, and apartment, condominium and commercial buildings crowded the hotels until the density along a 10-block stretch of Kalakaua Avenue, the main Waikiki street, has become that of a metropolis, not of a resort.

More as a measure to improve the economy of the Outer (now called "Neighbor") Islands than as a signal of environmental distress, the State of Hawaii, then brand-new, in 1959 commissioned an "action program" for development of new "Visitor Destination Areas" in the five major inhabited is-

lands. But the effect of the program— actually a broad-scaled, statewide study of the potentials for resort development —has been environmental as well as economic. For a part of the study included recommendations for "First Stage Plans for Public Improvements," prepared by Belt, Collins & Associates of Honolulu, engineers, planners and landscape architects. These plans set forth the improvements which would be necessary at the sites selected for possible development and which the state should provide— water (always a problem) and roads, parks, marinas and other open recreation areas—as incentives and stimuli to developers. But the plans also suggested the character that would be appropriate for development of each site.

The VDA study was a valuable tool to the state in fostering development, especially in the Neighbor Islands, little known to developers and investors. Of the 10 Neighbor Island sites, some development has taken place at seven; plans are under way at a different location (which had not seemed feasible in 1959); planning is under way on one, and nothing has yet happened at the last. The increased number of rooms, the growing variety of accommodations at resort areas, the much-needed choices of activities (few tourists really want the desert-isle syndrome for long; they want people and action) have attracted visitors in economically-encouraging numbers to these outer locations.

With the economy on the upgrade in these various places, it is fair to ask, What of the environmental quality?

The VDA, in its necessarily general terms, pointed the way toward quality in both planning and building design. And Hawaii's two pioneering tools, the State General Plan and the Land Use Law (Hawaii was the first state to enact such legislation) have respectively done much to set goals and high standards for development and to set the boundaries for the state's four zoning categories. But so far nothing provides specific design criteria for the selected sites in the Visitor Destination Areas, and it is these that Hawaii so greatly needs.

Fortunately, however, a series of Environmental Studies, just completed, was commissioned last year by the State's Foundation on Culture and the Arts. These provide the detail of carefully considered criteria for the particularly sensitive areas in the state. Excerpts are included on the following pages. These— and, hopefully, others of similar scope and depth—can become yet another pioneering tool and, if made policy, a means toward assuring environmental quality and economic viability.

Protection of natural beauty—at best a fragile thing—and enhancement of the economy are not necessarily mutually exclusive goals. Hawaii's far-sighted economic planning for tourism needs to be matched by far-sighted planning for the quality of its environment. Each island has its own character and capacity for use. The state needs an inventory of such natural resources and an estimate of their capacity for use. The General Plan sets Environmental Quality as one of its goals, and Good Design as another, but these are only a beginning. As landscape architect Garrett Eckbo, whose firm will make the first five-year review of the Hawaii General Plan, says, "Hawaii is the test for the landscape of tourism."

Dilemma in paradise: Must success prove fatal? Can Hawaii protect its loveliest places by increasing densities in already-urbanized areas? Or should it also extend protection to small but growing towns on outer islands? If it does, where will it house the millions of tourists expected in the next few years? Tourist tastes range widely, from Waikiki's congestion (near right) and many choices to remoteness and isolation (center), and in between, to small, quiet resorts (far right) with some choice.

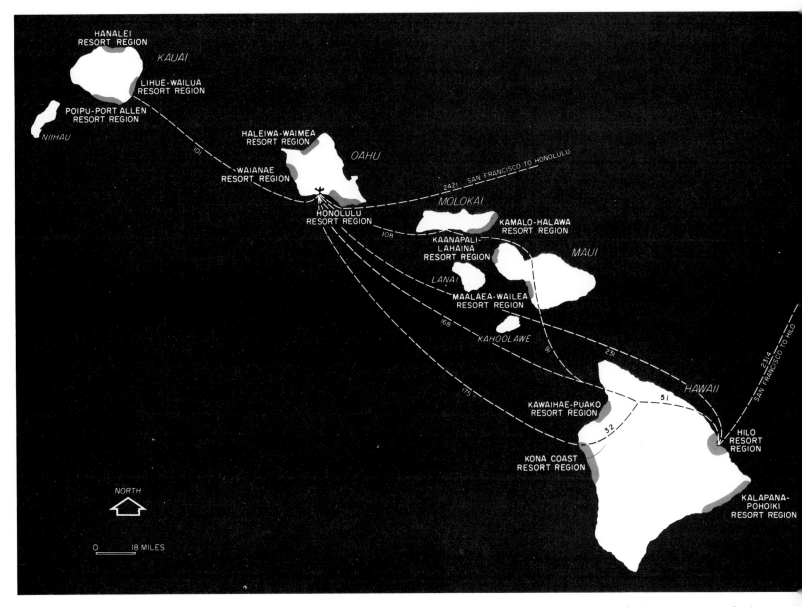

Visitor destination areas in each of its five major islands were selected in 1959 by the new state of Hawaii to spread benefits of growing tourism on Oahu to outer islands. VDA is defined as a place capable of "independently attracting and motivating travel to itself." Within a VDA, resort regions offer a variety of recreation and entertainment. State's "action program" made promise that outer islands would maintain "image" of Hawaii even with greater density in Waikiki.

Mauna Kea Beach Hotel, Skidmore, Owings & Merrill, architects   R. Wenkam   *Waiohea, Vladimir Ossipoff, architect*

OAHU

Waikiki: concentrating people, buildings and activity makes for choice—and planning problems

Waikiki, "playground of the world," is every tourist's destination at some time during his visit to Hawaii. Even now that it is no longer the inevitable first destination of every visitor—the Hilo airport was expanded to take jets late in 1967—it still is the overwhelming favorite of Hawaiian resorts. Part of its lure is no doubt the image of Diamond Head, for so many years the visual symbol of Hawaii. More important is the fact that Waikiki has a choice and contrast of activity that is hard to match in other resorts: all sorts of shops, hotels, nightclubs, restaurants; apartments; water sports, boat trips. Most of all, it has people, and they mean action, for a broad spectrum of tastes and backgrounds. But Waikiki's popularity has created a serious environmental problem: congestion. Buildings crowd the waterfront, each wall nudging its neighbor's wall. The vistas from Kalakaua Avenue, the main street, to the ocean are gone. Except for the bright muumuus and aloha shirts, it is difficult to believe this is Hawaii. It seems more like a new-built city, anywhere. To newcomers this problem is less acute than to returning visitors and residents. But it is not hopeless. The street is handsome, if crowded, and public opinion has been aroused to the need for long-range planning—comprehensive and uncompromising. Planner Aaron Levine and architect William Grant of the Oahu Development Conference, commissioned by the Foundation for Culture and the Arts to study the Honolulu waterfront, urge a "bold new approach" with land use, public works and architectural control as the working tools.

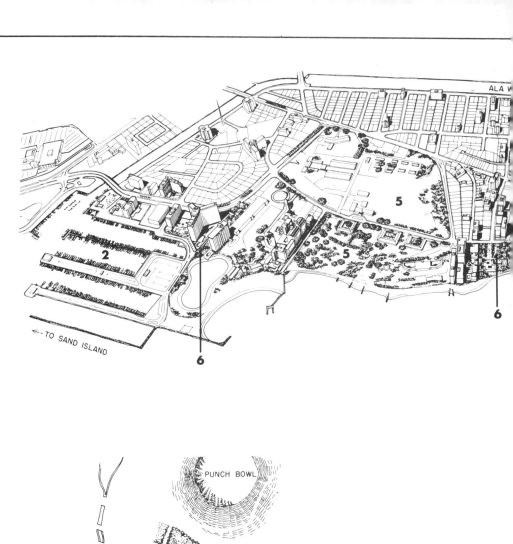

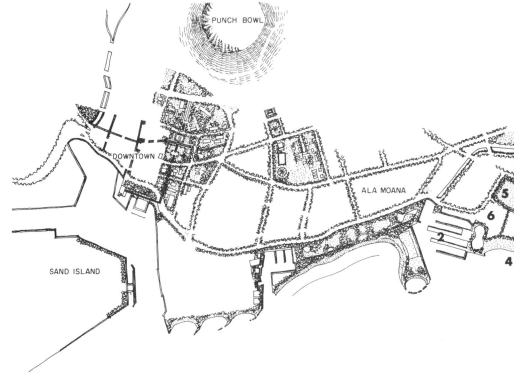

Hawaii Visitors Bureau

1960 (left): Some ocean-front sites were still open; 1968 (right): Only low-density uses afford relief from "concrete jungle" and plans indicate increasing density even for them.

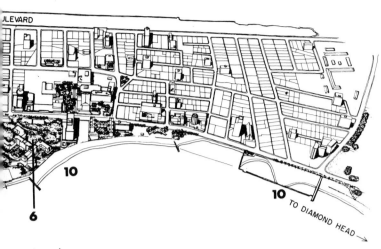

WAIKIKI TODAY

Legend

1. Surfing sites
2. Yacht harbor
3. Beach promenade
4. Beach reclamation
5. Open space, Fort deRussy
6. Low-density areas
7. Pedestrian mall
8. One way street system,
   Kalakaua Avenue-Ala Wai Boulevard
9. New by-pass boulevard
10. Beach park
11. Extension of existing park to Diamond Head

Nelson Zellers

"The Jungle," Waikiki's blighted area of bungalows and duplexes, will be redeveloped as a park-resort by Liliuokalani Trust to "re-establish the feeling of a relaxed tropical resort once characteristic of Waikiki." Raised pedestrian mall, with parking below, will form base for hotel and apartment buildings sited to preserve ocean view.

Belt, Collins & Associates, engineers, planners and landscape architects

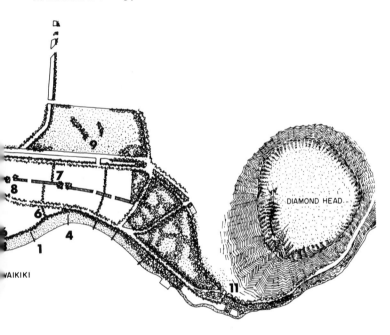

Urban Design Plan/1968: Environmental Study of Honolulu Waterfront

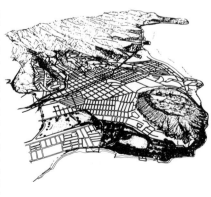

Diamond Head, "a fragile design element in the urban landscape" increasingly threatened by development on its lower slopes, appears safe now that city action (in response to unprecedented public expression against further building at its base) and designation as a National Natural Landmark have given it special status. But city's new 350-foot height limit and present high-rise buildings threaten many views of it. Recommendations of Environmental Study for Waikiki include relief of traffic congestion, more open space and emphasis on larger area for Waikiki.

Aaron Levine, planner, William Grant, architect

Camera Hawaii

Ala Moana Shopping Center, John Graham and Company

Academy of Arts, Bertram Goodhue, architect

B Honolulu's **unique character** as crossroads of the Pacific makes it a Visitor Destination Area in itself. Multi-cultural in aspect as in population, a mixture of sophistication and naturalness, set between the ocean and the mountains, its variety is apparently endless. Waikiki is only one part of the city; the other parts have their charm and interest also: Downtown with its fine older business buildings (below left) and new handsome office complexes (below right), its world-famous Academy of Arts (above) and mammoth Ala Moana Shopping Center (top). New hotels and apartment buildings in Ala Moana district will further link this area with Waikiki.

Financial Plaza, Leo S. Wou and Victor Gruen Associates, associated architects

Alexander & Baldwin Building, C. W. Dickey, architect

228

Honolulu, with many tourist attractions and new resorts north and west, will reduce pressures on Waikiki

The island of Oahu has some of Hawaii's most beautiful beaches and most dramatic scenery, but until such attractions as the semi-scientific Sea Life Park and the Polynesian Cultural Center on the Windward side of the island, the average tourist had no experience of Oahu besides Waikiki (except for Honolulu). With the development of Makaha Valley as a luxury resort, and of the magnificent North Coast, and with new and improved roads, the more adventurous visitors, at least, will spread to these outer areas.

Camera Hawaii

D **Makaha Valley,** one of Oahu's most dramatic and beautiful places, is one of three Visitor Destination Areas on the island. Although development came to it slowly, the Valley is fast being transformed into a luxury resort community. The VDA recommended 200 hotel units for the Valley; already 200 units are under way as the first of six hotels. It has been master-planned to respect—as much as so large a building program can—the landscape: tall apartment buildings are to be ranged along the base of the mountains; smaller-scale buildings will be in the open center; residential buildings will be on the ocean front. Planning and architectural controls are to be enforced on new work.

C **Oahu's North Shore,** not one of the original Visitor Destination Areas, is now scheduled for development as a resort community, with some 20 hotels planned for an 11-mile stretch of coast between Kawela Bay and Kahuku, provided zoning changes (from "agricultural" to "urban") are approved. Other changes in the wild and beautiful coastal area will occur with closing of a large sugar plantation at Kahuku.

N

FARM AND GRAZING LANDS

BEACH PARK

SCENIC DRIVE

MAKAHA

WAIANAE

MARINA

POKAI BAY

BEACH PARK

BEACH PARK

▓ RESORT HOTEL OR APT.
▢ PARK AND RECREATION

State Of Hawaii Visitor Destination Area Study

Camera Hawaii

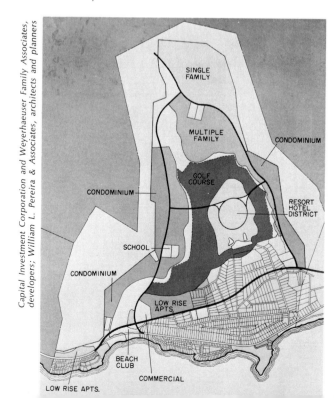

Capital Investment Corporation and Weyerhaeuser Family Associates, developers; William L. Pereira & Associates, architects and planners

SINGLE FAMILY

MULTIPLE FAMILY

CONDOMINIUM

CONDOMINIUM

GOLF COURSE

RESORT HOTEL DISTRICT

SCHOOL

CONDOMINIUM

LOW RISE APTS.

BEACH CLUB

COMMERCIAL

LOW RISE APTS.

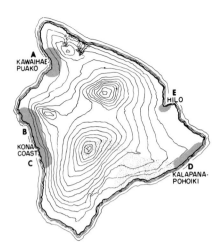

HAWAII

Transportation, land-use, design criteria: keys to future quality of Big Island's West Coast

West Hawaii is presently sparsely populated, partly because much of it is ranchland in private ownership, but mainly because roads are all but non-existent in the north section, and inland along the south Kona Coast. The new jet airport on the coast north of Kailua (B) and the new road linking the north (A) and south coasts have had effects on the whole coast, shifting and increasing its population, raising land values and increasing the pressures for more intense and denser development. It is an area of vast vistas to mountains, lava fields, lush vegetation and great potential. The area itself is not so much beautiful as it is rugged and wild, qualities which —at least along the coast—should be preserved and enhanced by whatever is man-made. State land use zoning has given the broad basis for future development, but still needed are detailed criteria of the scope of the Environmental Studies, and a process which would coordinate public works programs with private development plans. Also important to coordinate with development plans is the preservation of historic sites (like City of Refuge, below) in which the West Coast abounds.

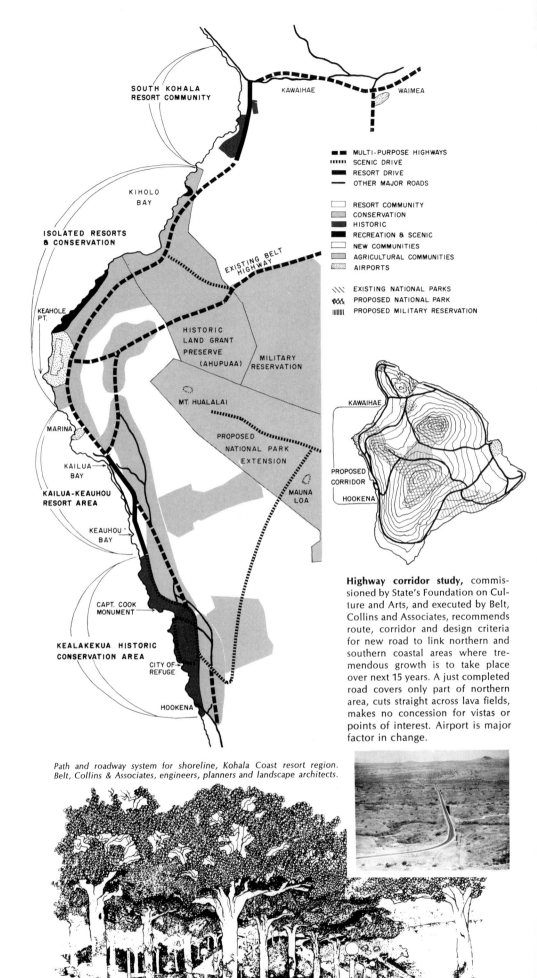

MULTI-PURPOSE HIGHWAYS
SCENIC DRIVE
RESORT DRIVE
OTHER MAJOR ROADS

RESORT COMMUNITY
CONSERVATION
HISTORIC
RECREATION & SCENIC
NEW COMMUNITIES
AGRICULTURAL COMMUNITIES
AIRPORTS

EXISTING NATIONAL PARKS
PROPOSED NATIONAL PARK
PROPOSED MILITARY RESERVATION

Highway corridor study, commissioned by State's Foundation on Culture and Arts, and executed by Belt, Collins and Associates, recommends route, corridor and design criteria for new road to link northern and southern coastal areas where tremendous growth is to take place over next 15 years. A just completed road covers only part of northern area, cuts straight across lava fields, makes no concession for vistas or points of interest. Airport is major factor in change.

Path and roadway system for shoreline, Kohala Coast resort region. Belt, Collins & Associates, engineers, planners and landscape architects.

Mauna Kea Beach Hotel, Skidmore, Owings & Merrill, architects

A **Kohala Coast** will be developed by Dilrock-Eastern Corporation (Dillingham Corporation, Laurance Rockefeller, Eastern Airlines) as $250-million resort community which will eventually include a new town, a range of hotel types, residences, public recreation and restored historic sites. Master plan (bottom) provides land uses compatible with existing Mauna Kea Beach Hotel, and conserves scenic and recreational resources.

Vacation villa: Thomas O. Wells, architect

Residence: Vladimir Ossipoff, Architect

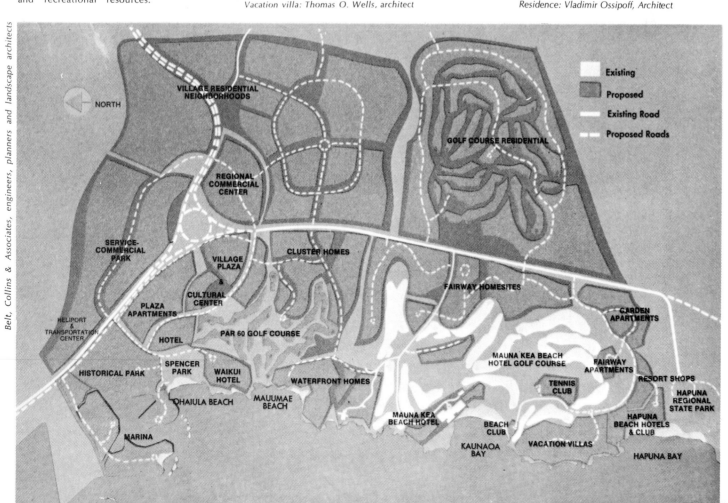

Belt, Collins & Associates, engineers, planners and landscape architects

Existing
Proposed
Existing Road
Proposed Roads

NORTH

VILLAGE RESIDENTIAL NEIGHBORHOODS

GOLF COURSE RESIDENTIAL

REGIONAL COMMERCIAL CENTER

SERVICE-COMMERCIAL PARK

CLUSTER HOMES

VILLAGE PLAZA & CULTURAL CENTER

FAIRWAY HOMESITES

GARDEN APARTMENTS

PLAZA APARTMENTS

HELIPORT & TRANSPORTATION CENTER

HOTEL

PAR 60 GOLF COURSE

MAUNA KEA BEACH HOTEL GOLF COURSE

FAIRWAY APARTMENTS

HISTORICAL PARK

SPENCER PARK

WAIKUI HOTEL

WATERFRONT HOMES

TENNIS CLUB

RESORT SHOPS

OHAIULA BEACH

MAUUMAE BEACH

MAUNA KEA BEACH HOTEL

BEACH CLUB

VACATION VILLAS

HAPUNA BEACH HOTELS & CLUB

HAPUNA REGIONAL STATE PARK

MARINA

KAUNAOA BAY

HAPUNA BAY

Kona Hilton Hotel Wimberly, Whisenand, Allison & Tong, architects

Big Island's Kona Coast knows pressures of rapid growth and great potential as tourist area, and seeks means to control quality of development

B **Kailua is center of Kona Coast** population, commercial activity and at present, hotels. But it is still a village (below) in size, scale and urban resources. In the rush toward tourism, Kailua's height limit, once three stories (as at old Kona Inn, right) was raised to seven stories, permitting height limit hotels (like Kona Hilton, above) to be built. Recent concern for future attractiveness of town as Visitor Destination Area led to lowering of limit to four stories. To realize its aspirations Kailua also needs well-planned, well-designed, man-made charm.

The Island of Hawaii—the Big Island—has four extinct or dormant volcanoes and one, Kilautea on the slopes of Mauna Loa, whose continuing activity is almost legendary. The miles of lava that cover much of the island become a part of its particular attraction, and resorts built on these lava fields are like oases. The great scale of the vistas from all parts of the island are its special beauty. Except for the resort area of Hilo on the East Coast (D), and the small village of Kailua on the Kona Coast (B) there is no tourist activity center on the island. As the new resort communities in the north and south—Kawaihae and Keauhou—develop, and as Kailua itself grows, as it will, and the new road becomes actuality, the tourist can choose among a great many recreational and sport activities.

Small isolated resorts like Kona Village (left) are at opposite extreme from large in-town hotels in Kailua. Low-density Kona Village is accessible only by air; the new road would make this and other suggested resorts of similar type easier to reach but would still permit isolation which is their special attraction. Presently only two or three such isolated resorts exist in Hawaii, but recommended land use plan (across page, bottom) suggests additional sites along North Coast. Scale and size of such resorts does not disturb landscape.

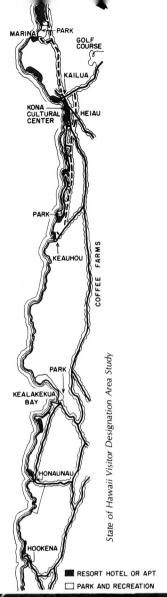

State of Hawaii Visitor Designation Area Study

■ RESORT HOTEL OR APT.
□ PARK AND RECREATION

C **Keauhou,** the $180-million residential and resort "Community of Leisure" now being developed on Keauhou Bay, is the historic playground of Hawaiian royalty. The new community will change the present small fishing port on the Bay by making it into a marina, with a plaza intended to become the focal point for the community and for tourist activities. The master plan contains four sites on which nine hotels can be located (three are already in planning). It will feature clustered residences of various types, and apartments.

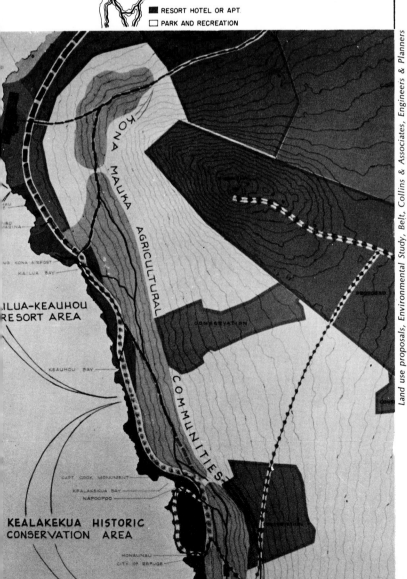

KONA MAUKA AGRICULTURAL

KAILUA-KEAUHOU
RESORT AREA

COMMUNITIES

KEALAKEKUA HISTORIC
CONSERVATION AREA

Land use proposals, Environmental Study, Belt, Collins & Associates, Engineers & Planners

H. Peter Oberlander & R. J. Cave, Community Planning Consultants, Inc.

KAANAPALI-LAHAINA — A

MAALAEA-WAILEA — B

MAUI

Second-largest island Maui is scenic, historic, and the site of the most successful Visitor Destination Area to date

Diverse, historic, beautiful, completely different from the Big Island, Maui is known as the valley isle because of the isthmus that joins its two volcanic masses, one derived from huge Haleakala, the other from smaller Puu Kukui. As a place, its beauty is more delicate than Hawaii's and stronger than Kauai's. Thus the impact of development on it can be disastrous if not carefully done. How it is done, where it is permitted to happen, and how the pressures for increased density are handled will be of utmost importance in its future. Since Maui is the site of the most successful Visitor Destination Area to date—Daanapal 12—that development serves as both example and caution. Siting and orientation can be significant factors in the quality of the environment, and at Kaanapali, where the openness of the site and the landmark Black Rock were its most noticable attributes, the scale could be bold and strong. But Black Rock has been obscured by a hotel, and whatever scale the place will have must come from siting, height and design. Kaanapali's hotels and choice of recreation offer the tourist the necessary variety, and Lahaina, an old whaling villiage south of the resort area, complements this with historic buildings, night clubs and restaurants.

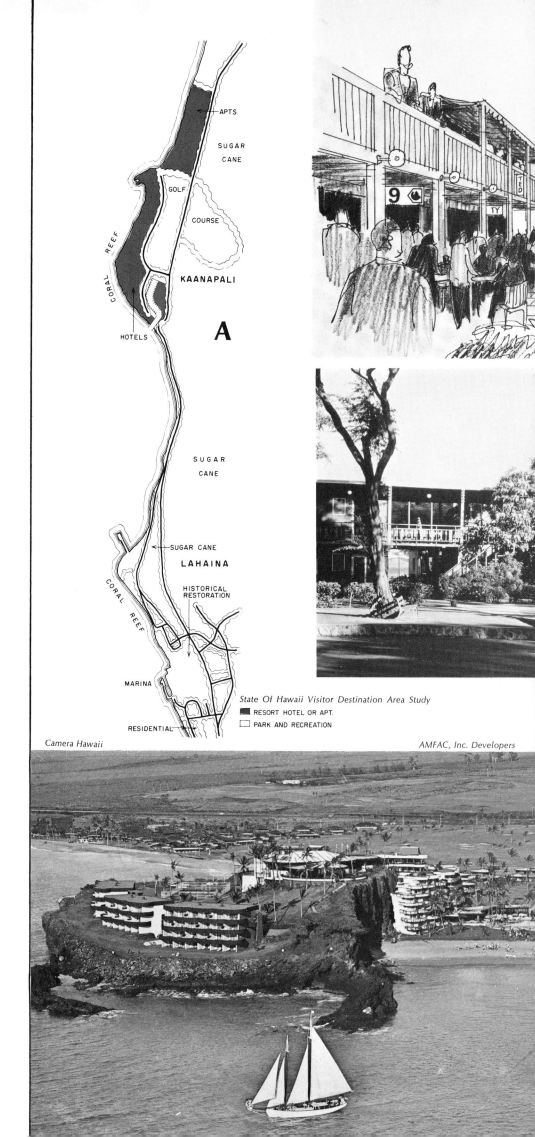

APTS.

SUGAR CANE

GOLF COURSE

CORAL REEF

KAANAPALI

HOTELS

A

SUGAR CANE

SUGAR CANE

LAHAINA

HISTORICAL RESTORATION

CORAL REEF

MARINA

RESIDENTIAL

State Of Hawaii Visitor Destination Area Study
■ RESORT HOTEL OR APT.
□ PARK AND RECREATION

Camera Hawaii

AMFAC, Inc. Developers

Lahaina, one of Hawaii's most historic towns, is being restored as an important tourist attraction. Keeping its vitality as a town while bringing visitors to its narrow streets is a design problem tackled by Environmental Study; how to make new buildings, inevitable for the town's growth, compatible visually and spatially, is another. Above, Hale Aloha church as focus.

Napili Kai resort on the north shore attracts long-staying, repeat patronage, and has a high occupancy rate. Small, comparatively remote, its patrons have similar tastes and backgrounds, enjoy similar activity (or non-activity).

Kaanapali (A), resort community proves validity of its selection as a VDA. Five hotels and a condominium have been built within its boundaries, with a range of accommodations and variety of activities. It meets the VDA definition of a destination area by having at least 1500 rooms, restaurants, golf courses, white sandy beach (one of the best). It will also have a large resort-oriented shopping center, Whalers' Village, now under construction at the Lahaina end of the beach. One of its problems—easy transportation into Lahaina—will be solved if proposed railroad with excursion train goes into operation. This would permit non-drivers (or those who could not rent a car, or those on tours) to make independent excursions into town for sightseeing or shopping.

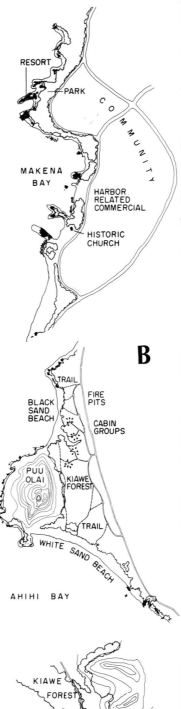

B

John Carl Warnecke and Associates, architects

Environmental Study of undeveloped coastal area below selected Visitor Distination Area was undertaken as commission from State Culture and Arts Foundation to determine how to prevent over-building and disfigurement of so sensitive an area, and to provide resident-oriented recreation facilities.

Makena, an old Hawaiian settlement, a town under missionaries, then a busy port, could be revived as a recreation-related town, Environment Study suggests. For residents' use, parks and beaches should be developed, it recommends.

At Puu Olai, study suggests keeping its two beaches—one white sand, the other black—as a natural park, with minimum development. Simple cabins and camping areas—which local people could use—could be located under trees along shore.

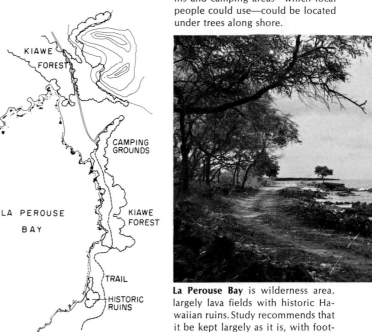

La Perouse Bay is wilderness area, largely lava fields with historic Hawaiian ruins. Study recommends that it be kept largely as it is, with footpaths to historic sites, but no other development.

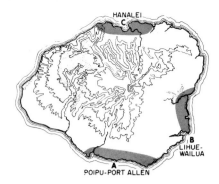

KAUAI

Kauai's natural beauty makes all of it a Destination Area and especially sensitive to development.

Kauai, oldest and, to many, loveliest of the islands, is so generally beautiful that the whole island was designated a Visitor Destination Area, with three regions (two of them—(A) and (C)—among the island's most exquisite) signaled out for resort development. Some development has taken place on all three sites, with varying degree of environmental success and respect for the fragile beauty they make their setting. That resorts do not have to intrude on the natural beauty of a place is clear in one of Kauai's older resorts, the phenomenally successful Coco Palms (B). This resort usurps no natural beauty, but transforms an ordinary

Coco Palms, Wimberly & Cook, architects

site into an extraordinary experience. Its atmosphere may be synthetic, but the flair with which it is done is undeniably effective and in so using an ordinary site, other sensitive places can be preserved in their natural state. Another way to do this is the high-rise hotel. Fortunately on Kauai there is a choice.

Kauai Surf, Frank Robert, architect

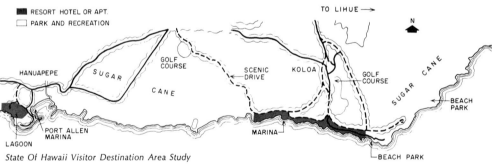

State Of Hawaii Visitor Destination Area Study

A **Environmental study** by Donald Wolbrink & Associates, landscape architects and planners, calls Poipu-Koloa area (A) "a world of its own" whose scale and character should derive from factors like indigenous housing, a 100-year-old mission church, vegetation like monkeypod tree.

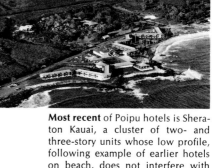

Most recent of Poipu hotels is Sheraton Kauai, a cluster of two- and three-story units whose low profile, following example of earlier hotels on beach, does not interfere with view to mountains. Scale of individual buildings is such that with more vegetation, relation of this resort to beach could be no more intrusive than is Waiohea, yet its openness and access to beach could be retained.

Camera Hawaii

Sheraton Kauai, Wimberly, Whisenand, Allison & Tong, architects

Waiohea, Vladimir Ossipoff, architect

Waiohea, a quiet resort on one of Poipu's small crescent beaches (A), evolved from two beach cottages, retains their scale and unobtrusive character. Environmental study warns that Poipu's beauty is "fragile, readily compromised, minimized or ignored"; that climate and location could turn it into another Waikiki unless land use and design controls are used.

MOLOKAI

Undeveloped, unspoiled, a unique opportunity to demonstrate quality in resort development

Molokai's first resort community is being developed at the opposite end of the island from the site selected by the Visitor Destination Study in 1959. Private enterprise, in the form of Molokai's largest land owner, Molokai Ranch Company, did not wait for the stimulus of public works, as the study proposed on the eastern end (A), but is forging ahead with development of a resort and second-home community on the west end (B). Here the beaches are superb and varied in type, from broad and sandy to small and rock-enclosed. The master plan (by Belt, Collins & Associates) uses the character of the beaches in its land use proposals: the small beaches for the intimate type of resort, the great beach for a public beach park, with a sports center and a golf course as part of the park: an exceptional demonstration of public conscience, and of particular importance now. Beach access, especially in resort areas, is often all but non-existent, yet all beaches are in public ownership. This great park opens the magnificent beach to the public, and suggests that the developers are concerned with the environmental quality of the new community. As yet no design criteria for the hotels and residences have been announced. These will be an important part of the implementation of the master plan.

Hotel Molokai, Frank Robert architect

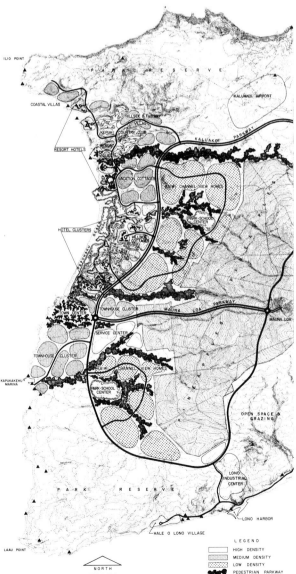

B Molokai's west end is completely undeveloped; most of the land is open range. It is dry and parched but wildly beautiful. The master plan envisions an eventual community of 30,000 population. Its proximity to Honolulu (15 minutes by air) indicates potential as a second home community as well as a resort. The amount of open space provided is unusual but appropriate to the rural quality of the island. Most permanent residents would live in the hills above the resort area. Hotels will be of two types: large, located near the park, and smaller luxury resorts located on semi-private beaches. Rezoning (from agricultural to urban) has been granted by the State Land Use Commission for 1460 of the proposed 6800 acres.

LEGEND

HIGH DENSITY
MEDIUM DENSITY
LOW DENSITY
PEDESTRIAN PARKWAY
PUBLIC PARK
ARCHAEOLOGICAL SITES

NORTH

GRAPHIC SCALE

DATE: AUGUST, 1967

Index

A

Aalto (Alvar), 199
Abend, Stephen, 139
Abrams, Benjamin, 46
Abrams, Poley, Corporation, 46
Academy of Arts, Honolulu, 228
Aga Khan, 34
Aguirre, Luis, 161
Ahlstrom, Lee, 136
Airpark Lodge, Reelfoot Lake State Park,
    Tiptonville, Tennessee, 206–208
Ala Moana Shopping Center, Honolulu, Hawaii, 228
Alameda, California, 66–67
Alderman, Britt Jr., and Associates, 10
Alexander and Baldwin Building, Honolulu, Hawaii, 228
Allen, Edward, 150
Allen Organization, The, 190–195
Alta Canyon, Utah, 150–151
Aluminum Corporation of America, 13
Amathus Beach Hotel, Limassol, Cyprus, 64–65
Amathus Navigation Company, Ltd., 65
American Restaurant, Kansas City, Missouri, 136–137
AMFAC, Inc. Developers, 234
Amis, James J., 114
Anderson, David W., 152
Anselevicius, Helen, 21
Ansteth, Ltd., 60
Architects:
    Atelier d'Architecture, 82–87
    Bohlin and Powell, 190–195, 198–203
    Breuer, Marcel, 78–81
    Bull Field Volkmann Stockwell, 88–93, 94–95
    Campbell, John Carden, 186–187
    Campbell and Wong and Associates, 66–67
    Caudill Rowlett Scott, 22–30
    Colakides and Associates, 64–65
    Copelin and Lee, 165
    Davis Brody and Associates, 216–217
    de la Torre, Jose, 52–53
    Dinsmore, Kulseth and Riggs/Architecture One, Ltd., 185
    Dreyfuss and Blackford, 42
    Drummey Rosane Anderson, 152–153
    Enteleki Architecture, Planning Research, 150–151
    Field, John Louis, 168–169
    Foster, Richard, 162–164
    Franzen, Ulrich, 220–221
    Gassner/Nathan/Browne, 206–207
    Goodhue, Bertram, 228
    Graham, John, and Company, 228
    Grant, William, 227
    Gruen, Victor, Associates, 228
    Jacobsen, Hugh Newell, 44–45, 144–145
    JV VIII, a joint venture of Koetter, Tharp and Cowell,
        Caudill Rowlett Scott, Neuhaus & Taylor, 22–30
    Killingsworth Brady and Associates, 96–103
    Koetter Tharp and Cowell, 22–30
    Kroeger, Keith, 142–143

Architects (*Cont.*):
    Lapidus, Alan H., 37–41, 52, 123–127, 188
    Lapidus, Morris, and Associates, 2, 37, 52–55, 123, 125, 126,
        188–189
    Millar, C. Blakeway, 134–135
    Morgan, William, 68–71
    Neish Owen Rowland and Roy, 132–133
    Nemeny, George, 166–167
    Neuhaus & Taylor, 22–30
    O'Dell/Hewlett and Luckenbach, Inc., 43
    Ossipoff, Vladimir, 60, 231
    Pereira, William L., and Associates, 229
    Perfido, Leonard, 142–143
    Platner, Warren, 136–137, 140–141
    Polshek, James Stewart, 178–181
    Portman, John, and Associates, 2, 4–11, 34, 35, 36
    Rameau, Charles, 56–59
    Riani, Paolo, 146–149
    Robinson and Mills, 154–155
    Rockrise, George T., and Associates, 114–116
    RTKL, Inc., 208–209
    Salsberg and Leblanc, 46–47
    Singer, Donald, 158–161
    Skidmore, Owings and Merrill, 225, 231
    Stein, Richard G., and Associates, 212–213
    Storrs, John, 117–122
    Tabler, William B., 34–36
    Taege, Robert L., and Associates, 106–107
    The Architects Collaborative (TAC), 64–65, 174–177
    Toscanini, Walfredo, 178–181
    Unthank, Seder and Poticha, 204–205
    Urban Architects, 138–139
    Warnecke, John Carl, and Associates, 112–113
    Warner Burns Toan Lunde, 56–59, 72–75
    Weese, Harry, and Associates, 16–21
    Wells, Thomas O., and Associates, 48–49, 231
    Wimberly Whisenand Allison and Tong, 61, 62–63
    Wolff Zimmer Gunsel Frasca, 182–184
    Wolff Zimmer Gunsel Frasca Ritter, 108–111
    Wong, Worley K., 186–187
    Wou, Leo S., 228
    Yamasaki, Minoru, and Associates, 2, 12–15, 36
Architectural Record, 1, 44
Arizona, 185
Asilomar, Pacific Grove, California, 112–113
Astor Foundation, 178
Atelier d'Architectural, 82–87
Athay and Nonus, 122
Atlanta, Georgia, 38–39
Atlantic Beach, Florida, 68–71
Avoriaz, France, 82–87
Avoriaz Ski Resort, Avoriaz, France, 82–87

B

Baer, Morley, 66
Bahamas, The, 125
Bahus, P., 83

Balasz, Harold, 110
Balys, E. A., 17
Barnes, Edward Larrabee, 17
Barron, Harris, 177
Barron, Ros, 177
Bartush, Daniel, 43
Basil, Frank E., 65
Bedford Stuyvesant Community Pool, New York City, 188–189
Bellows, W. S., 30
Belluschi, Pietro, 109
Belt, Collins and Associates, 224–238
Bend, Oregon, 114–116
Benjamin and Zicherman Associates, 181
Bennett, A. J., 122
Bennett, Eugene, 121
Bennett and Drake, Inc., 48
Bernardston, Massachusetts, 152–153
B.E.R.U. (Bureau d'Etudes et de Realizations Urbaines), 80
Biel, Lee English, 83
Birmingham, Michigan, 43
Bliss, David, 181
Bliss, Donald, 17
Blume, John, 10
Bohlin, Annie, 194
Bohlin, Peter, 194, 202
Bohlin and Powell, 190–195, 198–203
Bolt Beranek and Newman, Inc., 13
Borel Restaurant, San Mateo, California, 154–155
Boston, Massachusetts, 142–143
Boston Madison Square Garden Club, Boston, Massachusetts, 142–143
Bowsted, John, 188
Bradshaw, Richard, Inc., 62, 154
Bragstad, Jeremiah, 168
Brahern, J. L., 83
Brener, Stephen W., 36
Breuer, Marcel, 78–81
Bridgers and Paxton, 150
Brody, Van, 178
Brooklyn, New York, 188–189
Bruce, H. C. Jr., 94
Brunzell Construction Company, 94
Bull, Henrick, 92, 93
Bull Field Volkmann Stockwell, 84–85, 88–93
Burnside Photography, 195
Butterfield, Donald, 165

C
Caesar's Palace, Tokyo, Japan, 146–149
Caldwell Scott Construction Company, 161
California:
        Alameda, 66–67
        Lake Kirkland, 94–95
        Los Angeles, 12–15
        Mill Valley, 168–169
        Pacific Grove, 112–113
        Point Reyes National Seashore, 186–187
        Sacramento, 42
        San Francisco, 4–11
        San Mateo, 154–155
        Tahoe, 88–93
Camera Hawaii, 61, 228, 229, 234
Camino Real, 17
Camp Lane, Mapleton, Oregon, 204–205
Camp Louise, Girl Scouts of America,
        Columbia County, Pennsylvania, 198–203
Campbell, Donald, 154
Campbell, John Carden, 186–187
Campbell and Rocchia and Associates, 186
Campbell and Wong and Associates, 66–67
Camston, Ltd., 132
Canada, 132–135
Cannon Construction Company, 150
Capital Investment Corporation, 229
Carter, Robert Herrick, 13
Caudill Rowlett Scott (CRS), 22–30
Cave, R. J., 233
Century City, Los Angeles, California, 13
Century Plaza Hotel, Los Angeles, California, 2, 12–15, 36
Chamonix, France, 78–81
Charleston, West Virginia, 40
Checkman, Louis, 219
Chenault and Brady, 30
Cherg, James K. M., 88, 95
Christian, Erwin, 63
Church and Shiels, 114
City Hall, San Francisco, 5, 36
Clinton Youth and Family Center, New York City, 178–181
Clydes Bar, Washington, D.C., 144–145

Coal Street Pool, Wilkes-Barre, Pennsylvania, 190–195
Cochise Visitor Center, Willcox, Arizona, 185
Coco Palms, Kauai, Hawaii, 236
Coffeen, R. S., and Associates, 17
Cohen, Mark, 191, 192, 194, 199, 201
Cohn, Melvin, and Associates, 106
Colakides, Fotis J., 65
Colakides Associates, 64–65
Coleman, Prescott, 182
Collins, F. L., and Son, Inc., 72
Columbia County, Pennsylvania, 198–203
Con Ed Park and Visitor Center, New York City, 214–215
Concordia Management Services, 17
Confederated Tribes of the Warm Springs Reservation, 109
Connell, David, 136
Copelin and Lee, 165
Cornell Howland Hayes and Merryfield, 102
Corum, E. A., 42
Cousins, Tom, 38
Crow, Trammell, 6, 35
Crown Center Hotel, Kansas City, Missouri, 16–21, 34
Crown Center Redevelopment Corporation, 17
Crown Zellerbach Building, San Francisco, 5, 36
Cybarco, 65
Cyprus, 64–65

D
D'Addario, Vincent, 152
Dames and Moore, 92
Danielson, Robert, 42
Davis Brody and Associates, 216
Davis, Edwin, 144
de la Torre, Jose, 52–55, 127
de Zarraga, Gaston, 161
Dell'Abate, Ralph, 188
Dember Construction Corporation, 181
"Designing the Urban Landscape, New concepts in the work
        of M. Paul Friedberg and Associates," 214–221
Diamond Head, Waikiki, Hawaii, 224–229
Dickey, C. W., 228
Dinsmore Kulseth and Riggs/Architecture One, 185
Dohrmann Company, 122
Dolton and Dunn, 165
Downtowner Motor Inn, Kansas City, Missouri, 138–139
Drake's Beach Facilities Building,
        Point Reyes National Seashore, California, 186–187
Dreyfuss and Blackford, 42
Drummey Rosane Anderson, 152–153
Dubose Gallery, 30
Duc, Ngo Manh, 83

E
Eagleson Engineers, 112
East Hampton, Long Island, New York, 166–167
Eckbo Dean Austin and Williams, 88–93
Eckbo, Garrett, 224
El Conquistador Hotel, Punta Gorda, Puerto Rico, 52–55, 127
Eldridge and Son Construction Company, Inc., 17, 136
Elkhorn at Sun Valley, Sun Valley, Idaho, 96–101
Elkhorn Valley, Idaho, 96–103
Elkus, Howard, 177
Elliot, Barbara, Interiors, 102
Elsesser and Associates, 186
Elster's, 10
Embarcadero Plaza (San Francisco), 11
Englehart Buettner and Holt, Inc., 43
Enomoto, Junko, 149
Enteleki Architecture Planning Research, 150–151
Environmental Systems Designs, 80

F
Faion, F., 136
Fealy, Barbara V., 122
Feder, Abe, 188
Fein, Phil, and Associates, 42
Fenway North Motor Hotel, Revere, Massachusetts, 46–47
Ferguson, Franklin T., 150
Ferguson Sorrentino Design Incorporated, 152
Ferris and Hamit, Inc., 48
Fibreboard Corporation, 88
Field, John Louis, 168–169
Financial Plaza, Honolulu, 228
Fishbach, Joseph, 167
Fitzmeyer and Tocci, 177
Flaine, France, 78–81
Flaine Ski Resort, Chamonix, France, 78–81
Flamm, Roy, 42
Flanagan, W. M., 17

Fletcher, Norman C., 177
Florida:
    Atlantic Beach, 68–71
    Plantation, 158–161
Foster, Richard, 162–164
France:
    Avoriaz, 82–87
    Chamonix, 78–81
    Flaine, 78–81
Francis Associates, 72
Franzen, Ulrich, 220
Frasca, Robert, 109, 182
Frazier, Jack L., 152
Freiwald, Joshua, 8, 10, 112, 186
Friedberg, M. Paul, and Associates, 214–221
Fuller, George A., Company, 13
Fung, Peter, and Associates, 106

G

Garris, Michael J., and Associates, 61
Garnett, J. B., 109
Gassner/ Nathan/Brown, 206–208
Georges, Alexandre, 6, 25, 53, 71, 137, 140, 159
Gendler, G. L., 114
GFDS Engineers, 114
Gilbert Forsberg Diekmann and Schmidt, 92
Gillen, William V., 152
Gillum, Jack, and Associates, 17
Gleneden Beach, Oregon, 117–122
Goldberg, Albert, 10
Golden Gateway Redevelopment Area, San Francisco, 6
Goodhue, Bertram, 228
Graham, John, and Company, 228
Grant, William, 227
Green, Ron, 220
Gruen, Victor, Associates, 228
Gulfstream Land and Development Corporation, 158
Gunsel Brooks, 109

H

Hacking, Arthur, 177
Hall, Robert W., 152
Hallmark, 34
Hampshire Construction Company, 112
Hara, Elizaburo, 146
Harding Miller Lawson and Associates, 10
Harlem River Bronx State Park, New York City, 214–216
Harper and George, 17
Harrison, Morris E., and Associates, 10
Haskell, Preston H., Company, 68
Hatala, J., 83
Hawaii:
    Coco Palms, Kauai, 236
    Island of, 230–233
    Honolulu, 224–229
    Kaanapali, Maui, 235
    Kailua, 232
    Kauai, 236–237
    Keauhou, 233
    Kona, 232
    La Perouse Bay, Maui, 235
    Makena, Maui, 235
    Maui, 234–235
    Molokai, 238
    Napili Kai, Maui, 235
    Oahu, 226–229
    Poipu Beach, Kauai, 60, 236
    Puu Olai, Maui, 235
    Waikiki, 224–229
    Waimea, 48–49
    Waiohea, 225, 237
Hawaiian Dredging and Construction Company, 48
H.D.H. Mechanical Designers, Inc., 61
Hedrich-Blessing (Harr), 106
Heineman, Paul T., 209
Helmsley-Spear, 36
Henderson, Richard, 167
Hennigan Construction Company, 140
Hershberger, Ed and Carol, 109
Hilton, 34, 56
Hilton Head, South Carolina, 165
Hirsch and Gray, 94
Hirschberger, Ed, 183
Hoffman, Ace, 192
Hoffman, Jay K., Presentations, 218
Honjigo, S., 60
Honolulu, Hawaii, 224–229
Hopper, Bruce, 48

Hotel des Dromonts, 84
Houston, Texas, 22–30
Houston National Company, 22
Huntsinger, Ronald W., 194
Hyatt Regency Hotel, Houston, Texas, 22–30
Hyatt Regency Hotel, San Francisco, California, 4–11, 36

I

Idaho:
    Elkhorn Valley, 96–103
    Sun Valley, 96–103
Intercontinental, 34
Inwood Hill Park Nature Trails, New York City, 212–213
Island Development Corporation, 72

J

Jacaranda Country Club, Plantation, Florida, 158–161
Jacobson, Bernard, 167
Jacobsen, Hugh Newell, 44–45, 144–145
Jacoby, John, 102
Jamaica Hilton Hotel, 126
Janders, Heinz, 109
Janders, Henry, 121, 122
Janin Company, 56
Janss, Bill, 96
Japan, 146–149
Jaros Baum and Bolles, 13, 56, 140
Jenkins and Blaine Construction Company, 139
Jewish Community Center, Portland, Oregon, 182–184
Jewish Community Center of Baltimore, 209
Johns-Manville Corporation, 96
Jones-Allen-Dillingham, 10
JVIII, a joint venture of Koetter, Tharp and Cowell,
    Caudill Rowlett Scott and Neuhaus & Taylor, 22–30

K

Kaanapali, Maui, Hawaii, 235
Kah-nee-ta Lodge, Warm Springs, Oregon, 108–111
Kailua, Hawaii, 232
Kansas City, 16–21, 136–137, 138–139
Kauai, Hawaii, 236–237
Kauai Builders, 60
Kauai Surf, Kauai, Hawaii, 236
Keauhou, Hawaii, 233
Kenchiku, Kyoritsu, 149
Kendorf, Robert D., 92
Kennedy and Brown, 194
Killingsworth, Edward, 98, 100
Killingsworth Brady and Associates, 96–103
King of the Road Motor Inn, Nashville, Tennessee, 44–45
Kirkwood Meadows Lodge, Lake Kirkwood, California, 94–95
Klein, William, Engineers, 154
Kleister, Haley W., 68
Kivett, Paul, 139
Kodama, Steven Y., 92
Koetter Tharp and Cowell, 22–30
Kona Hilton Hotel, Kona, Hawaii, 61, 232
Kona Village, Hawaii, 232
Kroeger, Keith, 142–143
Kruchek, Keith, 122
Kure, T., 60

L

La Perouse Bay, Maui, Hawaii, 235
Labro, Jacques, 83
Lahaina, Maui, Hawaii, 235
Lake Geneva, Wisconsin, 106–107
Lake Kirkwood, California, 94–95
Lam, William, 10, 30
Lamb, Charles, 209
Landscape Associates, 17, 19
Lane Country (Oregon) Parks Department, 205
Lapidus, Alan H., 37–41, 52, 123–127, 188
Lapidus, Morris, 2, 188
Lapidus, Morris, Associates, 37, 38, 52–55, 123, 125, 126, 188–189
Lardiere, A., 83
Larson, Gary, 109
Lautman, Robert, 44, 144
Lawrence, Charles, 29, 30
Lawson Construction, Inc., 109
Le Messurier and Associates, 142
Le Monde Restaurant, TWA, JFK, New York City, 140–141
Lee, Edmund Y., 115
Lee and Praszker, 154
Len Koch Company, 92
Levin, Stuart, 152
Levine, Aaron, 227
Levy, Robert, 10

Lindsay, Robert, 204
Lippert, Tom, 90, 91
Lombard, P., 83
Los Angeles, 12–15
Luckenbach/Durkee and Associates, 43
Luss/Kaplan and Associates, 163

M

McAdoo Contractors, Inc., 207
McCoster, James, 188
McElfresh, Donald, 106
Mackel, John E., and Associates, 61
MacMahon, Douglas V., Ltd., 62
Macomber, George B. H., Company, 177
McWilliam and Kechonen, 43
Maeda, T., 60
Magierek, Paul, 106
Makena, Maui, Hawaii, 235
Makihi Nursery, 61
Malpass, Charles A., Sons, 194
Mansion Inn Hotel, Sacramento, California, 42
Manson-Smith, Peter, 132
Mapleton, Oregon, 204–205
Marion-Cerbatos and Tomasi, 92, 94
Maris, Bill, 142
Marks, Steve, 97
Marshall and Brown, 17
Martin, John A., and Associates, 48
Martin and Fladd, 202
Martinique, French West Indies, 56–91
Martinique Hilton, Martinique, French West Indies, 56–59
Maryland:
        Reisterstown, 208–209
Massachusetts:
        Bernardston, 152–153
        Boston, 142–143
        Revere, 46–47
Matsuyama, Makoto, 149
Maui, Hawaii, 234–235
Mauna Kea Beach Hotel, Hawaii, 225, 231
Maxwell, Donald E., 202
Mayer, Moshe, 34
Meagher, Zoldos, 163
Mechanical Design Incorporated, 106
Medwadowski, Stefan, 112
Menehan, Patrick J., 152
Menscher, Stan, 181
Meyers and Locker, 188
Michigan:
        Birmingham, 43
Mid Gad Valley Restaurant, Alta Canyon, Utah, 150–151
Mill Valley, California, 168–169
Mill Valley Tennis Club, Mill Valley, California, 168–169
Millar, C. Blakeway, 134–135
Milldale Camps, Reisterstown, Maryland, 209
Minden Construction Company, 182
Missouri:
        Kansas City, 16–21, 136–137, 138–139
Mitchell, Jill, 136
Modrall, A. William Jr., 30
Molitor, Joseph W., 165, 199
Molokai, Hawaii, 238
Molokai Hotel, 238
Montauk Golf and Racquet Club, Montauk Point,
        Long Island, New York, 162–164
Montauk Improvement, Inc., 163
Montauk Point, Long Island, New York, 162–164
Moore, G. E., Inc., 165
Moore, Walter P., and Associates, 30
Morgan, William, 68–71
Morton, Peter W., 65
Mountain Marketing Services, 92
Mullen, William F., 102
Munro Burns and Jackson Brothers, 61
Murchison Construction Company, 92
Myers, J. Matthew, 114

N

Napili Kai, Maui, Hawaii, 235
Nashville, Tennessee, 44–45
Neilson Engineering, 150
Neish, William J., 132
Nelson, Howard, 205
Nemeny, George, 166–167
Nemer, Basil, 43
Neuhaus & Taylor, 22–30
New York:
        Brooklyn, 188–189

New York (Cont.):
        East Hampton, Long Island, 166–167
        Montauk Point, Long Island, 162–164
        New York City, 140–141, 178–181, 214–231
Newport, Rhode Island, 72–75
Nixon, Sandy, 192, 195
Noodles Restaurant, Toronto, Ontario, Canada, 134–135
Norman, Vern, Associates, 177
Northstar-at-Tahoe, California, 88–93
Nortec, Inc., 109, 182

O

Oahu, Hawaii, 226–229
Oberlander, H. Peter, 233
O'Dell/Hewlett and Luckenbach, Inc.
        (successors to Luckenbach/Durkee and Associates), 43
Oldman, Inc., 13
Olin, William F., 114
Olin Corporation, 34
One Shell Plaza, Houston, Texas, 22, 23
Orbeck, Arvid, 109
Oregon:
        Bend, 114–116
        Gleneden Beach, 117–122
        Mapleton, 204–205
        Portland, 182–184
        Warm Springs, 108–111
Orzoni, Jean-Jacques, 83
Ossipoff, Vladimir, 60, 225, 231, 237

P

Pacific Bridge Company, 66
Pacific Grove, California, 112–113
Page Construction Company, 168
Painter, Michael, 112
Palace Hotel, San Francisco, California, 5, 36
Palmetto Dunes Clubhouse, Hilton Head, South Carolina, 165
Panda Associates, 133
Papeete, Tahiti, 62–63
Paradise Island, The Bahamas, 125
Paradise Island Hotel, The Bahamas, 125
Parker Ranch, Waimea, Hawaii, 48
PBNL Architects, Inc., 17
Pennsylvania:
        Columbia County, 198–203
        Wilkes-Barre, 190–195
Pennsylvania Society of Architects, 193
Pereira, William L., 229
Perfido, Leonard, 142–143
Perrin, Robert, 182
Perron, Robert, 109, 135
Phases Restaurant, Bernardston, Massachusetts, 152–153
Phoenix of Atlanta, 38, 39
PIC Realty Corporation, 6, 22
Pickering Engineering, 207
Pierson, James G., 122
Place by the Sea, The, Atlantic Beach, Florida, 68–71
"Planning hotels that pay," by William B. Tabler, 34–36
"Planning hotels that work," by Alan H. Lapidus, 37–41
"Planning successful resort hotels," by Alan H. Lapidus, 123–127
Plantation, Florida, 158–161
Platner, Warren, 136–137, 140–141
Playboy, 106, 107
Playboy Club, 106
Playboy Resort Hotel, Lake Geneva, Wisconsin, 106–107
Playground, private, 220
Plaza, The, New York City, 36
Point Reyes National Seashore, California, 186–187
Poipu Beach, Kauai, Hawaii, 60, 236
Polshek, James Stewart, 178–181
Portland, Oregon, 182–184
Portman, John, and Associates, 2, 4–11, 34, 35, 36
Pregnoff and Matheu, 168
Prince, Neal A., 62
Prudential Life Insurance Company, The, 22
Puerto Rico, 52–53
Punta Gorda, Puerto Rico, 52–53
Puu Olai, Maui, Hawaii, 235

R

Rado-Orzoni, G., 83
Rameau, Charles, 56–59
Reardon and Turner, 142
"Record Interiors of 1971," 44
Reens, Louis, 46, 57, 73
Regency Hyatt Atlanta, Atlanta, Georgia, 34
Reis and Manwaring, 154
Reiser, Debora, 167
Reisterstown, Maryland, 208–209

Revere, Massachusetts, 46–47
Rhode Island:
    Newport, 72–75
Riani, Paolo, 146–149
Rigger, Ira C., 209
Robbins, Donald A., 13
Robert, Frank, 236, 238
Robinson and Mills, 154–155
Robinson Neil Bass and Associates, 44
Rockefeller, David, and Associates, 6
Rockefeller, Laurance, 34
Rockrise, George T., 114–116
Roeder, Wallace, 182
Rosen, Harold, Associates, 163
Rosenthal, Joseph, 61
Rotary Club of New York, 178
Rowe, Terry, 158, 161
Roxbury Branch, YMCA, Boston, Massachusetts, 174–177
Royston Hanamoto Beck and Abey, 114
RTKL, Inc., 209

S
Sacramento, California, 42
Salbosa, A., 49
Salishan Lodge, Gleneden Beach, Oregon, 117–122
Salishan Properties, Inc., 122
Salsberg and Leblance, 46–47
San Francisco, California, 4–11
San Mateo, California, 154–155
Sasaki Walker Associates, 96–101
Sato Construction Company, 102
Scherr, Herman, Associates, 188
Schmidt, Fred, and Associates, 92
Schnall, Ben, 162
Schneider, Joseph, 46
Setziol, LeRoy, 121
Severud-Perrone-Fischer-Sturm-Conlin-Bandel, 56
Shaheen, Robert L., 19
Shannon and Wilson, 109
Sheraton, 34
Sheraton-Islander Inn, Newport, Rhode Island, 72–75
Sheraton Kauai, Kauai, Hawaii, 237
Shulman, Julius, 22
Sikes, Charles R. Jr., 30
Singer, Donald, 158–161
Sleeping Shelters, Camp Lane, Mapleton, Oregon, 204–205
Smith and Boucher, 139
Société-Hotelière et Touristique Martiniquaise, 56
Skidmore Owings and Merrill (SOM), 22, 225, 231
Sonesta, 34
Sousa and True, 177
South Carolina:
    Hilton Head, 165
Soverns, Wayne Jr., 64
Sox, Marion, 60
Speyer, Lars, 99
Stadler, Allan, 136
Statler, 34
Stecher, Leonard, 42
Stein, Richard G., and Associates, 212–213
Steinberg, Stanley, 10
Stockwell, Sherwood, 94
Stoller, Ezra, 189
Storrs, John, 117–122
Stouffer, 34
Strausser Construction, Inc., 202
Sun Valley, Idaho, 96–103
Sun Valley Corporation, 96
Sunriver Lodge, Bend, Oregon, 114–116
Swinerton and Walberg Company, 62
Szykman, Vincent B., Inc., 194, 202

T
Tabler, William B., 34–36
Taege, Robert L., 106
Taege, Robert L. and Associates, 106–107
Tahara'a Intercontinental Hotel, Papeete, Tahiti, 62–63
Tahiti, 62–63
Tahoe, California, 88–93
Tandy and Allen, 163
Taylor Robert, 134
TEC, 17
Tenneco Building, Houston, Texas, 22, 23
Tenneco Realty, Inc., 22
Tennessee:
    Nashville, 44–45
    Tiptonville, 206–207
Tennis Club, East Hampton, Long Island, New York, 166–167

Tern Construction, 188
Texas:
    Houston, 22–30
The Architects Collaborative (TAC), 64–65, 174–177
Thorn, Wayne, 99, 103
Times Square Hotel, New York City, 36
Tiptonville, Tennessee, 206–207
Tokyo, Japan, 146–149
Toronto, Ontario, Canada, 132–133, 134–135
Toronto Squash Club, Toronto, Ontario, Canada, 132–133
Toscanini, Walfredo, 178
Travelodge, Motel, Pacific Marina, Alameda, California, 66–67
Trimont Land Company, 88
Tucker, Marc, 29, 30
Turner Construction Company, 142
Twentieth Century Fox, 13

U
Unger, Charles F., Construction Company, 42
United Air Conditioning Corporation, 61
Unthank Seder and Poticha, 204–205
Urban Architects, 138–139
Utah:
    Alta Canyon, 150–151

V
Video Park, New York City, 218–219
Village Inn Motor Hotel, Birmingham, Michigan, 43
Vincent and Williams, Inc., 152

W
Waikiki, Honolulu, Hawaii, 224–238
Waimea, Hawaii, 48–49
Waimea Village Inn, Waimea, Hawaii, 50–51
Waiohea, Hawaii, 225, 237
Waiohai Resort Hotel, Poipu Beach, Kauai, Hawaii, 60, 237
Waitz and Frye, 68
Walker, Peter, 102
Wall Street Plaza, New York City, 218–219
Walters, George, 48
Ward's Island Park, New York City, 220–221
Warm Springs, Oregon, 108–111
Warnecke, John Carl, and Associates, 112–113
Warner Burns Toan Lunde, 56–59, 72–75
Washington, D.C., 144–145
Watertown East Development, Watertown, Massachusetts, 214–215
WBTL-Jacques-Durham, 56
WEBcor Builders, Inc., 154
Weese, Harry, and Associates, 16–21
Wells, Thomas O., 50–51, 231
Wenkam, R., 225
West Indies:
    Martinique, FWI, 56–59
West Virginia:
    Charleston, 40
Western International Hotels, 17
Western Supply and Service Company, 13
Weyerhaeuser Family Associates, 229
Wheel-Garon, Inc., 13, 56
Wick Construction Company, 102
Wilkes-Barre, Pennsylvania, 190–195
Willcox, Arizona, 185
Williams, John, 182
Wilsey and Ham, 88
Wimberly Whisenand Allison and Tong, 61, 62–63, 232, 237
Wimberly, George J., 61
Wimberly and Cook, 236
Wisconsin:
    Lake Geneva, 106–107
Wolbrink, Donald, and Associates, 236
Wolff Zimmer Gunsel Frasca, 182–184
Wolff Zimmer Gunsel Frasca Ritter, 108–111
Wong, Worley K., 186–187
Wong and Brocchini and Associates, 186
Wooten Smith and Weiss, 207
Worthington Skilling Helle and Jackson, 13
Wou, Leo S., 228
Wujeck, A., 83

Y
Yamasaki, Minoru, and Associates, 2, 12–15, 36
Yanow, Daniel, 66
Yeomans, Paul H., Inc., 194
YMCA of Greater New York, 178
Yoshpe, Daniel, 42
Yves-Gillemaut, 79

Z
Zinke, Paul, 88